Women and Theatre in the Age of Suffrage

Also by Katharine Cockin

EDITH CRAIG (1869–1947): Dramatic Lives

Women and Theatre in the Age of Suffrage

The Pioneer Players, 1911–1925

Katharine Cockin
Lecturer in English
University of Hull

Consultant Editor: Jo Campling

palgrave

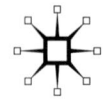

© Katharine Cockin 2001

All rights reserved. No reproduction, copy or transmission of this publication may be made without written permission.

No paragraph of this publication may be reproduced, copied or transmitted save with written permission or in accordance with the provisions of the Copyright, Designs and Patents Act 1988, or under the terms of any licence permitting limited copying issued by the Copyright Licensing Agency, 90 Tottenham Court Road, London W1P 0LP.

Any person who does any unauthorised act in relation to this publication may be liable to criminal prosecution and civil claims for damages.

The author has asserted her right to be identified as the author of this work in accordance with the Copyright, Designs and Patents Act 1988.

First published 2001 by
PALGRAVE
Houndmills, Basingstoke, Hampshire RG21 6XS and
175 Fifth Avenue, New York, N. Y. 10010
Companies and representatives throughout the world

PALGRAVE is the new global academic imprint of
St. Martin's Press LLC Scholarly and Reference Division and
Palgrave Publishers Ltd (formerly Macmillan Press Ltd).

ISBN 0–333–68696–9

This book is printed on paper suitable for recycling and made from fully managed and sustained forest sources.

A catalogue record for this book is available from the British Library.

Library of Congress Cataloging-in-Publication Data
Cockin, Katharine, 1963–
  Women and theatre in the age of suffrage : the Pioneer Players, 1911–1925 / Katharine Cockin.
     p. cm.
  Includes bibliographical references and index.
  ISBN 0–333–68696–9
  1. Pioneer Players (Theater group : London, England)—History. 2. Feminist theater—England—London—History—20th century. 3. Women in the theater—England—London—History—20th century. I. Title

PN2595.13.W65 C63 2000
792'.082'09421—dc21
                                                                00–033341

10	9	8	7	6	5	4	3	2	1
10	09	08	07	06	05	04	03	02	01

Printed and bound in Great Britain by
Antony Rowe Ltd, Chippenham, Wiltshire

For John Cockin (1932–1999)

Contents

List of plates viii

Acknowledgements ix

1 Introducing the Pioneer Players 1
2 The Costs of a Free Theatre 16
3 The Feminist Play of Ideas and the Art of Propaganda 41
4 Pioneers Perform Politics 67
5 Working Women 88
6 Outside Marriage 112
7 The Luck of War 135
8 Towards an Art Theatre 166
9 On the Verge 188

Appendix I: Pioneer Players' Productions 199
Appendix II: Subscription Performances – Plays and Dramatists Statistical Analysis of Data from Annual Reports 204
Notes 206
Bibliography 219
Index 230

List of Plates

Plate 1   Ellen Terry, Harcourt Williams and Miriam Lewes rehearsing at the King's Hall for the Pioneer Players' production of Hrotsvit's *Paphnutius* (The Drama of a Soul in the Home of Boxing, *Daily Graphic*, January 1914).

Plate 2   Printed envelope for the sale of *The Theatre of the Soul*, The Play that was stopped at the Alhambra.

Plate 3   Actors performing in *The Conference*.

Plate 4   The Pioneer Players' Mi-Carême Ball (*Tatler*).

Plate 5   Actors in *A Pageant of Great Women* (*Daily Mirror*, 13 September 1909).

Plates 6 and 7   Actors performing in *Pan in Ambush*.

Plate 8   Play programme cover, designed by Pamela Colman Smith, for special matinée arranged by Lady Randolph Churchill.

Plates 1, 2, 4, 5 and 8 are reproduced by kind permission of the National Trust.

Plates 3, 6 and 7 are held at the Brynmor Jones Library, University of Hull.

Acknowledgements

The research for this book began with my PhD thesis at Leicester University, funded in 1988–90 by a British Academy Major State Studentship. A Society for Theatre Research Award in 1990 enabled me to make numerous visits to London libraries. I am grateful to Dr Philip Dodd, Dr Jane Aaron, Professor Joanne Shattock, Dr Richard Foulkes and, Professor Clare Hanson who, at different stages, supervised my research at Leicester University and to Professor Susan Bassnett and Professor Martin Stannard, the examiners of my PhD thesis. I am indebted to the National Trust, especially to John Chesshyre, Historic Building Representative for Kent and East Sussex and Margaret Weare, Custodian of the Ellen Terry Memorial Museum, Smallhythe Place, Tenterden, Kent, for encouraging my work on the Edith Craig Archive and giving permission to quote from material in the archive. Since 1989 I have worked on the archive as a volunteer for the National Trust and for a short period in 1995 on a freelance basis supported by funds raised by local National Trust members. I was pleased to report on the work by giving a lecture at the Barn Theatre, Tenterden, Kent in September 1997. I am indebted to Raymond Mason who lent me for the duration of this research a Pioneer Players scrapbook (now held at University of Hull). I am grateful also to Dr Laurie Wolf who generously gave me a copy of her PhD thesis on the Pioneer Players.

During the course of my research on the Pioneer Players and Edith Craig many people have helped me by replying to letters of enquiry, by talking over ideas and, in the case of the late Athene Seyler (an acting member of the Pioneer Players) and Sir Donald Sinden, by providing an interview. I would also like to thank, for their help in many ways, Professor Gabriele Griffin, Dr Claire Tylee, Dr Maroula Joannou, Professor June Purvis, Professor Angela John, Professor Laura Doan, Dr Lucy Bland and the late Dr Leah Leneman. My appointment to the Elizabeth Howe Research Fellowship by the Open University in 1997 allowed me to make substantial revisions to the thesis in order to prepare the manuscript for this book. Dr Lizbeth Goodman gave me the opportunity to test out an early version of Chapter 1 on members of the Open University's Gender in Writing and Performance Research Group.

Librarians at the following institutions have been most helpful: Leicester University, Open University, British Library, Bodleian Library, x *Acknowledgements*

Theatre Museum, Mander and Mitchenson Theatre Collection, British Theatre Association and the Fawcett Library.

I am grateful for the opportunity of giving conference papers which have helped to shape the research for this book: Other as Self: Women's Writing in the Modernist Period, Nene College, Northampton 1991; Women's History Network conferences in 1992 and 1993; Women's Studies Network (UK) Conference 1993; Shakespeare on the British Stage 1900–45, Leicester University 1994; Charlotte Perkins Gilman: Optimist and Social Reformer, Liverpool University 1995; Seeing Through Suffrage, University of Greenwich 1996; Women, Drama & the First World War, Brunel University, 1997; International Federation of Theatre Research Congress, University of Kent 1998.

My views of women's suffrage drama have been influenced by responses from postgraduate students at Nene College MA Women's Studies 1992–94, University of Hull MA Women and Literature 1998–2000 and the first cohort of undergraduate students 1999–2000 on my module Suffragettes and Citizens: Writing for the Vote, University of Hull.

I would like to thank my colleagues at the University of Hull, in particular, Dr James Booth for reading the manuscript and Dr Veronica O'Mara for advice on Hrotsvit, and Jo Campling, Consultant Editor, for advice and assistance with the manuscript.

1
Introducing the Pioneer Players

'Drama in the Home of Boxing' was one headline in January 1914 when the Pioneer Players society was about to produce a tenth-century play in the King's Hall, at the National Sporting Club (Plate 1). *Paphnutius*, translated from the Latin especially for this performance,[1] was written by the nun Hrotsvit, said to be the first female dramatist. The press enjoyed the juxtaposition of boxing, nuns and women's suffrage, the political movement with which the Pioneer Players had strong affiliations. In this play, the abject figure of the penitent whore Thais, punished by close confinement and extreme privation, is profoundly misogynistic. However, her imprisonment and salvation may have had unusually empowering resonances for hunger-striking suffragettes. In the event, and characteristic of the precarious nature of single performances in borrowed or hired venues, the play was transferred at the last moment to the Savoy Theatre. Against all the odds, it was a success. Earlier, the launch of this small, London-based, play-producing subscription society at the Kingsway Theatre in May 1911 had been reported with great interest in national newspapers. True to their name, the Pioneer Players were ahead of their time. They were responsible for historic performances in women's theatre history including not only the first performance of the play by Hrotsvit but also two plays, *Trifles* and *The Verge*, by the American dramatist Susan Glaspell. The director of these plays was the society's founder, Edith Craig,[2] an experienced actor and director with well-established connections in the theatre.[3] Before the First World War, the society had promoted topical issues and campaigns, women's writing for the stage and unorthodox representations of gender. The Pioneer Players were committed to organising the performance of plays new to a British stage, in translation if necessary.[4] Increasingly, Edith Craig's productions were praised for visually

1

impressive effects contrived within a limited budget. The innovative lighting equipment at the Little Theatre, London was identified by a number of reviewers as enabling Craig to create characteristically subtle visual effects. As a theatre of slender means the Pioneer Players frequently achieved the impossible. Craig often worked with minimal props and scenery, making use of public halls such as the King's Hall, Covent Garden or theatres borrowed at short notice. But although the productions were reviewed in newspapers in Britain, Spain and France at the time, theatre histories have tended to overlook their work.

In 1981 the Pioneer Players were rediscovered as a 'women's company', involved with women's suffrage drama and providing a precedent for the women's theatres of second-wave feminism in Britain (Holledge 1981: 165). However, although the Pioneer Players showed an interest in female authorship and women's history similar to that of women's theatre groups of the 1970s, they were subject in the period of their activity (1911–25) to very different commercial, theatrical and political pressures. At this time, public performances of plays in London theatres were regulated (or censored), but not subsidised by government. The theatre was a precarious field of work, particularly for women, who faced the financial burden of providing their own wardrobe of costumes as well as the likelihood of sexual harassment during the casting process. Performers experienced unpredictable conditions of employment which conflicted with the responsibilities of caring for dependants, a role traditionally associated with women. A standard contract of employment did not exist until the Actors' Association took action in 1919; and it was not until 1929 that actors had their own trade union, Equity. Dramatists had achieved some limited protection over the copyright of their plays and would expect to publish a successful play in order to reach a literary market. The actor-managers of theatres were being supplanted by profit-minded entrepreneurs, and the need for standardised training coincided with the increasing prestige of acting as a profession. Experimentation was being recognised as a commercial and political necessity for the revival of theatre and for the development of a national drama. Eventually it was also recognised that experimentation required institutional support and government funding rather than the precarious subsidy of theatre practitioners' goodwill and unpaid work. These material conditions had an immediate effect on the ways in which the women involved in the Pioneer Players could work, over and above the significant fact that they could not vote in general elections for most of the society's lifetime. In the 1970s women's theatre groups could apply for sponsorship or gain access to a state-subsidised venue.

The obstacles overcome by the Pioneer Players, who had neither opportunity, make the longevity and success of the organisation all the more remarkable.

The Pioneer Players share more political ground with those who have questioned the category of gender in the 1990s than with the 'women's theatres' of the 1970s. The Pioneer Players, unlike the short-lived Woman's Theatre (1913), chose neither to define themselves nor to operate as a women-only organisation. Like the feminist in Jackie Fleming's cartoon, the Pioneer Players (women and men alike) disguised themselves as human beings. The demand for equality based on a redefinition of humanity extended to women was, in fact, a common and long-standing feature of the discourse of women's suffrage. During debates on the 1832 Reform Bill the use of the generic masculine pronoun to represent women was discussed, and, in 1867, John Stuart Mill attempted to replace the word 'man' in the second Reform Bill with 'person' in order to include women in the franchise. Nevertheless, suffragists who demanded women's enfranchisement on the same basis as that of men – even in the name of 'human' rights – were supporting specific groups of (propertied) women, and generally disregarded working-class, younger and propertyless women. Where support for women's suffrage was aligned with demands for women's rights in other areas, it uneasily accepted that some women would be speaking on behalf of others. Karen Offen has explained that such 'individualist feminism... emphasized more abstract concepts of individual human rights and celebrated the quest for personal independence (or autonomy) in all aspects of life' (Offen 1992: 76). This form of egalitarianism has been dismissed as merely demanding women's inclusion in patriarchal structures and as privileging different groups of women, specifically those claiming a place within the dominant group on racial and class grounds. Consequently, arguments for women's enfranchisement drew strength from the discourses of imperialism, Social Darwinism and eugenics. The worth of white, middle-class women was asserted, while that of people of colour, working-class people and the other routinely disenfranchised groups – the 'insane' and the imprisoned – was ignored. However, while suffragists' use of the category 'woman' risked denying diversity, the expectation of inclusion had its unsettling effects on structures founded on difference and hierarchy. The demand for inclusion consequently exposed the exclusivity of the existing 'democratic' structure, in that its elected representatives spoke on behalf of others. It also made it possible for some to look beyond enfranchisement towards a more thoroughly feminist revision of society.

It was this very respect for other, ordinarily marginalised, voices that made the Pioneer Players a politically ambiguous organisation. Tensions between sex and class framed the society's appeal to women and to a predominantly middle-class group. The Pioneer Players did not, and perhaps could not be expected to, resolve the conflicts between these groups which had been politically urgent during the crises of Edwardian Britain. These were demands for universal suffrage, challenges to the authority of the House of Lords and campaigns for colonial independence. The complex activities of the Pioneer Players and the unusual and changing coalition of members show that this was not a 'women's theatre' in any literal sense of the word. The Pioneer Players were exceptional and successful, surviving against the odds, adopting contradictory positions, refusing to define or categorise their work. Even what might be called the Pioneer Players' new 'manifesto' in 1915 appeared almost as an afterthought, printed in a play programme for a one-off, non-subscription performance. The Pioneer Players were devoted to diversity and to novelty. In a sense their identity was Romantic and modernist as much as it was feminist. The Pioneer Players challenged the liberal position they appeared to adopt. The Prime Minister, Herbert Asquith, if not the entire Liberal Party in government, was effectively opposed to women's enfranchisement. Occupying the position of devil's advocate, the Pioneer Players gave voice to the 'Other', even when, on one occasion, that same marginalised other voice was speaking for impartiality: an otherwise proscribed position in England at the time of the Easter Rising in Dublin. During a period of crisis and division the voice of the middle ground can appear to be revolutionary.

The Pioneer Players have justifiably attracted interest from feminist critics concerned with the drama produced by the women's suffrage movement,[5] and concerned with constructing a tradition of feminist theatre (Aston 1995) or the women's theatre movement (Davis 1994: 83). The significant contributions to women's history made by the Pioneer Players' translation and performance of a play by Hrotsvit and the performance of plays about women lost to androcentric history, such as Margaret Hughes, Irena Macrena and Queen Caroline, have provoked some critical discussion (Apter 1996; Case 1988; Ferris 1995). The production of plays by famous male dramatists, such as Kori Torahiko and George Bernard Shaw, has prompted author-centred discussion of the work of the Pioneer Players (Chiba 1996; Fisher 1995). The society may be guaranteed similar attention from theatre historians since they performed the work of a number of canonical male dramatists, including Paul Claudel, Herman Heijermans, Nikolai Evreinov,

Leonid Andreiev and Anton Chekhov. However, the society did not confine itself to the performance of plays by specific authors, whether exclusively women or famous men. As I will show, the context in which the society worked explains the rationale for play selection. The performance context, the relationships between the society's constituency and its commitment to diversity through innovative, controversial and topical plays, are mapped out here for the first time. The Pioneer Players' membership and audience were overlapping, but not identical, groups. This is demonstrated by a case study which considers the discourse of the newspaper review, its formal characteristics and strategies of evaluation, as well as investigating claims of gender bias in reviews of the Pioneer Players' performances (Dymkowski 1992: 224). This exploration of the 'reception and interpretation' as well as the genesis of the Pioneer Players is influenced by developments in the 'recent turn to history' in literary criticism (Hawthorn 1996: 47; 52).

Favourably reviewed in the *New Statesman* by Virginia Woolf and Desmond MacCarthy, the Pioneer Players' work was credited with ensuring 'the liveableness of life in London' during the First World War. Although Virginia Woolf seems to have missed the Pioneer Players' peak in 1916, she appeared to compliment the society in 1919, in terms reminiscent of the Futurists or Theatre of Cruelty, for its effect on the audience, who should expect to be 'scraped and harrowed' by a Pioneer Players performance (Woolf 1988: 207). Saint-Georges de Bouhelier placed the Pioneer Players in the context of a European struggle against naturalism (Adlard 1949: 61). The development of anti-realist dramatic forms has often been represented in terms of liberation. The Pioneer Players have been associated with this kind of Romantic narrative. Yet, as Julie Holledge has shown, the society's pre-war productions were more closely (though not exclusively, as will be seen later) concerned with issues arising from the women's suffrage movement. While the Pioneer Players' work was widely reviewed in the national and international press and often by suffrage newspapers, responses to the productions were unpredictable. The Pioneer Players were neither consistently condemned by the national newspapers nor consistently praised by suffragists and feminists. Thus, Rebecca West condemned the Pioneer Players on the grounds that their work was not artistic, while major national newspapers such as *The Times* routinely reviewed their productions without reference to any political context. A principal concern of this study is thus the institutional life of the Pioneer Players: precisely how they functioned in relation to other organisations and to what extent the plays produced were indeed expressive of the women's suffrage movement's, or other, concerns. The representation of gender and the dramatic form of the plays actually performed are situated in the processes of production, specifically the relationships between performance, audience and venue.

At the outset the women's suffrage movement was a significant influence. The Pioneer Players developed from Edith Craig's work for women's suffrage theatre, specifically her productions of *How the Vote Was Won*, co-written by Cicely Hamilton and Christopher St. John, and *A Pageant of Great Women*, devised by Cicely Hamilton and Edith Craig. These plays, subsequently placed in the canons of British 'suffragette plays' by Dale Spender and Carole Hayman (1985) and by Viv Gardner (1985), were originally performed under Craig's direction by a group of actors named on occasions 'the Pioneer Players'. Before the First World War and during the years of increasing militancy in the women's suffrage movement, the Pioneer Players produced numerous works exploring, in ways largely unavailable to other cultural forms, issues of concern for suffrage feminists. These included: women as workers; women's position in, and especially out of, marriage; prostitution; and women's history. Many of these plays do not conform to formal definitions of 'suffragette drama' as realist, 'agit-prop', female-authored plays with suffragist characters or plot-lines (Cockin 1998b; Hirschfield 1985, 1987, 1991; Stowell 1992). The political motivations of the Pioneer Players as an organisation assumed to have been 'feminist' prove rather to have been complex, shifting and pragmatic, employing parody and self-referential humour. They were oppositional to the extent, on a few occasions, of openly defying the law. But, while women always formed a majority of the society's members at all levels, it placed no restrictions on men's membership. Although Christine Dymkowski has claimed otherwise, a majority of women in the Pioneer Players' – or any organisation's – membership does not guarantee its 'feminist basis' (Dymkowski 1994: 222). The society's membership appears to have been drawn predominantly from the middle and upper-middle classes. Through the work of its director, Edith Craig, and members such as Miles Malleson,[6] the Pioneer Players constitute a link between the women's suffrage movement and other 'political theatres' in Britain, otherwise usually regarded as autonomous, namely the socialist theatres of the 1930s (Samuel *et al.*, 1985).

The Pioneer Players' engagement with political issues surprised and threatened some reviewers, who claimed that they were subversive, deliberately misrepresenting the political agenda and manipulating their audience: 'We had walked in so innocently, imagining that the pioneering of the Pioneer Players was to be dramatic, not (if we may be pardoned the ugly word) feministic' (*The Times*, 9 May 1911: 13). This anonymous female reviewer feared that women involved in the cultural politics of women's suffragism were becoming alert to new possibilities, appropriating new cultural forms and spaces in which their arguments could take hold. Edith Craig informed the suffrage newspaper, the *Vote*, that drawing-room meetings were being organised by suffragists specifically in order to attract women who would never attend a political meeting. The theatre, drawing-room meetings, the costume ball and other middle-class social and cultural forms were appropriated by suffragists. The 'openness' of the Pioneer Players, their determination to produce plays representing a broad range of views, including political ones, were perceived by their critics in opposite terms: as a manipulative liberal strategy masking a more directive, yet undisclosed, agenda. In fact, in the annual reports and in the announcements made before the Pioneer Players were launched, the society acknowledged an interest in women's suffrage *and* in any other current movement of interest. Like any annual report, that of the Pioneer Players' was selective, with a view to constructing a specific public image. But, significantly the Pioneer Players' concern to produce 'propaganda' was an explicitly stated aim of the society published in its annual reports rather than, as Dymkowski suggests, 'inferred' by critics.[7] However, the instability of the term 'propaganda' is indicated by the fact that the Pioneer Players' propagandist function was favourably reported in the women's suffrage press while national newspapers invariably used 'propaganda' as a derogatory term.

Contemporary newspapers rarely referred to the society as 'Edy Craig's Pioneer Players'. This more recent retrospective image of the society begs questions about the society's structure, its practices and the relationships it made possible between members. Edith Craig's role in the development of the society was significant. Her directorial acumen was in evidence in most of the society's performances and received critical attention from the press. She had a great deal of experience of commercial theatre, having worked in the Lyceum Theatre, and elsewhere, as a costumier and actor. When she founded the Pioneer Players in 1911, Craig was 42 years old and in mid-career. She had toured extensively as an actor with the Lyceum Company in America and with the supporters of Ibsen's drama – Charles Charrington and Janet Achurch – in Britain. She worked as stage-manager/producer for her mother, Ellen Terry, in America and in Britain, and Terry became president of the Pioneer Players and appeared in several plays. Terry's and Craig's contacts in the theatre world were invaluable to the Pioneer Players, enabling theatres to be borrowed, often at short notice, from sympathetic theatre managers. Craig also involved her talented partners, the writer Christopher St. John (d. 1960) and the artist Tony (Clare) Atwood (d. 1963), in translating, writing, making props and administration.

Over and above the Pioneer Players' support of women writers for the stage, their support of women working in other areas of production has been identified as a radical development in the history of 'feminist performance' (Aston 1995: 31). However, evidence for the repeated assertions that women worked 'in all areas of production' in the Pioneer Players (Dymkowski 1992; Ferris 1995; Holledge 1981) derives from Margaret Webster's description of the Actresses' Franchise League (AFL) from which the Pioneer Players developed (Webster 1969: 249). Women *were* involved in key areas but, with the exception of Craig's work as director, this was never identified as a characteristic of the society's work. It may have been an unspoken aim, but the Pioneer Players did not think it sufficiently important to record all those involved. Christopher St. John appears to have taken the view that feminism and female authorship were essentially linked. When asked whether Hrotsvit was a feminist, St. John referred to the Pioneer Players' production of *Paphnutius*: that women were responsible for writing, producing, translating the play and arranging the plainsong music. It would surely not have been necessary for the society to announce its female-centred working practices nor its commitment to feminism if these were implicit features of the society's work, and understood by its membership. The kind of feminism with which the society appears to have been interested was not defined in separatist terms. Men were numbered amongst. the plays' directors as well as dramatists. St. John's assertion that Craig lacked 'complete control' in the Pioneer Players must also be considered in relation to the society's formal structure (Adlard 1949: 26), not least because of the institutional constraints on women working in the theatre.

Even the most collaborative ventures tend to be associated with a single person. In the case of the Pioneer Players, the society's work has become synonymous with Edith Craig. Yet she was answerable to a hierarchical committee structure drawn from, and formally reporting to, the membership at the annual general meetings and through the published annual reports. During the Pioneer Players' lifetime she also worked independently of the society on several productions. The advisory committee, later working with the council of the society established in 1918–19, met once or twice a month. It consisted of 14 members elected at the annual general meetings to manage the society.

Sub-committees were set up to organise publicity and to cast the plays. The society produced annual reports and accounts. The two main types of membership – ordinary and acting – were differentiated by function and price. The lower subscription rate of 1 shilling for acting members acknowledged the society's reliance on their unpaid labour. This debt was later noted when greater prosperity enabled the payment of rehearsal expenses. The Pioneer Players were therefore more of an actors' society than a writers' society, although relatively more attention was paid to producing new plays (or plays new to a London stage) than to new actors or writers. Only a few dramatists had more than one play performed by the society and most plays were performed just once, or occasionally twice. New drama was actively sought. They promoted new writing, going to the lengths of researching and, if necessary, translating plays. Many of the dramatists, researchers and translators were also actors.

By contrast, the Pioneer Players' competitor, the Stage Society, was not associated with one director and seemed to favour writers, sponsoring, for instance, performances of plays by George Bernard Shaw. The Pioneer Players differed from the larger Stage Society by providing actors with a special membership status and favourable subscription rate. However, both organisations adopted the subscription society structure. This form of organisation was similar to that of the mutual societies of the co-operative movement in which members had a sense of ownership of the organisation. The Pioneer Players was neither a 'theatre company' (Holledge 1981: 103), nor an 'ensemble' (Case 1988: 35). It could not rely on a group of performers to be consistently available for hire to perform its plays. As a play-producing subscription society its audience and performers were drawn from its membership. Some joined in order to act in a specific play, and whilst most of the society's performers did rely on acting for their income, others were either amateurs or gaining experience in performance at the start of their careers.

The Pioneer Players' relationship with its actors had implications for the kinds of innovation, the society was able to make. It was not possible to develop a style of acting when the pool of available performers was always fluctuating. The society seems to have chosen the play first and then cast performers for the roles. The Pioneer Players appear to have been generally less exploitative of actors than other subscription societies. Although they produced many plays written by actors, they were not associated with individual actors or writers. The annual reports did not list all performances and did not attempt to characterise the work of the society. Christopher St. John claimed that 150 plays had been performed

(Adlard 1949: 10), but the annual reports recorded only 64 plays produced for subscription performances. These were authored by 62 dramatists. Only four plays were given repeat performances. Inevitably, then, locating and assessing the Pioneer Players' plays has been a principal objective of this study.[8] The difficulty in defining the Pioneer Players' work is significant, specifically because it was an organisation committed to change, to promoting social change and to responding to it, by engaging with controversial current events such as court cases, political campaigns and new legislation. This reactive aspect of the Pioneer Players' work resembled the responsiveness of the later 'Living Newspaper' of the American Federal Theatre Project (1935–9). However, the Pioneer Players also made plans for future productions, which were announced in their play programmes or newspapers though some of these were never fulfilled.[9]

In 1915 the Pioneer Players' production of an expressionist play by one of Russia's renowned modernist dramatists, Nikolai Evreinov,[10] marked a turn to art theatre. By 1920 Virginia Woolf was describing the effect of a Pioneer Players' performance on its audience in modernist terms. Modernism in the theatre has, of course, been notoriously hard to define, and drama has been generally omitted from literary studies of modernism.[11] Feminist critics are just beginning to explore the nexus of modernism, feminism and suffrage writings. Modernist drama developed in Germany, Russia and France, reaching the British theatre in translation; otherwise, as Christopher Innes has suggested, it appeared to pass Britain by (Innes 1993: 2). Initially, the Pioneer Players aligned their work with the 'play of ideas', associated with dramatists such as Bernard Shaw and Ibsen and formally with naturalism, with the 'new drama' and the 'free theatres'. The Pioneer Players were interested in combining a number of types of performance and art-forms. In addition to performing scripted plays, the society also staged a mime dramatisation of a ballad, three lectures, two costume balls and one harpsichord concert. The 'shock of the new' can, of course, be relentless. The number of innovative plays staged by the Pioneer Players is overwhelming, yet these historically significant productions are conspicuously absent from theatre histories.

Author-centred criticism has predisposed theatre history to study an individual dramatist's or actor's body of work, or the plays associated with an individual theatre building. The work of a society such as the Pioneer Players has therefore been difficult to place. Their eclectic approach was characteristic of modernist thinking, and reached a peak at a time of intense cultural change. The subscription society was, perhaps, a form of organisation flexible enough to respond rapidly to the political events and aesthetic whims associated with modernism; the financial overheads of a theatre building demand longer-term planning and commitment to economic success. Theatre societies such as the Pioneer Players have been described as 'testing grounds' or 'laboratories' (Orme 1936), where experiments were staged at little cost in anticipation of a successful run at a commercial theatre where greater investment would be forthcoming. For actors, as well as dramatists and investors, such experiments were deemed to be worth the risk (and the costs of unpaid labour): they provided a 'shop window' for the talents of actors and writers, advertising their abilities to write and perform unusual and technically demanding roles.

The experimentation of the Pioneer Players is, in retrospect, most evident in their selection of plays, which took a range of dramatic forms (naturalist, expressionist and poetic). Unconventional subject matter and forms were drawn from the drama of many countries. For other subscription societies the 'new drama' was specifically defined as new *English* drama and was associated with the movement for a national theatre as much as with the 'avant-garde'. As Josephine Guy (1991) has argued, the avant-garde is characterised by contingency rather than by formal definitions and mounts a reaction against a historically specific, moribund 'tradition' or past. It is therefore significant that, in spite of the Pioneer Players' persistent claim to represent the 'new', they achieved some continuity in their ideological positioning. The Pioneer Players were supportive of the theatre practitioner, of politically controversial issues and of innovative or newly discovered drama. They made space for women to experiment, developing acting and production skills with challenging roles and demanding mise-en-scènes. The Pioneer Players made significant steps in training practitioners, by extending the repertoire of available plays.

Supportive of women's writing for the stage generally, the Pioneer Players performed some plays by women in their first few years, which attracted considerable publicity. Yet the society also performed plays written by men (see Appendix II) and the annual reports show that, of the total number of plays performed in the subscription productions, the work of significantly more male than female dramatists was performed. The drama performed by the Pioneer Players cannot therefore be assessed exclusively as women's writing for the stage. However, in the context of their performance for the Pioneer Players' membership, some of the male-authored plays engage with gender in a provocative manner, as Edith Craig argued in a newspaper interview. The Pioneer Players prioritised performance, unafraid of cutting or adapting a play, challenging the authority of the author. The society's interests appear to have been iconoclastic. The diverse plays explored controversial issues, often representing women negotiating what were perceived as the 'separate spheres' of public and private life. Recurrent images of women in the roles of dancer, artist or worker confronted the sexual politics of the women's suffrage movement. The Pioneer Players' alignment with 'the foreign' during the First World War, for instance, manifested through the production of plays in translation, was defiant and signified the artistic freedom of non-combatants to continue to engage with current international work despite the conflict. Indirectly, this stance represented the attitude of women determined to continue their work during war-time; the disruption by war was rejected or denied. The ways in which the Pioneer Players' work developed through the women's suffrage movement and war-time are significant and difficult to interpret in that the Pioneer Players' response, typically, was unconventional, providing the exception to the rule presented by histories of war-time culture in Britain. But they are representative of the difficulties faced by women as workers and artists in the war and by men as unwilling combatants.

The Pioneer Players' story is exceptional. Their extraordinary history raises questions generally relevant to a number of different aspects of theatre history: the under-researched processes of production; the relationships between institutions, audience and reception; the significance of researching the exceptional rather than the commonplace. Such questions derive from feminist cultural materialist concerns in which theatrical production is regarded as a social practice taking place in historically specific moments. My analysis of the Pioneer Players' performance of gender in drama draws on new material from the Edith Craig Archive, the archives of the Lord Chamberlain in the British Library, the Theatre Museum, and also published autobiographies of actors and writers. Some basic questions needed to be explored. How were the Pioneer Players organised? What role did Edith Craig perform as founder and director of the society? Who were the Pioneer Players? What significance did the performances of their plays have for contemporary audiences?

The published membership lists and annual reports are the main sources of evidence for the Pioneer Players' declared agenda and constituency. A database has been used here in order to analyse for the first time the profile of the membership in terms of sex, membership status (acting or ordinary) and duration. The actual audiences for any of the society's performances were not recorded but left ephemeral traces when a reviewer happened to name individuals or when names for subscription ticket sales were recorded on a theatre seating plan. The Pioneer Players operated at a time when middle-class women, including suffragists, were being identified as a new commercial market. As one of many London-based play-producing subscription societies, the Pioneer Players needed to attract sufficient members to facilitate its continued existence. This depended on the Pioneer Players' projecting an attractive and coherent public image of itself as an organisation. This was organised by the society's own press agent and publicity committee. The practice of issuing press releases may partly explain the extensive range of newspapers that reviewed the society's productions.

Advertising space in Pioneer Players' play programmes was sold and the income generated was recorded in the society's accounts. These advertisements indicate the expected interests of the society's constituency. Advertisements for women's suffrage newspapers, such as the *Vote* or *Votes for Women* are juxtaposed with those for women's clothing from the department store Debenham and Freebody. The visual field of women's suffrage was analysed by Lisa Tickner (1987), while the specific relationships between the women's suffrage movement, theatre and fashion have been analysed by Joel Kaplan and Sheila Stowell (1994). More recently, Barbara Green (1997) has focused on the 'spectacularity' of suffrage activism as a site of strategic performances. However, positions in the processes of consumption and the gaze are unpredictable. In some of the Pioneer Players' plays, women are agents as well as objects of the gaze, and in their play programmes, advertisements for small businesses run by women interpellate women as producers as well as consumers in this new market. The effect of conflating political activist and feminine woman was destabilising: not merely ironic or exploitative but impossible within the terms of gender ideology.

The reception of the society's plays may be analysed through the newspaper reviews of the time. The interdisciplinarity of the methods used in this study derive from reading performance in terms of cultural representation, exploring the contexts and possibilities of performance, to consider in what ways the women who worked in the Pioneer Players were able to do so. Consequently, as Tracy Davis suggests for methods in feminist historiography, an examination of the institutional contexts in which women have, or have not, worked in theatre may provide a disruptive new perspective on theatre generally (Davis 1989). The Pioneer Players has been described as a 'women's theatre company' (Holledge 1981: 103), earning a place in the history of 'feminist performance' (Aston 1995: 31), through its egalitarian deployment of women. However, this study shows that the society's working practices challenged, in an uneven and complex fashion, the dominant categories of the amateur/professional and the aesthetic/political. This history of the Pioneer Players shows the difficulties facing women in the theatre and demonstrates some of the compromises as well as the strategies used to overcome them, such as working informally, autonomously or collaboratively, outside or between institutions. This will be a narrative attentive to the Pioneer Players' failures and compromises, as well as their achievements.

The Pioneer Players produced plays new to a British stage for its membership. A subscription fee guaranteed each member a seat at five productions year in whatever theatre or public hall had been borrowed or hired for the occasion. As a theatre society without a permanent building, the Pioneer Players shared this precarious form of organisation with other 'free theatres' in Britain, France and other western countries. Chapter 2 considers the Pioneer Players' place in this movement and namely, 'The Costs of a Free Theatre'. Issue-based drama and the Pioneer Players' relationship to a developing dramatic form are explored in Chapter 3: The Feminist Play of Ideas and the Art of Propaganda and Chapter 4: Pioneers Perform Politics. The society developed from the success of Edith Craig's nationwide productions as freelance director of plays in support of women's suffrage and from her work with the Actresses' Franchise League (AFL). In contrast to the AFL, the Pioneer Players did not define themselves in terms of any single political movement or group. The Pioneer Players' constituency was drawn from a middle-class, theatre-going audience, women and supporters of women's suffrage and other political movements: groups which overlapped but which occasionally voiced their differences. The society engaged with contemporary gender issues, discussed in Chapter 5: Working Women, and in Chapter 6: Outside Marriage. The development of the society is charted in Chapter 7: The Luck of War. As Chapter 8: Translating Art Theatre, shows, the Pioneer Players successfully performed plays in translation and plays which spoke to women's suffrage and other campaigns. When the break was made in 1915 to establish itself as an 'art theatre', the Pioneer Players did not acknowledge any inconsistency in their activities. The way in which these changes came about, provoked unresolved tensions in the Pioneer Players' work and a persistent discomfort in their critics. Conforming to the pragmatism of women's suffrage politics and embracing diversity, the Pioneer Players rejected the prevailing principles of literary culture, which regarded the political and the aesthetic as separable and which revered the author's text above all else. In this rejection lies the destabilising force of the Pioneer Players in literary history.

2
The Costs of a Free Theatre

Raymond Williams has argued that the crisis of the 'transitional' period towards the end of the nineteenth century generated a renaissance in drama through the 'free theatre movement' (Williams 1983: 171). The Pioneer Players' contribution to this movement has received little attention (Watson 1970; Stokes 1972; Woodfield 1984). It has been associated rather with figures such as George Bernard Shaw, John Galsworthy and Harley Granville-Barker. The free theatre movement was organised by a progressive fraction of the middle class outside of, but dependent on, the commercial theatres and concerned with class and national identities.[1] However, within this group a female subset emerged. The 'new drama' promoted by this movement was not only concerned with representations of a dissident femininity, notoriously characterised by Nora in Ibsen's *A Doll's House*, but was also driven by real dissident women working in the theatre; women such as Janet Achurch, Florence Farr and Elizabeth Robins. Feminist critics have begun to explore the contribution of such individual women to the English 'free theatre' movement, as actors, but especially as managers and promoters of plays (Gardner and Rutherford 1992; John 1995; Litz 1996). Female actors and male writers were the prime movers in Britain.

The movement had a place in the process of constructing a national identity, and of challenging those cultural representations permitted by state regulation or censorship. Matthew Arnold's injunction to 'organise the theatre' in England responded specifically to performances by French theatre practitioners in London in 1882. Arnold was generally concerned with a middle-class audience and a selective dramatic canon rather than any kind of popular forms or audience. The formation of national or popular theatres in England and France constituted an assertion of national unity in response to the crisis posed by diverse groups pressing for democratic representation (Kruger 1995). The Pioneer Players shared with the other free or independent theatres in England their hostility to the legal restrictions in the theatre which, it was widely claimed, amounted to censorship. Experimentation was couched in Romantic terms of novelty, freedom and pioneering for the 'free theatres'. It was the Pioneer Players who appropriated the colonial subjectivity of the 'pioneer' for feminism. In this and in other significant ways, they differed from the other free theatre societies, as this chapter will demonstrate. An analysis of the organisational structure of the society and its differences from the larger Stage Society establishes that it was unique in its support of women in the theatre and in its fundraising role for the women's suffrage movement and other political campaigns.

In this context, the Pioneer Players' challenge to the censorship of the stage was oppositional rather than alternative, linked to an increasingly decisive political movement for women's enfranchisement. As Martha Vicinus (1985) has argued, many women motivated by greater access to education and economic independence towards the end of the nineteenth century were recognising the limitations of existing institutions and beginning to organise their own. Such a context was significant for the establishment of the Pioneer Players. The organisation was also emulating the play-producing subscription society, associated with the European free theatre movement, particularly the *Théâtre Libre* inaugurated in 1887 by André Antoine. This form of organisation was relatively informal and relatively autonomous. Without a theatre building and with a fluctuating membership, economic restrictions were minimised.

In Britain, the challenges to the Theatre Licensing Act 1737 gave rise to general debate about censorship. The free theatre movement therefore attracted liberal reformers interested in the wider issues of freedom of expression rather than specifically theatrical experiment (Knowles 1934). The most vociferous campaigners for a free stage were not theatre practitioners but journalists and writers. One repeated complaint concerned the covert and inconsistent approach to the process of assessing plays. Between 1737 and 1968 a copy of the script of a play had to be submitted to the Lord Chamberlain's Office prior to public performance in theatres. The play would then be read, licensed, refused a licence or returned with recommendations for alteration. During the period of this study, the readers for the Lord Chamberlain were Charles Brookfield, Ernest Radford and G. S. Street. Since the play-producing societies were performing plays for their membership, sometimes in public halls rather than theatres, their performances were technically private and therefore did not require a licence. The Shelley Society exploited this loophole for its unlicensed production in 1886 of *The Cenci*, a precedent followed by many subscription societies, including the Pioneer Players. Infamously, the Independent Theatre gave an unlicensed production of Ibsen's *Ghosts* (1891). It has been assumed that it was the reference to a genetically-acquired sexually transmitted disease which made the play so controversial. However, Tracy Davis has shown that it was the exploitation of the subscription society as a means of organising the production of the play that was innovative (Davis 1990: 448). The powerlessness of the law to prevent its staging to a large theatre audience rather than the theme of the play provoked anxiety.

It was often the actions of the female characters in the 'new drama' which led to a licence being refused. In the 1892 Select Committee Report, the Examiner of Plays' objection to Ibsen's plays on moral grounds seems to amount to a rejection of any challenge to conventional gender roles:

> I have studied Ibsen's plays pretty carefully, and all the characters in Ibsen's plays appear to me morally deranged. All the heroines are dissatisfied spinsters who look on marriage as a monopoly, or dissatisfied married women in a chronic state of rebellion against not only the conditions which nature has imposed on their sex, but against all the duties and obligations of mothers and wives; and as for the men they are all rascals or imbeciles.
>
> (Woodfield 1984: 113)

Ibsen's *Ghosts* had been performed in England thanks to the efforts of Kate Santley, manager of the venue, and J.T. Grein, founder of the Independent Theatre (1891). The history of women's place in the free theatre movement provides an appropriate context in which to understand the work of the Pioneer Players. The society was developing the efforts made by individual women in staging such plays and doing so with the benefit of a wide network of cultural organisations established by women committed to women's enfranchisement.

The Pioneer Players overtly challenged the Lord Chamberlain's control of the theatre in the first few years of their activities. They performed 'privately' several unlicensed plays and through their affiliation to the women's suffrage movement had a particular interest in challenging the censorship of representations of women. One such example was Laurence Housman's play, *Pains and Penalties*, about Caroline of Brunswick (1768–1821), tried for adultery in the House of Lords in 1820 at the instigation of her husband, George IV (Smith 1993; Fraser 1996).

At the end of the Pioneer Players' production of *Pains and Penalties*, reviewed in *The Times* under the heading 'Incident at the Savoy' (*The Times* 27 November 1911: 8), the new Joint Examiner of plays, Charles Brookfield (1857–1913), was named and indicted in a debate (Housman 1937: 248; Woodfield 1984: 100). Brookfield's appointment had proved controversial because of his involvement with frivolous revues. Harley Granville-Barker, at Elizabeth Robins's request, made a speech.[2] It seems that the audience was invited to take part in a post-performance vote. Granville-Barker proposed a resolution – carried carried unanimously – that the Lord Chamberlain was out of touch with the theatre (Housman 1937: 248). The Caroline Society was thus formed 'to preserve the memory of Queen Caroline...from the oblivion designed for it by the Lord Chamberlain' (Findlater 1967: 118). The theatre building and the occasion of a private performance had become a forum for debate, the stage a platform for lobbying.

Laurence Housman (1865–1959) was an artist and writer who became actively involved in a number of political campaigns for civil liberties, including women's suffrage and anti-censorship. He had referred to the plot of *Pains and Penalties* as a hypothetical case in his testimony at the 1909 deputation to debate the Theatre Licensing Act (Knowles 1934: 98). It was to have been the first performance at Gertrude Kingston's Little Theatre. Housman gave readings of the play at the Beckstein Hall on 29 October 1910 (*Vote* 15 October 1910: ii). In his autobiography he acknowledged that it was the unorthodox representation of a monarch which transgressed the licensing regulations (Housman 1937: 244). He pursued this relentlessly by writing numerous plays about Queen Victoria.

Two months after the 'Incident at the Savoy', the Lord Chamberlain was consistent in his refusal to license the Pioneer Players' non-subscription performance in January 1912 of *The Coronation* by Christopher St. John and Charles Thursby. This play concerned the political awakening of the king on the day of his coronation, under the influence of a working-class woman. The controversial aspects of the play include the representation of a monarch manipulated by politicians and prepared to intervene in the government and the representation of a working-class woman who is both articulate and politically effective. Since *The Coronation* was one of the Pioneer Players' fund-raising productions, the Lord Chamberlain's refusal to license it had an impact on the organisation for which funds were being raised.[3] In this case the International Suffrage Shop was deprived of a large, paying audience:

As however, [the play] has been judged to be unfit for public performance, the money which had been paid for the tickets had to be returned, and the audience were present at a dramatic At Home as invited guests, and were therefore regarded, by a polite fiction, as a collection of private individuals.

(*The Times*, 29 January 1912: 10)

The Pioneer Players exploited this publicity to further the anti-censorship campaign, and the audience was invited to join the Coronation Society (Findlater 1967: 119).

According to Lady Cynthia Asquith (1887–1960), such 'polite fiction' in evasion of the Lord Chamberlain's authority was a crucial function, even a characteristic, of the Pioneer Players. Lady Cynthia, married to the Prime Minister's second son, Herbert, left in her diaries a valuable record of her social milieu. She commented on her attendance of the Pioneer Players' dramatisation of Pierre Louÿs' The *Girl and the Puppet* which had not been submitted for a licence:

Alex called for me at four and we went off to see a play given by the Pioneer Society. It's a ridiculous bit of chicanery – the censorship being dodged by calling themselves a 'Society' and having tickets on the subscriber system. The performances are always on Sundays.

(Asquith 1987: 411)

Although this impression was mistaken as regards the restriction to Sunday performances, it was formed in 1918, at a time when the society was ostensibly less concerned with challenging the licensing laws. The 'chicanery' of the Pioneer Players' apparently covert operations emphasises the extent to which any of the theatre societies were challenging the law. In fact, each of the unlicensed performances given by the Pioneer Players was reviewed in national newspapers. As James Woodfield and Richard Findlater have noted, circumvention of the Theatre Licensing Act was to a certain extent tolerated. Challenges to the Theatre Licensing Law were posed in two ways: by performing plays without a licence; and by submitting for licence plays that tested the undisclosed criteria used for granting a licence. Even though the Pioneer Players did not *require* a licence for any of its subscription performances, the society sought one on many occasions.[4] Submission of a play for a licence may have encouraged theatre managers to produce it for public performance, earning the Pioneer Players some royalties. Presumably when extensive cuts or the outright refusal of a licence were anticipated, the society adopted a different strategy. On at least two occasions, one of which was the production witnessed by Lady Cynthia Asquith, plays were not submitted for a licence. This was a strategy which Edith Craig admitted in an interview with Dorothy Knowles, historian of theatre censorship. The Pioneer Players had thus proceeded with productions of A. D'Este Scott, *The Daughters of Ishmael*, and Pierre Louys and Charles Frondaie, *The Girl and the Puppet* (Knowles 1934: 161–62).

The society sometimes chose a venue over which the Lord Chamberlain had no jurisdiction. If the unlicensed play were privately performed in a public building or theatre, the management could face action under the Theatre Act 1843 when attempting to renew the licence for the building. This happened at the Grand Theatre, Islington after its unlicensed production of *Ghosts* (Woodfield 1984: 44). On many occasions the Pioneer Players made use of the King's Hall in the National Sporting Club in order that, as Craig said in an interview, 'there may be no fuss about any possible censoring' (*Pall Mall Gazette* 13 April 1912: 5). Craig's confident characterisation of the law as 'fuss' was influenced by the audacious law-breaking of the suffrage activists. Plays were performed in support of the women's suffrage movement in unusual spaces, including private homes and even (in at least one instance) in Eustace Miles' vegetarian restaurant, London.[5] For the Pioneer Players the priority was to stage the play for an audience rather than to stage it in a particularly elaborate manner which would require the facilities and acting space of a theatre.

When the Pioneer Players submitted plays for a licence it found itself in the same position as predecessors like the Independent Theatre Society. The Lord Chamberlain was still sensitive to references to women's independence, particularly in taking control of their own bodies, either in sexual intercourse outside marriage or in abortion. The representation of even the possibility that women might attempt to make decisions about reproductive and sexual choices challenged medical discourse and gender ideology. Specifically, constructing a choice for women regarding sexual activity and reproduction directly challenged the dominant notion that pregnancy was a natural and inevitable, if mysterious, event in a woman's life. The Lord Chamberlain's reports on two plays performed in 1915 by the Pioneer Players – Edward Knoblock's *Mouse* and Nikolai Evreinov's *The Theatre of the Soul* – demonstrate that attitudes were changing towards the representation of pregnancy outside marriage. The context of such representations has a direct relationship to the meanings it generates. As Jonathan Dollimore says of the censorship of Renaissance drama:

what makes an idea subversive is not so much what is intrinsic to it or the mere thinking of it, but the context of its articulation – to whom, and to how many and in what circumstances it is said or written.
(Dollimore 1989: 22)

Thus the Lord Chamberlain was concerned with what he perceived to be the central thesis of a play, with the way in which the reference to a 'problematic' issue functioned within the text, and with the expected audience for the play. In 1915, G. S. Street, the Reader of Plays, demanded that the Pioneer Players delete the reference to abortion in Edward Knoblock's *Mouse*, with the following explanation:

It is certainly a strong play, well written and well arranged and the character of Elsie, in its defiant selfishness, is especially well drawn. It is also 'strong meat' and undoubtadely [sic] not a play to ban, as some years ago it would have been banned, and in my opinion it should it should [sic] be licensed. The physical fact is that the girl is going to have a baby and *in a serious play* [my emphasis] I think there is nothing wrong in that. I would cross out, however, a passage Act II, p. 20 in which Elsie tells Paul a doctor had 'refused to listen' to her: that points to the idea of abortion and should come out.
(ADD LCP 1915/32; BL)

The play, ending with the public denunciation of the pregnant woman and a reconciliation of the other characters through marriage, conforms to the plot structure of the well-made play. Ian Clarke has suggested that in such plays 'transgressions against the dominant code eventually will out and those who, according to that code, deserve stricture, will be dealt with appropriately' (Clarke 1989: 35). The Reader permitted the representation of an illegitimate pregnancy but would have censored any discussion of abortion. He concluded that abortion was not the central theme of *Mouse*:

Otherwise it is not a play like 'Waste',[6] which was concerned with abortion and banned for that reason, and though I can quite understand that another view might be taken, it is recommended for license.
(G. S. Street, ADD LCP 1915/32; BL)

The acknowledgement of diverse opinions was disingenuous. The authority to regulate performance resided with the Reader of Plays.

In the same year, the Pioneer Players submitted Nikolai Evreinov's *The Theatre of the Soul* for a licence. This was partly to test the Lord Chamberlain's response against that of André Charlot (1882–1956), the manager of the Alhambra, who had already withdrawn his permission for the play to be performed.[7] Lady Muriel Paget (1876–1938) had invited the Pioneer Players to perform the play as part of a charity matinée to raise funds for aid to Russia. She organised medical aid for Russia during the First World War, opening the Anglo-Russian Hospital in the Dmitri Palace, Petrograd in January 1916 (Blunt 1962). Much to Paget's embarrassment, without reason or warning Charlot rejected the play. The play was published by Henderson's, advertising itself provocatively as 'The Bomb Shop' a reference to its subversive literature. This edition of the play, translated by Christopher St. John and Marie Potapenko, was sold in an envelope bearing the slogan, 'The play that was banned at the Alhambra' (Plate 2). St. John's introduction claimed, accurately, that it had been passed by the Lord Chamberlain for licence, but she failed to mention that this was subject to deletions regarding the reference to abortion. The report stated:

> I have marked on p. 9 a phrase which seems to refer to abortion, 'kill them for the sake of their precious figures': perhaps that should best be cut out, though in a *serious play* [my emphasis] as this, I should hesitate to do so.
>
> (ADD LCP 1915/31; BL)

The apparently conciliatory tone of this report, with the implication that some negotiation was possible, belied the force of the law. Yet as the Lord Chamberlain's reports of this period demonstrate, pragmatism and uncertainty characterised the discourse of censorship.

These extracts from the Lord Chamberlain's reports on plays performed by the Pioneer Players indicate the society's role as a pressure group for law reform and demonstrate the unstable borders of permissible dramatic representations. The different criteria imposed by the Lord Chamberlain on 'a serious play' signify the assumptions regarding the class composition of the expected audience for dramatic art. This was distinguished from popular forms in music halls that were beyond the jurisdiction of the Lord Chamberlain's powers (Woodfield 1984: 115), and often challenged the narrow limits of 'decency' imposed on theatres. The can-can craze (1870–4), and the suggestive performance of Bessie Bellwood, Marie Lloyd and Kate Harvey, demonstrated that, as Tracy Davis suggests:

the difference between the moral regulation of theatres and music halls was not so much a matter of audience standards, repertoire, or protection of the public good, but rather a question of the authorities' habit, ability, and inclination to recognize certain types of problems and repress certain types of performance.

(Davis 1991: 118)

This pragmatism produced some inconsistent decisions, but the Lord Chamberlain's decision was final. In the case of the Pioneer Players' treatment by André Charlot, Christopher St. John demanded a public apology and explanation for his defamatory actions. St. John wrote a letter on behalf of the society in the strongest, potentially litigious, terms. It is likely that Charlot objected to *The Theatre of the Soul* on the same grounds as the Lord Chamberlain licensed it, precisely because it was a 'serious play'. In the opinion of J. Fisher White, a member of the Pioneer Players, Charlot considered that the play was too serious for an Alhambra audience (unpublished letter from Fisher White to Edith Craig, 21 November 1915; 3.762, ECCF). The Alhambra, originally a music hall, had, under Charlot's management, staged Ballets Russes in 1911 but was more generally associated with spectacular revues.

The Pioneer Players were manipulating the common belief that the Lord Chamberlain's licence was an index of a play's respectability. This is exemplified in the reviews of the Pioneer Players' first production of three one-act plays which were censured in spite of the fact that the Lord Chamberlain had licensed them. Margaret Wynne Nevinson's play *In the Workhouse* criticised the law of coverture, exposing the logical consequences of the legal status of women as men's property. Nevinson had a legal background, working as a Poor Law Guardian and later becoming the first female Justice of the Peace. Since the play includes a mother and baby and is set in a women's ward in a workhouse, many reviewers and some recent critics have assumed that it was set in a maternity ward (Holledge 1981: 127; Wolf 1989: 178). This elision of women and motherhood exposes the dominant expectations of women's role which writers such as Nevinson had to challenge. The representation of women as subjects needed to overcome the automatic objectification of women in performance which has been theorised as the 'male gaze'. This was no easy task as Peggie Phelan's analysis of the difficulties of representation indicates:

Representation is almost always on the side of the one who looks and almost never on the side of the one who is seen.... Visibility and invisibility are crucially bound; invisibility polices visibility and in this specific sense functions as the ascendant term in the binary. Gaining visibility for the politically under-represented without scrutinizing the power of who is required to display what to whom is an impoverished political agenda.

(Phelan 1993: 25–6)

The central image of women talking was therefore invisible to most of the reviewers. The perceived (but inaccurate) setting of the scene – in a maternity ward – dominated. In her article 'A Bewildered Playwright', published in the *Vote*, Nevinson wrote: 'The criticisms are strange and bewildering; only about five percent, have at all understood the point of the play.' The conflict of ideological positions occupied by dramatist and critics was marked. Significantly, Nevinson discussed it in terms of visibility, alert to the mimetic conventions employed by the critics and the ideological effects of concealment and repression that those conventions serve:

Many papers accuse me of immorality and defying the Censor, but this latter is not true, for In the Workhouse is officially licensed.... The Press adopts a kind of Christian Science attitude: 'There is no evil as long as it is not mentioned, however dark the foul places of the earth. For God's sake, let us keep them dark; let us draw a veil'.

(Nevinson 1911: 68)

Since the play had been licensed it had received official sanction but the critics could not, or would not, address themselves to the issues the play was debating: that of the legal status of women, and ways in which women were oppressed in marriage, work or prostitution. However, some reviewers appear to have been shocked by the play because they believed that it condemned marriage as such. Although this is a possible interpretation of the play, it is one that Nevinson rejected.

The 'free theatre' was therefore envisaged as free from censorship and from the commercial theatre's insistence on profitable productions. Such freedom derived from Locke the idea of independence and from Rousseau ideas of autonomy and political liberty (Merquior 1991: 116). The cultivation of a theatre for a minority audience along these lines has been described in terms of a controversial stance. The free theatres were, in Raymond Williams' terms, alternative cultural formations in that they offered to produce drama ordinarily ignored by existing institutions (Williams 1983: 70). They can be considered to be 'oppositional' only to the extent that their productions were 'raised to active opposition to the established institutions, or more generally to the conditions within which these exist' (Williams 1983: 70). The Pioneer Players, and organisations such as the Independent Theatre (founded in 1891) and the Stage Society (founded in 1899), were oppositional in the public campaign against stage censorship. In addition, to the extent that the Pioneer Players' drama represented the interests of women and the organised political campaign for women's suffrage, it challenged the established patriarchal institutions of both theatre and parliament. In this respect the Pioneer Players was oppositional in a way which distinguished them from the Stage Society. This was written into the Pioneer Players' constitution, the first objective being: 'To produce plays dealing with all kinds of movements of interest at the moment' (*PPAR 1911–12*: 3).

The Pioneer Players' constituency reflects the changed class composition of the acting profession which, from the late nineteenth century, drew many middle-class women, some of whom had engaged in political action for women's suffrage. For many female theatre practitioners the issue of 'freedom' in the free theatre movement was not confined to challenging the Lord Chamberlain. Cicely Hamilton (1872–1952), suffrage activist and prolific writer, was one of many actors to write in her autobiography of the oppressive conditions endured by women in the theatre. In addition to inequalities of pay, Hamilton recalled the nepotism of male theatre managers casting their lovers in prime roles, the considerable expense of providing elaborate costume and the unpredictable quality of lodgings when on tour. Theatre societies such as the Pioneer Players provided an opportunity to challenge practices adopted by the commercial theatres, and the other avant-garde theatres which, either by accident or design, did not encourage women working within them.

The extent to which the Pioneer Players challenged such practices and supported women working in the theatre may be measured by considering the Pioneer Players' organisational structure, constituency and modes of operation. The rest of this chapter will therefore provide a general account of the Pioneer Players' institutional context, identifying the tensions at play and concentrating on how the Pioneer Players worked rather than what they performed. It is precisely this kind of analysis that tends to be marginalised in favour of an attention to the play, its staging, and the dramatist.

The Pioneer Players had a formal elected membership and sub-committees, held annual general meetings, and presented annual reports and accounts. The society was hierarchical; it had an annually elected advisory committee, which precluded the dominance of any single individual including Edith Craig. The advisory committee was later renamed the council, possibly emulating the Stage Society which had a council of management rather than an executive. The Pioneer Players' advisory committee or council changed from year to year. Throughout the society's life the sex ratio of its membership was 15:51 female to male (see Appendix II).[8] The aristocratic constituency of the society's advisory committee was female. Five women, Edith Craig, Gabrielle Enthoven, Christopher St. John, Olive Terry and Ellen Terry, were members of the committee throughout the life of the society (1911–20) and brought invaluable skills. St. John was an historian and translator as well as a writer, having already proved herself as Ellen Terry's 'literary henchman'. As Edith Craig's partner since 1899 she was a keen collaborator in Craig's work in the theatre. Olive Terry, Ellen Terry's niece, was a performer. Gabrielle Enthoven became responsible for the record of the society's work, compiling collections of press cuttings.

The political affiliations of the ten members of the first advisory committee indicate some of the influences on the Pioneer Players' early work. A significant number were prominent figures from the broad spectrum of women's suffrage politics, both militant and constitutional organisations, with differing positions on party politics. Laurence Housman had already worked with Edith Craig, designing women's suffrage processions and working for the Suffrage Atelier. He was founder member of the Men's League for Women's Suffrage (and in 1917 founder with Edward Carpenter of the Society for the Study of Sex Psychology). Marie Lawson was editor of the WFL's newspaper, *The Vote*. Sime Seruya founded the International Suffrage Shop and (with Winifred Mayo) the AFL. It is likely that two members, Mrs Drummond and Mrs Auerbach, were suffragists: Mrs Flora Drummond was a famous activist in the WSPU; and Mrs Helena Auerbach was vice-president of the Jewish League for Woman Suffrage, a member of the executive and later treasurer of the NUWSS (1913–14). Gabrielle (Mrs Charles) Enthoven, Cicely Hamilton, Christopher St. John and Olive Terry were suffrage activists, drawn from Craig's circle of friends. Charlotte (Mrs Bernard) Shaw seems to have taken little part in the Pioneer Players, other than in name.

Members of the Pioneer Players' executive changed throughout the society's life, as did the name of its managing body. The Advisory Committee was later renamed the Executive. After the society's most successful year, 1916–17, the management structure of the society was changed in an attempt to consolidate this position. From 1917–18 a selected number of the much larger advisory committee formed the smaller executive committee which Lady Maud Warrender chaired. The officers of president (Ellen Terry) and honorary managing director (Edith Craig) remained constant throughout. The honorary treasurer and honorary secretary were subject to the most change. Some stability was achieved in 1915–16 when these posts were held respectively by Irene Cooper Willis and Christopher St. John. The position of hon. treasurer was held in the first four years by, consecutively, Lady Sybil Smith, Olive Terry, Hon. Mrs E. Fitzgerald and Nona Stewart. The position of honorary secretary was held by Florence Nordon (1911–12) and Geraldine L'Estrange (1913–14). The post holder was not named for two years (1912–13, 1914–15) and the reason was not given in the annual reports. From 1915–16 Christopher St. John was named as secretary, often in a temporary or honorary capacity. As suggested in the annual reports, members were loath to commit themselves to participation in the management structure, abdicating this responsibility to Craig and her friends. Marie Lawson held the office of honorary auditor from 1911 to 1916, after which time the auditor was not named. In naming an honorary solicitor, Arthur Veasey (1911–14) the society took an expedient measure considering the uneasy legal position regarding the 'chicanery' or 'polite fiction' of staging unlicensed plays.

Assumptions have been made about both the Pioneer Players' membership and its audience which need to be questioned. Although the society claimed to perform plays exclusively for its membership, tickets were made available to non-members, who were invited as guests. This practice explains how some individuals who were never members attended some of the Pioneer Players' plays.[9] Since it is unlikely that the entire membership was present at each performance, the membership lists do not represent the actual audience for each play. There is no record of the actual audience for any production, although there are some references to named (famous) individuals in newspaper reviews. The society's handbills prove that, at least for the production of *Mrs Warren's Profession*, tickets were obtainable from members. The membership of the society is recorded in its lists of ordinary and acting members, and these show that the society always had a majority of female members, but that the membership fluctuated. Some members left the society and later rejoined. Other members failed to sustain their subscription for financial reasons, but on at least one occasion members left the society disenchanted with the society's selection of a particular play: George Bernard Shaw's *Mrs Warren's Profession*.

The rates and types of membership available indicate the economic position of the Pioneer Players' expected membership. There were four different types of membership and rates of annual subscription: patrons 31s 6d; members 21s; associates 10s 6d; acting members 1s. The status and entitlements of these different forms of membership were not defined in the constitution, which merely states that annual subscription entitled the member to one seat at each subscription performance. The Pioneer Players' inclusion of 'patrons' in the highest rate of annual subscription recalls an earlier form of social relation in which artists were dependent on patronal support (Williams 1983: 44). While all the society's members could be considered patrons in one sense, the inclusion of this category of membership may indicate an ambivalence towards the market culture in which it was operating (Williams 1983: 48). State patronage was ultimately sought for theatre, culminating in the establishment of the National Theatre in England (opened in 1976) and in recognition through a higher education training and qualification. The lowest subscription was accorded to acting members, encouraging the large proportion of theatre workers which made up the membership. Other societies did not favour actors in this way. The Stage Society, for instance, did not list actors separately in its annual reports and did not grant them any special status in respect of different rates of subscription. The Play Actors differed in that they drew all of their members from the Actors' Association, producing several important plays written by women including Elizabeth Baker, Cicely Hamilton and Edith Ellis. The Pioneer Players may therefore have acknowledged the inequities of the system within which they were working by offering low subscriptions to actors who were otherwise subsidising the 'free theatre' by performing without pay.

Experimentation has its price: the subscription society's anti-commercial stance was problematic in relation to the pay of its actors. George Bernard Shaw and Nigel Playfair had reservations about this issue (Woodfield 1984: 61). The subscription society could not divorce itself from the commercial theatre which ordinarily employed most of its actors and provided them with a wage which unofficially underwrote the experiments of the avant-garde. In the Pioneer Players' first annual report it was announced that both professional and amateur actors would be used. Through the pre-war period, the membership of actors had remained fairly stable compared with that of the ordinary membership. The list of professional actors was impressive. Some like Basil Rathbone, applied, hoping for a part in the next production.[10] For actors, this was an opportunity to advertise their professional skills to potential employers in the audience. But there was some risk involved in acting in an unlicensed publicly performed play, as Jerome K. Jerome recalled: 'in those days the feeling against Ibsen was almost savage, and no player prominently connected with his plays was ever forgiven' (Jerome 1926: 157). At the same time, the subscription society's use of amateurs could be seen as a threat to the professional actor rather than as a radical step, as Tickner has suggested was the case with the Suffrage Atelier with which Edith Craig was involved (Tickner 1987: 24). J. T. Grein had been criticised for engaging an amateur in Ibsen's *Ghosts* (Orme 1936: 83).

Such hidden costs of the 'free' theatre were addressed in a play written by Rose Mathews and performed by the Play Actors society in June 1908 in aid of the debenture debt of the Actors' Association. In *The Parasites: A Story of the Seamy Side of Life*, the cast included 'Stage Aspirants', 'Extra Ladies who are paid to walk on' and 'Extra ladies who have paid premiums to walk on'. The *Stage* judged the play 'A vigorous and impassioned indictment of bogus agents and premium paying amateurs' (D131 ECD). But for actors in subscription societies a commitment to both the agenda of the subscription society and the play often seem temporarily to have taken precedence over their employment rights. This may have been tolerated by professional actors who did not rely on the subscription society for their income.

By 1917–18 the Pioneer Players were emphasising professionalism, a dependence on professional actors and the need to maintain high standards in spite of the war:

> the fluctuating fortunes of the commercial theatre have reacted on us in this respect. Plays have suddenly collapsed, and actors and actresses who had promised to play for us have had to resign parts in our productions owing to engagements which they could not possibly foresee.
> (*PPAR 1917–18*: 7)

It was only after the Pioneer Players' peak of success in 1916–17 that major changes in the society's procedure were introduced. At the beginning of the year an entrance fee came into force. There was a slight improvement in the society's financial situation. Paid secretarial help was secured from December 1918 and the payment of rehearsal expenses to actors was instigated, providing further evidence that the society was aware of this problematic relationship with its actors. As soon as the society's financial situation improved, it acknowledged the work of its actors with a token payment. This continued in spite of the introduction of the Entertainment Tax which imposed further financial constraints on the society to the extent of a loss of 12 per cent of its income.[11]

From a financial as well as a professional viewpoint, authors, like actors, were in a difficult position in the free theatre (Housman 1937: 260). An author would gain publicity from a Pioneer Players' production but little income, as the society's 'note for authors' shows:

> 4. The Society is responsible for the cost of production. No fees are paid to authors. The number of performances of each play is determined by the capacity of the theatre and the membership of the Society. More than two will not be given without the consent of the author or his representative.
> 5. The Society reserves the right to sell seats at one or more performances; the proceeds of such sale to belong exclusively to the Society.
> 6. Should any management in the British Empire or the U.S.A. accept for production of a play or translation of a play originally produced by the Pioneer Players within twelve months of the Society's performances, the author or translator shall pay to the Society one-fourth of the royalties received until the cost of production is refunded: or, if sold outright, the author or translator shall pay to the Society the amount of the cost of production, or one fourth of the purchase price, whichever is less.
>
> ('The Pioneer Players' Society. To Authors', nd; Theatre Museum)

Significantly, no specifications are given regarding the representation of women in the plays. The Pioneer Players had therefore chosen not to emulate the precedent set by Lena Ashwell's Kingsway Theatre, which explicitly insisted on good parts for women in plays submitted for performance (Knoblock 1939: 87). However, since most of the plays selected by the Pioneer Players conformed to this standard, it may have been an implicit criterion, understood by those submitting plays for production and implemented by the Play Secretary who read through the numerous plays submitted.[12]

The significance of the Pioneer Players in offering opportunities for female theatre practitioners should not be underestimated, but needs to be qualified. While it has been assumed that the Pioneer Players supported women's writing for the stage, a statistical analysis of the annual reports does not bear this out.[13] For four years of the society's existence, the sex ratio of dramatists' work performed was equal, while for the other five years more male than female dramatists' work was performed.

Indeed, in one year (1917–18) all the plays performed for the subscription performances were male-authored. As regards the directorial role, the Pioneer Players clearly supported its founder, Edith Craig. However, although she directed most of the society's plays she did so unpaid until, in 1917–18, an anonymous donation of £100 enabled the society to pay her a fee for each of the season's four productions (PPAR 1917–18: 8). Other individuals, including men, directed plays for the society. Cicely Hamilton was the only woman other than Craig to direct a play: her own, *Jack and Jill and a Friend*. Some male dramatists directed (or co-directed with Craig) their plays for the society,[14] while some male actors turned to direction.[15] Directors or 'producers' received little remuneration from the society, as Leon M. Lion's letter to Craig reveals:

> In respect of the Pioneer's [sic], it is rather difficult to quote terms for 'producing', as I presume, like the Stage Society, their work is mostly for honour and glory, and their material rewards commensurately scant.
> (Unpublished letter from Leon M. Lion to Edith Craig, 10 May 1915; 3.450. ECCF)

Subscription societies relied on commercial theatres as venues. This gave rise to an uneasy relationship between the overtly anti-commercial avant-garde theatres and the theatre managers who lent or hired their theatres. Some theatre managers were interested in supporting experiments for the sake of innovation and for profit; a successful experiment might turn into a long run if spotted early by a theatre manager. The Pioneer Players benefited from their royalties when a play was taken up by a commercial theatre. *Romanticismo* by the Italian dramatist, Gerolamo Rovetta (1851–1910), was staged at the Ambassador's Theatre after the society's production had 'secured for it a brilliant success' (*PPAR 1917–18*: 8). Most of the Pioneer Players' plays were performed in theatres lent to the society by theatre managers. The importance of contacts in theatre management became a decisive factor in the society's history because promised venues were withdrawn at the last moment. In 1914, when *Paphnutius* was transferred several hours before performance, Edith Craig was seen transporting props on a handcart across Covent Garden (Adlard 1949: 28). The society's annual reports give no reasons for the unexpected unavailability of theatres in which plays were to be performed. Theatre managers gave priority to the production of a commercial play from which they would profit.

The Pioneer Players, unlike the earlier Independent Theatre, never needed to resort to a competition in order to attract new plays. Their success was signified by the freedom to choose plays. In 1917–18, for instance, Clare Atwood as Play Secretary dealt with 122 plays: 'Of these 102 have been read, 10 have been passed, and 92 have been returned to their authors. Twenty are still under consideration' (PPAR 1917–18: 9). The society was nevertheless constrained in its selection by the direct relationship between the number of members and the plays produced. Since plays were produced for its membership in a technically private space, the subscription society's funds were derived solely from membership subscriptions. As such, the performance was not produced to make a profit. This was a widely approved method of supporting experimentation when commercial theatres tended to reject any play which did not promise financial reward. As the Pioneer Players acknowledged:

> The more subscribers we have the better the fare we can put before them. Money, of course, cannot always procure a good play; but the possession of a comfortable balance at the bank does ensure that a good play shall not be rejected on the grounds that its production would cost more than the Society can afford.
> (PPAR 1912–13: 8)

The type of play produced was also dependent on the society's funds. An elaborate play requiring expensive scenery would be discarded if funds dictated in favour of a less financially demanding play: 'Apart from this difficulty our freedom in the selection of plays has been restricted by the impossibility of procuring scenery and lighting necessary for their adequate production, and by the absence of facilities for proper rehearsal' (PPAR 1917–18: 7). This had repercussions on the quality of productions. Emphasising quality and selectivity, the society persuaded the membership to accept a smaller number of performances for the same annual subscription fee during the First World War:

> Those of our Members who have its future at heart, who hope to see it do better work when the violent activity of war has ceased to absorb all the best energies of this country, will no doubt stand by it, if it is forced as a temporary measure to adopt a system of rations.... The wiser course would seem to be to keep the venture honourably alive by giving one or two performances of high quality...
> (PPAR 1917–18: 10)

Although the Pioneer Players were based in London,[16] they had welcomed the idea of working in the provinces. In this respect, they compared with the earlier London-based Independent Theatre which had a Manchester branch and with the Stage Society which attempted to forge links with experimental theatre in provincial repertories by announcing bulletins of their work in the society's annual reports. The Pioneer Players offered to produce plays, probably from the stock for which Edith Craig held the acting rights:[17]

> The Pioneer Players are very anxious for provincial societies to understand that they are prepared to organise amateur performances, as well as to supply companies of professional players. The Pioneer Players possess the acting rights of many plays well suited to the needs of such societies, and are willing to give advice on the subject.
> (Advertisement, play programme, 21 April 1912; ECD)

The non-subscription performances of Cicely Hamilton's *A Pageant of Great Women*, which Edith Craig directed, were the only productions associated with the Pioneer Players to find a nationwide rather than metropolitan audience. Some of the London-based experiments, including that of the Pioneer Players, were later copied elsewhere. H. Hamilton Fyfe's *Race Suicide*, for instance, was performed by the Gaiety Theatre, Manchester five months after the Pioneer Players' London production.

The subscription society played an important part in disseminating cultural innovation from London to the provinces and thereby promoted a growing sense of national cultural cohesion. Many English subscription societies stated their intention to produce, not simply new plays, but new English plays. The difficult search for specifically English plays is indicative of a sense of national insecurity in this period. The Pioneer Players shared the class composition of the other free theatres, described by Raymond Williams as a 'class fraction' which 'emerged, within the dominant social order itself' (Williams 1983: x). The difference and dissidence manifested by the Pioneer Players can be introduced by examining the place of the avant-garde theatre in the construction of Englishness. Apart from the censorship debate, the free theatre movement became the focus for an increasingly fervent interest in national drama. As Philip Dodd has argued in his essay 'Englishness and the National Culture', the agitation for a national theatre in England emerged at the same time as the avant-garde theatre societies, some of which shared the aims of the proponents of a national theatre: to centralise and disseminate a national culture from the metropolis (Dodd 1987: 20). Although this movement was conceived as the 'free theatre', its exponents failed to identify exactly what they understood by such freedom. The campaigns against theatre licensing suggest that the free theatre was to be free from censorship, yet it was never conceived as a theatre open to all. By contrast, the Pioneer Players' affiliation with, and roots in, women's suffrage politics and its support of female theatre practitioners, placed it as the uneasy and illegitimate other within these 'other theatres'.

The extent to which the Pioneer Players could pose any significant challenge to the dominant groups rests with their constituency and significant links between oppositional cultural practice and the organised political opposition represented by the women's suffrage movement. These issues are central to the analysis of the ways in which the Pioneer Players differed from its male-dominated contemporaries, such as the Stage Society. The role of the Pioneer Players in the process of challenging dominant cultural forms has not hitherto been examined. The challenge to the Lord Chamberlain's regulatory powers was only one of the society's concerns. The freedom offered by the subscription society had always been limited, but, until the Pioneer Players was formed, it had also been confined to men. The Pioneer Players' support of women and the way it worked were unique contributions to the 'new' theatre. James Woodfield's assertion that the Pioneer Players was little different from the Stage Society and other earlier theatre societies needs now to be reconsidered (Woodfield 1984: 69).

The Pioneer Players differed from the male-dominated societies specifically as regards a commitment to an emerging national identity. The phenomenon of 'Englishness' adopted a peculiarly masculine expression perpetuated through institutions such as the public school and universities from which many of the Pioneer Players (as women) were excluded. Poggioli's characterisation of the avant-garde's conflict with 'the old generation, the generation of the fathers...the antithesis of "father-son"' (Poggioli 1968: 34–5) typifies the masculine preoccupations of the avant-garde (and its critics). Fears of the masses, the popular (and implicitly the female) are the unspoken tensions at work behind the psychological processes of constructing a national-masculine identity. Similarly, as Suzanne Clark (1991) argues, such fears form the basis for the masculine construction of modernism and the relegation of women's writing to the sentimental.

The Pioneer Players' relationship to women's writing changed during the course of their activities. Anxieties regarding a matrilineal tradition were common for women writing in the early twentieth century. Virginia Woolf's confident claim, 'We think back through our mothers if we are women', was the opposite of the view held by suffrage activists. The older female generation were seen as suffocating their younger suffrage rebels, and as complicit in their confinement within femininity. The nostalgia for the lost mother of a female literary tradition espoused by Woolf would have been rejected by the sharp critical pen of Cicely Hamilton. She argued specifically for a break with the mother. The Pioneer Players made a break in the kinds of plays they staged. Their naturalist plays diverged from much Edwardian drama by foregrounding female characters. *Waste* and *A Doll's House* had explored situations in which women resisted the limitations of femininity but they dwelt on the impact this had on the male characters. In addition, the Pioneer Players never identified the English play as their object; they were not concerned with differentiating themselves from the commercial theatres and in this respect differed from the male-dominated theatre societies. The major contribution of the Pioneer Players to the 'new drama' was an interest in gender, rather than national, identity. This is manifested in some of the Pioneer Players' drama which examines the difficulty of gendered subjectivity and the problems of forming and breaking with social or cultural groups.

A comparison of the organisational structure of the Pioneer Players with that of the Stage Society confirms the Pioneer Players' break with the male-dominated avant-garde. It shows how, in producing the specifically feminist play of ideas, the society was more effectively (although not entirely) resisting incorporation into dominant culture through its alignment of the theatrical avant-garde with a growing oppositional politics manifested in the women's suffrage movement.

Allan Wade's assertion that the Pioneer Players was not a *rival* of the Stage Society (Adlard 1949: 70), has framed the relationship between the two societies in personally antagonistic terms. The Pioneer Players was inevitably competing with the Stage Society and other organisations but was founded on different principles, with a gendered perspective on what freedom in the theatre might entail. The Stage Society, like many of its predecessors, was formed with no explicit agenda; the concept of a free theatre was based on liberal notions of freedom which ultimately erase cultural diversity. The Stage Society, more successful and larger than any other theatre society, was formed on 8 July 1899 with more than 300 members and an all-male management council. In its second year, a few women, including Edith Craig, were invited onto the council, but remained in a minority. By 1904 the Stage Society had changed remarkably; it had grown to over 1,000 members, resulting in a change of name and form of organisation. The

Stage Society became the Incorporated Stage Society and redefined its objectives which were:

> to promote and encourage Dramatic Art; to serve as an Experimental Theatre; to provide such an organization as shall be capable of dealing with any opportunities that may present themselves or be created, for the permanent establishment in London of a Repertory Theatre and to establish and undertake the management of such a theatre.
>
> (Woodfield 1984: 65)

The intention to found a permanent theatre for its work and to concentrate on 'Dramatic Art' distinguished the Stage Society from the Pioneer Players. While the Stage Society began with innovatory performances and defied the Lord Chamberlain, it quickly generated dissatisfaction in some quarters. By 1904, Shaw regarded the Stage Society as about ten years behind the times.[18] J. T. Grein suggested that its size may have threatened its status as an exclusively free theatre (Britain 1982: 174). The exclusivity of the 'free' theatre depended on a minority audience and therefore economic instability. As Tracy Davis has argued, the 'uncommercial theatre' is something of an oxymoron, revealing a fundamental denial of the realities of the market in which the free theatres existed (Davis 1990). Without subsidies or capital from patronage the experimentation of the free theatres depended on the gifts, charity or goodwill forthcoming from actors and managers of commercial theatres. The dependence of the 'free' theatre on the commercial theatre was largely unacknowledged by those claiming an alternative, autonomous, oppositional theatre. As the state of war affected the economy, any expenditure was scrutinised. Any charitable act was expected to have a war-related aim. A widespread utilitarian ethic affected theatre-going. Yet in spite of the extreme economic climate, the Pioneer Players prospered. In 1916–17, the year in which the Pioneer Players secured their greatest success and publicity and was producing plays which aligned them most closely with the Stage Society, the Stage Society redefined its objectives again:

> It will have been evident that the Society in the last two seasons has inclined to the production of plays of which the artistic merit is not in doubt rather than to plays of an immature or *propagandist* [my emphasis] nature. The Council feel that, as regards the freedom of the stage, the work of which the society was one of the pioneers is

practically accomplished, and its establishment may now well be left to others.

(*SSAR 1916–17*: 10)

Perhaps the Stage Society was conceding some ground to the Pioneer Players. In dispensing with 'propagandist drama' and 'the encouragement of younger and unknown dramatists' it was departing significantly from the earlier subscription societies' attempts to foster new talent in England:

> In future, then, the Council will make it their aim to study solely the artistic merits of a production, rather than to produce a play for ulterior motives however worthy.
>
> (*SSAR 1916–17*: 10)

The Stage Society thus distanced itself from the use of drama to sponsor any campaigns (including opposition to the censorship of the stage) and defined its agenda solely in terms of art.

The Stage Society had long sought a theatre building in which to ground its activities. Increasingly, and paradoxically, it saw itself as the leading avant-garde theatre society, encouraging experiments in the repertory theatre in particular and attempting to centralise the organisation of such experiment. In his brief summary of the Stage Society's later career, James Woodfield overlooks the ways in which the Stage Society changed its agenda. He states that by 1930, a motion to wind up the society was narrowly defeated: 'By then the Society had perhaps fulfilled its function of providing an outlet for new, experimental and non-commercial or censored drama (although censorship continued until 1968 it was much less inhibiting)' (Woodfield 1984: 71). The Stage Society's annual reports show that, as early as 1917, its support was confined to the experimental and the non-commercial, rather than new or unlicensed drama. Its oppositional stance had faltered. But it was favourably placed regarding the Lord Chamberlain's surveillance after 1913 when Stage Society dramatist, G. S. Street, had been appointed as Examiner of Plays.[19] This 'ushered in a more enlightened regime' (Woodfield 1984: 128). Woodfield's inaccurate description attributes to the Stage Society the role of 'an outlet', unproblematically open to all.

The Stage Society and the Pioneer Players differed in their attitudes towards propaganda. It is no surprise then that the Pioneer Players and the Stage Society shared very few members,[20] and according to contemporary reports, drew different audiences. Reviewers often described the

Pioneer Players' audience as predominantly female, whereas the Stage Society's was characterised by its exclusivity. William Archer regretted 'the aesthetic tea-parties of the Stage Society' (Watson 1970: 45), while Herbert Swears' description of a typical Stage Society audience suggests that members of the audience were more interested in being seen themselves than in watching the play:

> Early reactions to the new movement were rather amusing. Some people thought that Sunday playgoing was just a little naughty. 'Almost like being in Paris,' they chirruped. Very valuable support came from the pseudo-artistic set. At that time the males of the species wore unpleasant beards and nondescript clothes, and their women favoured clinging garments that fitted nowhere, in striking contrast to their Philistine sisters, who in those days were encased in whalebone corsets. The prevailing tint, I remember, was green.
> (Swears 1937: 101)

The natural vegetable dyes favoured by dress reformers provided observers with a taxonomy of unusual shades with which to categorise the unconventional (Wilson 1985: 214). Sybil Thorndike shared Swears' impression, noting 'a few of the so-called "Aubrey Beardsley aesthetic types", who tended to use the occasion as an opportunity to parade their own eccentric behaviour' (Watson 1970: 43).

The differences between the Stage Society and the Pioneer Players were significant. The Pioneer Players were, as one of its actors, Athene Seyler, recalled in an interview in 1989, 'more political' than the Stage Society. Measuring a 'political' public image is complex. The public statements issued by the Pioneer Players can be compared with the society's recorded activities. The Pioneer Players were explicit about their fund-raising function for organisations such as the International Suffrage Shop and the National Food Reform Association. A commitment to women's suffrage was acknowledged as one of their many current concerns. The refusal to compromise their work in the face of repressive practices during the First World War was unusal and set the Pioneer Players apart from the Stage Society. The Stage Society ignored the existence of the Pioneer Players until 1914 (*SSAR 1913–14:* 11). The societies were associated with different political organisations. While the Pioneer Players' affiliations were to the women's suffrage movement, the Stage Society was unofficially affiliated to the Fabian Society. The Stage Society made no attempt to grant its actors any special status. It tended towards dramatic 'art', distancing itself from the production of propaganda which characterised the Pioneer Players' early work. The 'play of ideas', for so long associated exclusively with male dramatists of the period such as Shaw, Galsworthy and Ibsen, many of whom the Stage Society had supported, was by 1911 specifically associated with an emerging feminist drama which the Pioneer Players helped to bring to the stage.

3
The Feminist Play of Ideas and the Art of Propaganda

The Pioneer Players' name was something of a Trojan horse, promising dramatic art, unexpectedly delivering feminism. The woman sent by *The Times* to review the first production felt tricked:

> We left the Kingsway Theatre yesterday afternoon feeling, if not... battered... chastened. We had walked in so innocently, imagining that the pioneering of the Pioneer Players was to be dramatic, not (if we may be pardoned the ugly word) feministic; and we found ourselves compelled to sit for two hours and see the weaknesses of our sex exposed.
>
> (*The Times*, 9 May 1911: 13)

At this time the term 'pioneer' had a range of meanings in religious, colonial and political discourses: as missionary, immigrant, coloniser and feminist.[1] The feminist resonance of the term 'pioneer' was having some effect. The Pioneer Players' operations were perceived to be covert, manipulating the audience:

> We went to the theatre all unsuspecting; but it very soon dawned on us that we were to be 'Trafalgar Squared,' for it would seem that the object of the Pioneer Players is to disseminate Suffragist teaching by means of the stage. The Society may have other objects, but this one is glaringly apparent.
>
> (*Daily Graphic*)

Concerned to expose the Pioneer Players' relationship to women's suffrage and feminism, these reviewers asserted that these plays consisted of 'propaganda' rather than 'art'. This chapter will therefore explore the stated and implied relationship between the Pioneer Players and 'propaganda', and the contributions they made to the emergence of the feminist play of ideas. An examination of the reception of the society's first subscription production will contextualise the Pioneer Players' production of issue-based plays and formally ambiguous plays which exemplify the feminist play of ideas deriving their force from strategies of reversal, mimicry and excess.

The WSPU newspaper, *Votes for Women*, described the Pioneer Players' aim as 'playing propaganda plays, chiefly those dealing with the woman's movement, as that is at present the most important'. This aim is not 'inferred' as has been suggested (Dymkowski 1992: 223), but stated eloquently in the Pioneer Players' first annual report:[2]

> It has more than once been suggested in the Press that we are a Society formed for the purpose of suffragist propaganda only; but this suggestion is a misleading one. It is obviously quite impossible nowadays to produce thoughtful plays written by thoughtful people which do not bear some traces of the influence of the feminist movement – an influence which no modern writer, however much he may wish it, can entirely escape. But those responsible for the selection of the plays that we have performed have never had either the wish or the intention of narrowing their choice to works dealing with one phase only of modern thought. All we ask of a play is that it shall be interesting; and if many of those who have sent us plays have found inspiration in various aspects of the feminist movement, we must conclude that it is because the feminist movement is, in itself, not without dramatic interest. This is confirmed by the fact that the leading provincial Repertory Companies have recently produced several new plays with a strong 'feminist' element.
> (PPAR 1911–12: 7–8)

The society's work was therefore not restricted to one type of propaganda. The claim that in 'modern thought' women's suffrage and the feminist movement had an inevitable place strategically relegated the anti-suffrage argument to an outmoded position. A suffrage cartoon had similarly depicted the anti-suffragists as a species of dinosaur. The simplistic opposition in the debate between 'art' and 'propaganda' was refused. Any play that engaged with 'feminist' ideas must be intrinsically 'dramatic'. Considering the evidence of their annual reports, headed notepaper and press releases, the Pioneer Players were often charged accurately with dealing in propaganda. The founder and director of the society, Edith Craig wrote on notepaper headed 'Suffrage Plays' and 'Propaganda Plays'. She freely admitted that this was the function of the society but, consistent with its first annual report, she emphasised the diversity of the propaganda:

> The Pioneer Players was started to produce propaganda plays. The propaganda is of all kinds. The most diverse views can be aired and explained. We do things all the way round, and are as a body possessed of an open mind on all problems
> ('"Little Interview": Miss Edith Craig at the Pioneer Players', *Pall Mall Gazette*, 13 April 1912: 12)

Craig explained that the society was unique:

> In the low price at which it is possible to join [sic]. For propaganda work you must reach every kind of person, and by varying the subscription to suit different pockets we can manage this. Our performance next Sunday closes the first half of our first season, and as we are a young society we are anxious to increase our membership. Though our actors and actresses give their services, and we get our plays for nothing, the expenses of production have to be met, and the office expenses, which keep on whether we are producing plays or not.
> ('"Little Interview"')

The political incongruity of getting something 'for nothing' and simultaneously claiming a radical position shows the contradiction within which Craig and other middle-class and aristocratic members of the Pioneer Players worked. Nevertheless, Craig did show some concern for the financial implications of the society's practices. In 1913 the Pioneer Players responded to further charges of propaganda:

> There are some who accuse us of being propagandists rather than entertainers; we ourselves have no desire either to preach dull doctrines or to provide dull amusement. Naturally our productions do not always please everyone. If they did, it would probably mean that they were negligible from the point of view of ideas; for it is in the nature of an idea to provoke antagonism as well as sympathy.
> (*PPAR 1913–14:* 8–9)

Antagonism was a characteristic of the Pioneer Players' play of ideas, provoking hostile criticism even in apparently radical papers such as the

Daily Herald[3] and the *Freewoman*.[4] The interrogative form of the society's plays raised many complex questions, not least about antagonistic relationships between class and gender, which could not easily be resolved.

Propaganda is invariably distinguished from art, as Lisa Tickner points out, in order to sustain an opposition between 'the ideologically saturated and the ideologically pure' (Tickner 1987: xi). If any image, form or cultural product is susceptible to appropriation for a political campaign, propaganda tends to be in the eye of the beholder, whether appreciative partisan or disgusted aesthete. A formal definition of propaganda is highly problematic. Histories of political theatre have tended to overlook the drama of the women's suffrage movement. Instead they identify the earliest propaganda plays in Britain as those of the 1920s Workers' Theatre Movement, which were influenced by the agit-prop of Russia and Germany (Samuel *et al.* 1985; Kershaw 1992). In their mixture of songs and sketches, they directly addressed a working-class audience through 'ideologically unambiguous' scenarios (Kershaw 1992: 79). Baz Kershaw has emphasised the formal closure of this dramatic form:

> The promotion of class solidarity required a theatrical language that was deliberately simple.... If the form dealt only in answers, rather than questions... then that was because the questions were all too patently inscribed in the situation of its intended audience.
>
> (Kershaw 1992: 80)

Catherine Belsey has similarly defined propaganda in terms of formal closure; the 'imperative text' explicitly exhorts the reader/audience to subscribe to a specific political campaign outside the text/play (Belsey 1980: 91). Sheila Stowell has taken issue with such 'ahistorical thinking' (Stowell 1992: 81), arguing that early twentieth-century realist drama was interpreted in diverse ways. Rather than produce a mystificatory representation and reinforcement of oppressive environments, the mimetic function of realism could expose oppression with revolutionary effect:

> Theatricalizing workrooms, drapers' establishments, law offices and (yes) drawing-rooms can have the effect of making visible traditionally invisible processes of capitalist production, exposing the usually hidden workings of an oppressive system, such staged revelations calling into question existing ideology's 'naturalized' view of the world, each one a call to action.
>
> (Stowell 1992: 85)

Realism and its radical contexts have been marginalised by modernism and formalism which have dominated the study of twentieth-century culture. Since second-wave feminists rejected realism rather prematurely, critics such as Stowell (1992) and Joannou (1995) have begun to reassess the feminist-historical contexts of realism. An attention to sexual politics helps to resituate Raymond Williams' account of the instability of naturalism at the turn of the century. The radical potential of naturalism lay in its allusion to the broader social determinants (always off-stage) which caused the events played out in a claustrophobic domestic interior. It is off-stage where significant changes can be made to the characters' lives. Naturalism risked appropriation. Deracinated, the room became merely the occasion for superficial curiosity. In Ibsen's *A Doll's House,* Nora rejects her doll-like role, leaving husband and house. Although the door closes on Torvald, the ending of the play resists a mystificatory closure. Nora's future does not appear to be easy. The causes of Nora's imprisonment and infantilisation by her husband are clarified in the audience's imagination at the end of the play. Such revolutionary potential was recognised when women's suffrage activists chose to perform this particular scene at political events.

The Pioneer Players' drama bears out the more complex account of realism suggested by Stowell and Williams. The society's plays tended to resist or undermine closure, rarely referring explicitly to the suffrage movement, often generating more questions than they answer. They explored the complexity rather than the simplicity of issues. In Kershaw's terms the Pioneer Players' drama was bad propaganda. It had a difficult job to do, in addressing its audience. This was not a 'class fraction' (Williams 1980), but rather a nexus of progressive political and social interests. Since the women's suffrage movement was mobilising as a group women from different social classes it could not appeal to 'class solidarity' (Kershaw 1992: 80). Christopher Innes argues that the avant-garde 'may repudiate existing social conditions and work for change', through ritual forms which 'seek to change the nature of the participants directly by irrational, often highly disturbing means' (Innes 1993: 11). Innes traces this tendency in avant-garde theatre from the symbolists and expressionists to the drama of Paul Claudel, all to be found in the Pioneer Players' productions. Yet Innes is not alert to the avant-garde as a space of feminist potential. For the Pioneer Players, with their feminist concept of the pioneer, the avant-garde and the politically committed theatre could not easily be distinguished. Although the Pioneer Players' relationship with 'women's suffrage drama' will be considered in detail in Chapter 4, some difficulties of definition facing the

Pioneer Players can be considered here from the reception and representation of the society's first production in May 1911.

It has been suggested that, in this context, the Pioneer Players' first production, a triple bill of three short plays, met with a biased response from reviewers (Dymkowski 1992: 223). In order to test this claim a case study of a collection of some 60 notices and 48 reviews of the first triple bill was made.[5] Surprisingly few reviews referred explicitly to suffrage or votes for women, feminism or propaganda.[6] The named individuals especially featured in these reviews were Ellen Terry (recently returned from America) and Cicely Hamilton (in the capacity of performer rather than dramatist or producer). Only one review (and 23 of the 60 notices) named Edith Craig as producer of the plays. Those reviews concerned with the political effect of the production and with the constituency of the society articulated this by means of a number of different strategies which served to dismiss, devalue and discredit the play or those involved with it.

The Pioneer Players' first three plays were dismissed by several reviewers on the grounds that they were simply not plays. They lacked the formal properties of a play. *The First Actress* was a vehicle for actresses' self-promotion, a 'semi-pageant or 'pièce d'occasion'. *In the Workhouse* was no more than a dramatised tract or pamphlet. Edith Craig had no problem with this. In an interview with the *Daily News and Leader*, she asserted, 'In short, our plays take the place of tracts'. Reviewers based their arguments on a presumed distinction between propaganda and art. One warned that propaganda and art was a 'dangerous mixture'. Another, alluding to Henry Irving's claim for the theatre as a 'temple of art', condemned the Pioneer Players for turning it into 'a temple for propaganda'. Aesthetic excellence was claimed as a male monopoly. The plot of Cicely Hamilton's *Jack and Jill and a Friend* – a woman wins a writing competition and finds her fiancé is jealous – was claimed to be a rare occurrence. Christopher St. John's *The First Actress* was rejected on the grounds of historical inaccuracy, or indeed as one reviewer put it, a 'violent perversion of the facts and dates'. Speculation ensued about candidates for the first actress on a Restoration stage, such as Mistress Sanderson or Anne Marshall in place of St. John's claim for Margaret Hughes.

Some reviewers projected their own confrontational stance onto the plays. One 'sex play' (*Daily Sketch*), purveying 'sex propaganda' (*Bookseller*), was charged with arguing antagonistically on what might now be defined as biological essentialist grounds. Indeed, reviewers claimed gender bias in the Pioneer Players' triple bill. Some engaged in parodic self-effacement, explicitly identifying themselves as culpably male. J. T. Grein and Herbert Farjeon deviated from the norm and signed their reviews. Grein was unafraid of political controversy. He had supported the production of Ibsen in England and been a prominent activist in the free theatre movement. But he was critical of the Pioneer Players. He claimed, like several other reviewers, that their drama was hostile, showing 'the weak side of man'. Another review asserted that the plays were committed to 'the glorification of women and the belittlement of man'. In order to support the contention that the Pioneer Players was an organisation with a partisan commitment to women one review even suggested provocatively renaming (and therefore sexing) the society, 'the new histrionic suffragettic body, The Pioneer Players – or Player-esses'. Other evidence of the Pioneer Players' bias towards women concerned claims about the audience. Plays written by women and performed to a reputed 80 per cent female audience were presumed to generate 'sex antagonism'. Christopher St. John's masculine name confused some reviewers, one of whom claimed of the author of *The First Actress*, 'Mr St. John was a traitor to his sex'. The sex of the dramatist was not of overriding concern to Edith Craig. In response to the suggestion that the Pioneer Players was 'anti-man', she said, 'some of the most strongly feminist plays were written by men'. Yet in this same interview she asserted that the first few productions of the society were propagandist. It is therefore rather the case that 'propaganda' was a category to which the Pioneer Players subscribed rather than a derogatory term used by others to dismiss their work.

A number of the plays produced by the Pioneer Players concern identifiable political issues or campaigns in terms of the plot and/or the performance context. Laurence Housman's *Pains and Penalties,* George Bernard Shaw's *Mrs Warren's Profession* and *The Coronation* by Christopher St. John and Charles Thursby were performed in the context of the campaign against the theatre censorship which the Lord Chamberlain's regulation of public performance in theatres constituted. *The Coronation* was also performed as a fund-raising venture for the International Suffrage Shop, founded by Sime Seruya. Campaigns against oppressive working conditions were supported by Cecil Fisher's *The Great Day,* which exposed the pressures facing insurance clerks following Lloyd George's social welfare legislation and by Edith Lyttelton's *The Thumbscrew,* which exposed sweated work in the clothing industry. Campaigns for legal reform were addressed by Margaret Wynne Nevinson's *In the Workhouse* which challenged the law of coverture,[7] and M. E. M. Young's *The Higher Court* which concerned the debate about divorce reform. Florence Edgar Hobson's *A Modern Crusader* was given a fund-raising performance for the National Food Reform Association's campaign week. It was this play which provoked the wrath of Rebecca West in the *Freewoman*:

> I am inclined to agree with the Anti-Suffragists in their opinion that 'there are some things which can safely be left to the men.' Writing bad plays is one of them. Therefore I regard Mrs J. A. Hobson's 'A Modern Crusader' as an unfeminine usurpation of man's sphere.
> (West 1912: 8)

West took this opportunity to condemn both the Pioneer Players and the Actresses' Franchise League. She saw no distinction between them; both organisations, in her view, dealt in propaganda rather than art:

> This is nonsense, such nonsense that it is rather funny; but it is also blasphemy. Words are sacred, pen and ink are sacred, because of the noble uses they have been put to by artists, and propagandists who mishandle them ought to be punished for sacrilege. The Pioneer Players and the Actresses' Franchise League are perhaps the most shameless offenders in the way of producing degradations of the drama written by propagandists, whom nothing but the fire of Prometheus could make into artists. It is untrue to say that these impertinences towards Art are innocuous by their own ineffectiveness. For the public taste has already been so perverted that dislocated Suffrage speeches, such as Miss Cicely Hamilton's plays, stand the chance of wide popularity.
> (West 1912: 8)

Although West supported women's suffrage she, like the editor of the *Freewoman*, Dora Marsden, was generally critical of the militancy of the WSPU (Glendinning 1988: 41). West was also clearly opposed to the use of drama rather than political speeches to promote the movement. The *Freewoman* would not have been averse to the ideas explored by the Pioneer Players' drama. It had a reputation for publishing controversial material and had, in its first issue, claimed a role model in Ellen Terry, the President of the Pioneer Players:

> Where are the women of whom and for whom you write who are free? Can they be pointed out, or named by name? There must be, say, ten in the British Isles. The question is pertinent enough, but it is

difficult to answer, because its answer must of necessity become personal. We might, perhaps, hazard the name of one Freewoman who has become a sufficiently national figure to make her mention impersonal – Ellen Terry. There at least is one, and for the rest the inquisitors must be content with being enabled to arrive at the conception of Freewomen by way of a description of Bondwomen.

(The *Freewoman* I.1 (23 November 1911): 1)

The hostility of West's review is therefore significant, other than as an indication of her antagonistic personal attitude either towards Cicely Hamilton or towards particular suffrage organisations. It indicates, rather, the extent to which contemporary debate insisted on opposing art and propaganda.

This debate had taken place in the first two issues of the *Freewoman* in a controversial exchange between Ashley Dukes and G. L. Harding only six months before the Pioneer Players' production of Hobson's play. The Pioneer Players may be the unmentioned referent in this debate. In his article, 'The Illusion of Propagandist Drama', Ashley Dukes attempted to define drama organised by feminists:

> The theatre of late has been the favourite hobby of reformers; the ideal hobby, intended to combine work and play. Suffragist *matinees*, political Sunday evenings, social Monday afternoons and the like tread upon each other's heels week by week. The output of propagandist plays has become immense. Ever since the time of Ibsen, Socialists, Feminists, and advanced persons in general have cherished the superstition that they are gifted from the cradle with a sort of *ex-officio* understanding of works of art; and, in particular, that the theatre is their natural perquisite as a medium of expression.
>
> (Dukes 1911: 13)

Dukes significantly named few playwrights; none was female. He suggested that the 'play of ideas' (the stated objective of the Pioneer Players) was already out of date and in any case inappropriate for the theatre, alluding to George Bernard Shaw's notable comparison between the theatre and church:

> For some time past we have heard that the theatre is taking the place of the church. This is only one of the superficialities of revolutionists who never go to church, and who imagine that there is nothing in the church but the sermon. The phase is passing, however. Just as the

demand for realism twenty years ago was due to a revolt against the prevailing condition of theatricality within the theatre, so the cry for propagandist views in the 'advanced' drama now springs from a revolt against political and social conditions outside. The method must be tried before it is found wanting. Our newer repertory theatres may transform themselves for the moment into parish council meetings, and debate Socialism or the Suffrage or the Poor Law Report to their head's content, but they will discover that life cannot be moulded in that way, and that the art upon which they depend goes deeper than opinion.

(Dukes 1911: 13)

A month later, G. L. Harding responded. In 'Feminism and the Propagandist Drama', he objected to the distinction between art and politics insisted upon by Dukes and to be sustained later by West in her review of the Pioneer Players' production of *A Modern Crusader*. Harding challenged the masculine bias of critics unable to find a vocabulary with which to assess the new drama:

The old familiar controversy in the drama between the 'art for art's sake' and the 'art for men's sake' schisms has lately been complicated by the animated assertion that there can also be 'art for women's sake'. It is not at all an unnatural claim. Here and there we have a few good feminist plays to give us the hint; on every hand we have the tokens of a stirring feminist movement to justify us with the sanction of honourable material. Why, then cannot this movement express itself, along the *pioneer* [my emphasis] lines already laid down, in a school of plays which should fairly be called a 'feminist drama'?

(Harding 1911: 76)

Harding assesses the arguments for and against feminist drama, aligning with the anti-suffragists:

the dramatic dogmatists [who] have undoubtedly constructed a profoundly consistent intellectual case against the drama of ideas.... What can be said against using the stage as a pulpit or as a platform for intelligent discussion can be said with equal reason and considerably more emotion against making the stage a tribune for the Suffragettes. It is the last straw which should break the back of the propagandist drama – it is, indeed, a *reductio ad feminem*.

(Harding 1911: 76)

By 1911 'Propagandist drama' and particularly 'the play of ideas' associated with Shaw and the male-dominated subscription societies, had become synonymous with feminist drama:

> Now I do not here propose to fight the battle over again for the drama of ideas. What I am concerned to point out is that if this style of drama belongs with propriety to the realm of art, and I believe it does, its claim rests to a far greater extent than is commonly considered on the dramatic expression it has given to feminism.... Ibsen, Brieux, Shaw, and Barker have earned the name of 'advanced' dramatist, for example, very largely through the attention they have paid to the 'advanced' woman. In fact, *feminism* is the only intellectual issue which the *drama of ideas* [my emphasis] has set forth in anything like common *accord*.
>
> (Harding 1911: 76)

This debate on the feminist play of ideas and propaganda drama signals the emergence of a new dramatic form which foregrounded female subjectivity in the naturalist play. Harding argues that it has developed because:

> [the] feminist movement represents a social and an individual question in one. It aims toward a moral change no less passionately concerned with personal than with social problems. It is bringing about an alteration of the soul of man through the recognition of the soul of woman.
>
> (Harding 1911: 76)

Liberal and feminist discourses are thus conflated, integrating women into a (re)vision of humanity. This is exactly what is demonstrated in the Pioneer Players' drama. It brought about what Harding called 'the recognition of the soul of woman', by insisting that the room reproduced in the naturalist play was, furthermore, loaded with significance as the site of domestic labour. In Spring 1911, when Ibsen's *A Doll's House* had played at the Court Theatre, Margaret Slieve McGowan noted particularly that it 'ends upon a note of hope'. The notorious ending, which saw Nora leaving her husband and children, was amenable to the suffragists' appropriation of Nora. McGowan recommended every suffragist to see it:

> Like the great of all ages, Ibsen the reformer was in advance of his time. But how badly would fare the laggards in life's journey did not

the lights of the pioneers make clear the path! It is difficult to realise that 'A Doll's House' was written over thirty years ago, since the ideas it expresses are so typical of the thought of to-day. Indeed it is only the 'advanced' of our time who have followed in the wake of Ibsen. The Doll's Houses of the world still, alas! are considered most desirable residences by a great number of both men and women. There is no need to describe the motif of the play, since every reader of *The Vote* has doubtless more than an acquaintance with such a splendid piece of feminist propaganda as 'A Doll's House'.

(*Vote*, 18 March 1911: 254)

It was *A Doll's House* which instigated the new perspective for Harding, and placed the feminist play of ideas (from the outset a male-authored drama) in 'the art of the theatre' :

But where the 'art for art's sake' breaks down utterly is where it fails to account for that no less legitimate art which challenges convention. The defiance of tradition is a subject just as proper to great art as its assertion and explanation. Surely the defiance of the tradition of woman's place and duty in the world is no trivial or abstract defiance; it is a passionate conflict of the highest dramatic possibilities. Let him who doubts this read his 'Doll's House' and consider whether there are many scenes in all the art of the theatre which conjure up in us more intensely the intimate magic of the drama than when Nora sits down opposite her husband and lays before him the things that have grown great in her desire which neither he nor the men who made his laws had ever counted on.

(Harding 1911: 76)

This scene had indeed become memorable for suffrage activists and was a common reference at suffrage events and in suffrage newspapers.[8] The naturalism of Ibsen, as Raymond Williams has shown, focused on the family and the individual in a domestic space, while indicating the wider social determinants of the action beyond that room (Williams 1977). All forms and images are available to competing discourses. Ibsen's play had been adapted by H. A. Jones and H. Herman as *Breaking a Butterfly on a Wheel* (1884), a reactionary revision of the plot, which saw Nora remaining in the doll's house. In society drama the potential for change which the off-stage space could promise in the naturalist play, was rarely articulated. The action, confined to the room, dissociated family and individual from their social roots.

However, conventions of the society drama were equally available to revision. The female protagonist of the feminist play of ideas appropriated the role of the *raisonneur*, who dominated society drama with worldly-wise opinion (Clarke 1989: 45–7). This enabled the play to foreground a female perspective and feminist issues by drawing on the authority and cultural status of the popular society drama. The construction of a rational subject position for the female protagonist contradicted the subjectivities available to women in dominant discourses.

The anti-suffragists' insistence on the biological irrationality of women is wittily illustrated by a contemporary cartoon showing a woman's head filled with trivia. Rational discourse had long been deployed by women to support their case for social reforms, as Chris Weedon has indicated:

> Nineteenth-century women had to lay claim to subject positions which implied rationality and physical strength in order to gain access to education.... Like women of all classes they had to discredit the hegemonic belief that they were naturally inferior, but in this case not just to men but to the middle and upper classes.
> (Weedon 1987: 95)

The strategies deployed in *Beastie, The Conference, The Patience of the Sea, Race Suicide* and *Idle Women* discussed below, consisted of the reversal or conflation of conventionally opposing images. Just as Nora left Torvald stupefied in the doll's house of his own making, the female character in the Pioneer Players' drama often acts as *raisonneur* to the astonishment of comparatively foolish male characters. The charge that the society's drama concerned 'the glorification of women and the belittlement of men' is to some extent accurate. Such a strategy had its limitations but it began to unsettle some of the gender stereotypes circulating in the debates concerning women's enfranchisement. In the Pioneer Players' feminist play of ideas the challenging conflations of the domestic and the political – the Womanly Woman as *raisonneur* and the New Woman as wife – defy the limited positions available to women in dominant gender ideology. Distinctions between the Womanly Woman and the Suffragette (or New Woman), which regulated and defined acceptable female behaviours, are presented as artificial. The naturalist play in particular offered an opportunity for the controlled collision and fusion of public and private spheres. The domestic space was being politicised, exposing the potential of the room to imprison and confine women. The private room (reproduced on stage) became the forum for the debate of political issues by, and relevant to, female characters who held the male antagonists in their gaze. These plays foreground the possibilities for women's independence and self-determination in reproduction and sexual relationships.

Significantly, the Pioneer Players unsettled conventional representations of the New Woman and the middle-class reformer most effectively through comedy. The destabilising force of comedy had been appropriated in cartoons, posters as well as drama of the women's suffrage movement. It was captured in a popular song, 'The March of the Women', written by Pioneer Players' dramatist, Cicely Hamilton to music by Ethel Smyth: 'Firm in reliance, laugh a defiance – / (Laugh in hope, for sure is the end)' (Norquay 1995: 94). 'Laugh a Defiance' became the title of the autobiography of Mary Richardson, the suffragist who famously slashed Velasquez' 'Rokeby Venus', in the National Gallery in 1914. A strategy of subversive comedy had been more obviously deployed in the visual artwork of the movement with the cartoon and poster caricatures of the anti-suffragists. Sheila Stowell has remarked on the uneasy tone of Cicely Hamilton's drama, and generally speaking, there has been a difficulty in categorising the writings of the women's suffrage movement in formal terms. Glenda Norquay has referred to the 'shaky plot structures' and 'hybridity of form' of narrative and poetry written in the context of women's suffrage (Norquay 1995: 30). This evaluation presumes an ideal which is formally cogent. Similarly, Virginia Woolf assumed that the anger intrinsic to politically motivated writing had a distorting effect on aesthetic form. Woolf expressed this view as early as 1916 in an essay on Charlotte Brontë. It coalesced famously in 'Women and Fiction' (1929) where the woman writer is urged to 'resist the temptation to anger', and to 'turn towards the impersonal' in order to 'look beyond the personal and political relationships to the wider questions which the poet tries to solve – of our destiny and the meaning of life' (Woolf 1979: 51). Woolf acknowledges the usefulness of comedy to expose misogynistic aporia but cautions against 'scorn and ridicule' (Woolf 1993: 82). Textual fissures can look like flaws when they are opening up new spaces from which repressed forces are released. Unreconcilable conflicts were created when competing groups were campaigning for social reforms. The tensions that these conflicts produced are apparent in the Pioneer Players' drama, where a destabilising comedy transforms sources of anger into a means of transforming 'personal and political relationships'.

In Hugh de Selincourt's one-act play *Beastie*, performed by the Pioneer Players in December 1912, the Womanly Woman is capable of confronting and demolishing the sexual double standard through the force of argument. Simultaneously, the uneasy contradictions in this play indicate the limitations imposed on the Pioneer Players by a middle-class perspective. When Jessie Grant insists that her husband Johnnie interview a candidate for the post of nurse and governess, he discovers that the interviewee is Ellen Smith, known to him as 'Gypsy', the servant with whom he has had an affair while an undergraduate at Oxford University. The ensuing discussion between the married couple about Ellen's suitability for the post reveals Grant as a man with a past. He claims to be representative of his class in flirting with servants. Jessie Grant is incredulous: 'The gardener's boy at home was quite a jolly chap, I never thought it fun to kiss him' (310). Johnnie's remorseful self-definition as a 'beast' is exposed by Jessie as a product of the double standard, whereby men idealise some women and are licensed to objectify and oppress others: 'I expect you only think yourself a beast in comparison with the little creature you stuck up on a pedestal in a glass case. The case is smashed' (314). Johnnie's confession is prompted by Jessie's searching look: 'She persists in looking at him, much to his dismay, in simple round-eyed astonishment' (311). The male character, caught by the female gaze in the domestic interior, is forced to confront the implications of his sexual double standard.

The imbalance of power between class, sex and colonialism is imbricated in the name of 'Gypsy', used by Grant and other Oxbridge students for their female servants. Male-dominated institutions were, as Laurence Housman astutely observed, responsible for propagating the anti-suffrage point of view:

> especially may any man be aware of the Anti-suffrage germ in his composition who has been through Public School and University or has entered on any career from which by law or custom women are expressly debarred.... Look at the inducement there is to every English public school boy to regard himself as a far more important factor of the community than his own sister.
>
> (Housman 1910: 238–40)

Class conflict remains unresolved in this, as in many other plays. Both Johnnie and Jessie Grant are uneasy about interviewing a servant. This embarrassment is contrasted with the business-like attitude of Ellen, the interviewee, who enters the room 'fairly at her ease'. The role of servants in middle-class life was changing. As Paul Thompson has noted, the numbers of servants employed in Edwardian households was declining during this period and servants' deferential attitudes to their employers were becoming more relaxed (Thompson 1992: 289). The contradictions emerging in the ideologies of gender and class in *Beastie* ultimately expose the materially different kinds of oppression facing women of different social classes. Although the dramatic focus falls on conflicts within the Grants' marriage, attention is drawn towards the exploration of different positions for wife and husband established in contrast to the fixed position of the servant. How would sympathy between these two women be possible? Within the terms of the play different class positions are understated but not negotiable. In the emancipatory writings of the women's suffrage, and other social reform movements of this period an imperial logic invariably underwrites the construction of a 'new' female subjectivity. Middle-class women are repeatedly seen to collude in the oppression of other women.

Jessie concludes that she now has two babies to look after, one of whom is her husband. Sexual difference is reinforced by Jessie's assumption of the adult (mothering) role and by her infantilisation of her husband. A visual allusion to Madonna and child occurs at the end of Cicely Hamilton's *Jack and Jill and a Friend,* and in Olive Schreiner's 'Three Dreams in a Desert' where man is the dependent child at Woman's breast.[9] The conventions of the society drama are reversed. The man with the past is not denounced but merely rebuked and then forgiven by the female character in the role of *raisonneur*. The power of rational discourse adopted by Jessie's arguments is moderated through femininity by her infantilism as a 'childlike (not childish)' (294) wife. The possibility that Jessie's understanding, rather than condemnation, of her husband's pre-marital affairs might lead to an open marriage for both Jessie and Johnny is not examined in the play. However, members of the Pioneer Players would have been aware that the author of *Beastie*, Hugh de Selincourt,[10] wrote the sensational novel about free love, *A Daughter of the Morning* (1912). Havelock Ellis described it as 'First Lessons in Immorality or a Child's Guide to Vice', which nevertheless 'ought to exert a wholesome influence' (Grosskurth 1985: 306).

Beastie conflates the Womanly Woman and the *raisonneur*. The world of the Womanly Woman was conventionally limited to domestic matters, protected from knowledge of sexual relationships. *Beastie* foregrounds the unconventional perspective of Jessie Grant and subverts the assumption that a married woman is ignorant of sexual relationships. But it does so by reinforcing sexual difference and marginalising the voice of the working-class woman. If *Beastie* challenges convention by showing that the Womanly Woman can argue against the double standard, *The Conference* and *The Patience of the Sea* subvert expectations by presenting the New Woman as choosing, rather than rejecting, marriage. In these plays the New Woman's decision to get married poses a threat to, rather than a restoration of, the existing order. Legal discourse accorded democratic powers to women depending on their marital status and on their status as property owners. In 1894 married women were allowed to vote in local elections. In 1918 property-owning women over age 30 could vote in general elections. Universal female franchise was granted in 1928. This enfranchisement of the younger woman attracted the title of the 'flapper vote'. The older woman's preferential treatment derived from the assumption that she was married and that her husband would guarantee her worthiness to operate in the public sphere. The New Woman's decision to marry would constitute an even greater threat than a rejection of marriage precisely because it challenged the long-standing law of coverture that elided husband and wife. One of the feminist arguments which was sometimes forwarded in support of women's enfranchisement was for women's independence. On some occasions this constituted a challenge to marriage; on others it posed a revision of the institution of marriage.

The Conference concerns three of the Edwardian crises: the rise of Labour; the challenge to the power of the House of Lords; and the women's suffrage movement. Written by an aristocrat, Lady Margaret Sackville, it was presented under the pseudonym Delphine Gray. An aristocratic family holds a conference to discuss effective measures for controlling the unorthodox behaviour of Barbara, the New Woman in the family. The conference is held in a room symbolising both the family's wealth and the constraints that this imposes. The family is seen to be anachronistic, cut off from the world outside, which ironically determines the dilemma it attempts to resolve (Plate 3).

The New Woman was typically represented as a middle-class female exhibiting a catalogue of unconventional but faddish behaviours (bicycling; smoking) and visible signs (key to the house; reading glasses) which detract from the more socially disruptive aspects of emancipated women (going out alone; choosing to study; refusing marriage). The faddishness has a serious import in that it implies that the New Woman is going through a phase that will inevitably end in her marriage. Barbara exhibits all the troubling characteristics of the New Woman, witnessed by members of the family: eating chocolates in the theatre; reading pamphlets by George Bernard Shaw; sleeping with the windows open at night. She has stopped going to church, rejected marriage and intends to live by herself. She has been involved in numerous societies and plans to speak at a suffrage meeting. Reading the novels of Mrs Humphry Ward (an anti-suffragist) had proven an ineffective antidote. Ward's novel, *Delia Blanchflower* (1915) was published only a year before this production. The innocent Delia is subject to the malevolent influence of the militant suffragette, Gertrude Marvell, whose 'hatred of men' is intense. It is the attack on an aristocrat's Elizabethan country house that the novel uses to symbolise the threat to Englishness posed by militant suffragism. The audience would have understood that Barbara was more of a Gertrude than a Delia.

The New Woman is particularly identifiable by her appearance. Barbara is especially threatening. She looks like a Womanly Woman but behaves like a New Woman. The family even suggests an extreme change of appearance – cutting her hair short and wearing 'Nature shoes' – in order to soften the impact of her unorthodox behaviour. Free thinkers such as members of The Fellowship of the New Life, to which Edward Carpenter (1844–1928) belonged, were committed to comradeship, a return to nature, an integration of art and life (Rowbotham and Weeks 1977). Sandal-making and vegetarianism were some of the attractions to Carpenter's small-holding at Millthorpe near Sheffield in the 1880s. The dress reform movement, as Elizabeth Wilson suggests, marked a 'shift from clothing as part of a social project to clothing as part of an identity [which] really launches it into its most 'modern' manifestations' (Wilson 1985: 218). By 1916, when the Pioneer Players performed *The Conference*, the New Woman had come to be seen as the object of ridicule, supporting Rosemary Hennessy's argument that the New Woman represented a commodification of feminism and a means of incorporating its challenge to dominant gender ideology. At this time the Edwardian crises had been overshadowed. The regulation of behaviour had become a routine matter. There was even talk of reintroducing the Contagious Diseases Acts because of fears about rising poverty and prostitution during wartime (Dodd 1993: 66).[11] Although Barbara proves that a beautiful New Woman is more conspicuous and in need of discipline, her deviation seems limited.

The comic resolution of the play is provided with the unexpected arrival of Barbara, already secretly married that morning to a Radical MP. This aspect of the plot compares with Granville-Barker's *The Marrying of Ann Leete* (performed by the Stage Society in 1902) in which Ann marries a gardener rather than accept an arranged and politically expedient marriage. Social mobility might even improve the dominant class. The gardener promises to revitalise aristocratic stock. As Ian Clarke says: 'The collapse of social distinctions does not so much argue for a real reorganisation of society as promote a certain construct of male vitality and sexuality' (Clarke 1989: 76). The significance of that vitality varied across social classes. The poor health of the working-class population became particularly visible to other classes when their services were required: at times of war. During the Boer War healthy recruits were hard to find and in 1916 when conscription was introduced only one third of the men examined were in 'normal' health (Thompson 1992: 9). 'Eugenics' or 'the science of improving stock' had developed in 1883 but as a movement become popularised in 1907 with the founding of the Eugenics Education Society. Eugenics attracted interest from the broadest political spectrum for differing reasons. The 'selective breeding' endorsed by eugenics appealed to the kind of feminism based on 'maternalist imperialism' but could equally be used to argue against women dissipating their energies in duties other than breeding (Bland 1995: 231).

In this context, Barbara's marriage to a political radical fuels rather than abates the family's fears, presenting on stage a comic embodiment of pressing concerns, as Suzanne Raitt suggests: 'Anxieties about the rise of socialism and the declining birth rate among the middle classes fed a deep-seated fear of the poorer classes and the threat of their domination' (Raitt 1993: 45). The acute deafness of every member of the family, indicates the decline of the aristocracy and their refusal to listen to new ideas (*Stage*, 10 February 1916: 23), as well as the inheritance of specific physical characteristics. The relative ineffectiveness of the male characters reflects the eugenic arguments underlying the play which emphasise the matriarchal power of the family.[12] As Laurie Wolf says, the men have the weakest voices in the play (Wolf 1989: 156). Cousin Everard's attempts to contribute to the discussion, for example, are thwarted by interruptions. The dominant class is exposed as operating an outmoded system of hegemonic control through arranged marriages, inherited wealth and ownership of land. *The Conference* demonstrates the findings of Leonore Davidoff: that throughout the nineteenth century the marriages of upper-class women were regulated rather than overtly arranged. To this end, the young woman's social life was closely supervised 'to ensure exclusion of undesirable partners' (Davidoff 1973: 49). In Barker's play the marriage was unconventional because of the social mobility implied by inter-class marriage, but as Clarke points out, 'in terms of the symbolic system of the play, Ann is validated and her decision vindicated by her potential for procreation' (Clarke 1989: 77).

The New Woman in *The Conference* is effective and decisive, threatening the dominant class through an unsanctioned marriage and promising a wholesale revision of marriage, if not other institutions. Politically radical couples, such as Emmeline and Frederick Pethick

Lawrence, had managed to achieve an egalitarian relationship within marriage. A reform of marriage is similarly presented through an unconventional representation of the New Woman in *The Patience of the Sea* by Conal O'Riordan.[13] The New Woman, Eva Fareworth, is conflated with the woman with a past. The taxonomy of the New Woman is given an ironic gloss. She is in middle age, has given up smoking, admits to false teeth and an illegitimate child. As a mother, Fareworth is successful from a eugenic point of view, but much of the play exposes the limitations and difficulties which motherhood poses in a patriarchal society, not least when those men keen to develop 'progressive' theories reveal their own psychological crises and inadequacies. Fareworth acts as the *raisonneur*, a role typically played by male actor-managers, and in this case performed by Gertrude Kingston, manager of the Little Theatre.[14] Although Fareworth has worked to support her illegitimate son, the play shows her pragmatism in marrying for financial security. Her new husband, Deering, coincidentally works in the same post which Fareworth had held, as secretary to Brown. Brown is a Fabian socialist philosopher. The allusion to George Bernard Shaw ends when Brown renounces vegetarianism.[15] The play exposes the disempowerment of women by Fabian idealism. It could also be interpreted as a criticism of the Stage Society which, as Jill Davis has argued, was an 'offshoot of the Fabian Society' which 'subscribed to eugenic ideas ... predicated upon the reduction of people to their sexual and reproductive roles' (Davis 1992: 18–20).

The idealism of the male characters is challenged through a sensational and comic series of events which expose the men as self-serving, narrow-minded and oppressive. The altruistic ideals of these men are revealed as hypocrisy in the scenes of violence. Fareworth is subjected to a violent assault from Deering when he discovers her in an embrace with Brown. Brown leaves the room apparently to commit suicide by drowning, following a thwarted duel with Deering. The competing interests of class and gender create a crisis for Brown, ironically represented by the setting. Brown's house is precariously situated on the edge of the cliff, overlooking the sea. For Brown the sea symbolises death or femininity, to which he dreams of yielding. Although both Brown and Deering have political objections to marriage, they are seen to idealise women. The effects of this prove to be destructive, as they were for the many suffragists who were routinely subjected to indecent assault when they demonstrated in public.

The reversal of the *raisonneur* role is accentuated by the allusion to H. A. Jones' *The Liars*. Deering shares the name of the *raisonneur* in Jones' play,[16] who rejects romance in favour of returning to duty as a pioneer in the colonies. In *Patience of the Sea*, O'Riordan presents Deering as foolish and irrational, representative of a destructive masculinity. The masculine reverence for the power of authorship is parodied. The manuscript of Brown's new and definitive book, *Patience (or The Soul of Socialism)*, is thrown into the sea by Deering. The characterisation is extreme, constructing profound sexual differences. As in some of the Pioneer Players' other productions,[17] in the *Patience of the Sea* the male characters are in the process of psychological disintegration, observed by a bemused female character. Fareworth, as *raisonneur*, remarks that Brown's solitude and obsession with work signifies a lack of humanity apparent in his writings. He is obsessed with producing grand totalising theories that bear no relation to his personal experience. While Fareworth has taken a pragmatic course in dealing with life as a single parent, Brown has withdrawn from the world, only able to function on an intellectual level.

The Lord Chamberlain's Reader judged that *The Patience of the Sea* was 'a very clever comedy with some real stuff of intellect in it. Many of the views expressed will shock the average playgoer'.[18] However, it is clear that, like Magdalen Ponsonby's *Idle Women* and Hamilton Fyfe's *Race Suicide*, it interpellates a particular social group through the allusion to contemporary events. The private membership of a subscription society meant that the constituency of the audience was familiar to the management and the performers. A degree of recognition could be guaranteed even though the actual audience was unpredictable. The small, intimate audience of the English theatre societies and the Russsian cabaret theatres had a tradition of self-parody. The Stage Society satirised George Bernard Shaw and Harley Granville-Barker in Gilbert Cannan's *Dull Monotony* (Holroyd 1989: 281). Allan Monkhouse's *Nothing Like Leather* performed the same funtion at the Gaiety Theatre.[19] At the end of the Glastonbury Festival in 1916 Rutland Boughton recalled the closing 'travesty play ... which guyed everything and everybody' (Hurd 1962: 61). Some features of *Idle Women* and *Race Suicide* similarly invite recongnition from the Pioneer Players' auidence. The object of the satire is not easily identifiable.

Race Suicide and *Idle Women* expose the ineffectiveness of organisations when the middle-class participants lack either commitment to their cause, or sufficient knowledge about the subject. In Raymond Williams' terms, the organisations featured in *Race Suicide* and *Idle Women* exemplify alternative, rather than oppositional formations (Williams 1981: 70). The threat was limited. Since the object of the comedy is the ineffective role of these organisations and their members, one may assume that the Pioneer Players distanced themselves from such incompetence, positioning the Pioneer Players as (at least) potentially or avowedly oppositional. Social reform was not merely a topic of idle conversation for the Pioneer Players. The strategy of self-parody marked the extent to which their pioneering was constrained, permitted and regulated by the dominant class to which many of the members in any case belonged, even if they wished to distance themselves from it.

Written by Hamilton Fyfe, a journalist and dramatist for the Stage Society,[20] *Race Suicide* satirises the eugenics movement, explicitly associating this with a disempowered masculinity and patriarchal institutions of industry, religion and the army. The Lord Chamberlain's report designated it, 'An amusing satire upon the futility of barking when you are not prepared to bite.'[21] The three male characters in the play, Mr Brown a manufacturer, a Church of England clergyman, and Colonel Flagg meet to form an association to disseminate their views on preventing 'race suicide', but these turn out to be muddled, hypocritical and contradictory. 'Race suicide' referred to the falling birth rate amongst the middle and upper social classes and also to the poor health of the working-class population: a dangerous degeneration of the nation's populace (Bland 1995: 226). The working class is erased by the term 'race'. The *Pall Mall Gazette* describes Fyfe's play as 'a light comedy, in which the attitude of parochial magnates on a serious social question suffers an amusing change when they are faced with putting their principles into practice' (*Pall Mall Gazette*, 13 April 1912: 5). Like the Fabian socialist in *The Patience of the Sea*, the men in *Race Suicide* are determined to discuss issues in extreme and abstract terms. Like Eva Fareworth, Mrs Brown insists on returning them to specific examples drawn from their own experience that proves to disturb them considerably.

The gendered differences in characterisation seen in *Beastie* are repeated here. Mrs Brown, the only female character, is the authoritative voice of practical reason in the play, contrasted with the misinformed bungling of the male characters. The emphasis is on dialogue rather than action. It is the men who are doing the talking and the audience is left in no doubt as to what nonsense it is. Turn-taking and interruption represent relationships of power as the men argue and the female character interrupts. The last words in this battle for air space are given to Mrs Brown when she mocks her husband who, she says, has had his chance to ring his little bell (if nothing else).

Her wit undercuts the men's claim to knowledge. She is quick to introduce Mrs Short, who turns up at the house asking for food, as an example of women burdened with more children than can be fed. The class prejudices underpinning the men's arguments for preventing 'race suicide' by marriage are revealed in discussion: their solution is marriage, but only of the 'fit' middle and upper classes. When a reviewer of *In the Workhouse* pointed out that the predicament of the 'idiot girl' with her third baby could have been prevented the unspoken issue, as in *Race Suicide,* was the use of contraception. Many eugenists feared that this practice would be adopted by the middle classes and it was not given publicity until Marie Stopes' campaign in the twenties. The Ministry of Health did not make advice on contraception available until 1930. Mrs Brown's angry exchanges with the vicar compare with Christabel Pankhurst's *The Great Scourge and How To End It* (1913), in which she attacked the church and others who conspired to put women at risk by concealing the facts about sexually transmitted diseases. Pankhurst argued that such diseases contributed to 'race suicide'. The appropriate response to this risk, she argued, was women's celibacy. She used available medical statistics to prove that 75–80 per cent of men were infected with gonorrhoea. Christabel Pankhurst and Cicely Hamilton in *Marriage as a Trade* (1909) argued, like Lucy Re-Bartlett, that the falling birth rate was caused by a 'silent strike' by women (Bland 1995: 247). *Race Suicide* is contemporaneous with the publication in the *Suffragette* of some of the individual articles compiled later in Pankhurst's book. *The Great Scourge* was endorsed by the Pioneer Players two years after this performance of *Race Suicide*, when it was advertised in a play programme.

Race Suicide posits profound gender differences. Mrs Brown at first knows nothing about 'race suicide' but gradually discovers that she knows more than the men on the subject. Her superior knowledge is rendered less threatening by her femininity. The stage directions, however, refer to her as 'blonde and buxom', 'genial', 'quicker than her husband, but happily not aware of that fact' (1). Like Jessie in *Beastie*, Mrs Brown is presented as conventionally feminine rather than a New Woman. She has compassion and understanding for those women who have many children and argues that her husband and his colleagues cannot appreciate these problems because they are men. In these respects, she may occupy the position of a morally superior motherhood compatible with eugenics. It may, perhaps, be the case that women such as Mrs Brown would be better equipped to expound upon the topic of 'race suicide'. At first peripheral, the female character becomes central to the play. The criticism of the destructive and dehumanising effects of patriarchal organisations was articulated by Cicely Hamilton (Hamilton 1935: 87) and dramatised in Hobson's *A Modern Crusader* in which the men-only debating society, appropriates 'ideas' as the exclusive property of men. In this context the Pioneer Players, with its agenda of the play of 'ideas' and a majority of female members, was challenging the masculine bias of the avant-garde theatre societies and, by extension, other patriarchal organisations. It does so by simultaneously reinforcing and challenging gender stereotypes. The problems that Jill Davis identifies with eugenics may explain the tensions within the plays examined in this chapter:

> Eugenic thinking therefore holds particular dangers for women: indeed I would argue its capture of social thinking in this period defeated much of the potential of early-twentieth century feminism, for its terms reassert the binary opposition of man/woman, mind/body, civilisation/nature which feminism was struggling to deconstruct.
>
> (Davis 1992: 20)

Although *Race Suicide* and *The Patience of the Sea* seem to challenge eugenics and the abstract social theorising of the Fabian Society which disempowered women, they do so by presenting their critique through a female character whose authority is confirmed by her motherhood. Thus Davis contends that while 'feminism was struggling to deconstruct' binary terms which disempowered women, many Fabian socialists and social reformers in social engineering were assuming that women would fulfill a reproductive role. The risk incurred in reversing dominant discourses was therefore the reinscription of binary oppositions.

While *The Conference* offered a critique of the aristocratic old order, it should be remembered that in Hobson's *A Modern Crusader* it was the intervention of an aristocratic woman which underwrote the younger generation's campaign for social reform. The role of wealthy philanthropists in social reform was well established by the time the Pioneer Players produced *Idle Women*. This play does, however, mock the superficial interests of some wealthy individuals and the dangers that their participation in alternative formations might pose.

Idle Women, subtitled 'A Study in Futility',[22] is a short play written by Magdalen Ponsonby, one of the few women active in the council of management of the Stage Society. In Lady Ditcham's drawing room in Grosvenor Square a committee meeting is held for the newly formed association for the dissemination of the religion of Bunginn Ga. This religion is based on the ideas of a Bhuddist philosopher, founded on the principle of *bienveillance,* and promoted by Tanno Matsuri, a Chinese boy said to be a reincarnation of Lao Tse. The allusion to the Theosophists' promotion of Krishnamurti, who arrived in London at Charing Cross Station in May 1911, is inescapable (Lutyens 1990: 13).[23] *Idle Women* takes the incident and works it into a comedy of mistaken identity. At the railway station a W. H. Smiths errand boy is mistaken for Matsuri. In scene two the real Tanno Matsuri arrives but is sent away since Lady Ditcham cannot face revealing her mistake. The second scene begins with the servants arranging the room with suitably oriental decorations in preparation for the arrival of Tanno Matsuri. The servants criticise their employer's fads, which include an interest in 'Apaches'. While the play satirises the superficial interest in other cultures it risks trivialising such cultural imperialism. However, the servants offer an astute and critical perspective on the activities of the house, drawing on a convention in plays such as *A Chat With Mrs Chicky*, where servants were depicted as suffragists before their employers.

The play presents a group of rich women trying to fill their time.[24] Lady Ditcham acknowledges her shortcomings. Unable to become involved in the suffrage campaign because it is 'too real', she has a merely 'amateur' interest in social issues and has therefore arranged a eugenics luncheon party. The characters discuss a cubist poem on the mystery of sex,[25] consider inviting Marinetti to write a futurist poem to sponsor the association, eat vegetarian food, talk of socialism and fancy dress balls. These topical references to the diverse cultural practices of this class fraction of reformers would be familiar to the Pioneer Players.[26] They had endorsed vegetarianism through their fund-raising production of Florence Edgar Hobson's play, *A Modern Crusader* in 1912 and held two fancy dress balls in 1913 and 1914. The Mi-Careme ball held at the exclusive Connaught Rooms in London on 19 March 1914 attracted photo-coverage in the *Tatler* (Plate 4). Nevertheless, the inscribed audience for *Idle Women* is 'active' rather than idle women, taking socialism and the suffrage movement seriously. *Idle Women* provides, like *Race Suicide*, a critique of organisational management. Women are named on the committee without their knowledge; those who do the work do not attend meetings. The dramatist clearly writes from an informed position regarding the occupations of aristocratic women. Although the committee to propagate the religion of Bunginn Ga includes men, the title of the play might have encouraged the misreading of the play by the *Stage* as 'an amusing skit on various Women's Societies and Committees' (25 June 1914: 22).

These comedies reverse and subvert conventions of both the society drama and the romantic comedy. In society drama, the woman with a past is exposed and either commits suicide or is sent into exile.[27] In the romantic comedy, all problems are resolved through the concluding marriage. The problem plays, typical of the earlier free theatres, were similarly transformed by the Pioneer Players. Characters become involved with social problems, exposing naivety and inexperience. The ensuing problematic situation is foregrounded comically. The romantic and idealist perspectives, endorsed by dramatists such as Shaw and Barker, are presented as complicit in violence, subjugation and destruction. The New Woman has grown older and has even become something of a joke. The concept of women's independence is given new treatment and it is through the figure of the pioneer that an 'active female subjectivity' is forming. Significantly, the Pioneer Players' feminist play of ideas is not necessarily female-authored. However, it is the favourable representation of women and the society's middle-class composition that engenders contradictions and unresolved tensions. As Stowell has argued, such realist plays address topical issues relating to social reform and identifiable contemporary political campaigns, raising more questions than they answer. Many of the plays offer a critique of gender stereotypes by foregrounding the perspective of the female characters. In this respect the category of the 'feminist play of ideas' is in some cases appropriate. However, the stable ideological position that these plays seem to offer is intelligible only in the address to a middle-class, rather than an exclusively female, audience. It is particularly in the comic form of these plays that the inscribed audience is discernible.

The Pioneer Players were purveyors of good drama and bad propaganda. The society's plays explored problems, provoked debate but refused inadequate solutions. As one of the 'free' theatre societies it was willing to try out possible solutions, to find a space in which to experiment with ideas and arguments. Although the private performances of such societies were exclusive, for many women the private space seemed to offer greater opportunities than the public stage. Some women had recognised the important influence of the theatre at this time and took up Matthew Arnold's injunction to 'organize the theatre', to engage not in the construction of a (male) national culture, but to represent themselves on stage and in the public arena. The Pioneer Players' intervention was successful in their challenge to the exclusivity of the English free theatres as regards gender but was limited in their treatment of class. The self-referential comedy demonstrates a sense of confidence in the position of women but insecurity in a middle-class and masculine identity. In retrospect, laughing at wealthy aristocrats did not improve the society's chances of patronage.

4
Pioneers Perform Politics

The seventeenth-century actress Margaret Hughes was hailed as a 'forgotten pioneer' at the Pioneer Players' inaugural performance in May 1911. In the last play in the triple bill that afternoon, Christopher St. John's *The First Actress*, actresses from the future, such as Madame Vestris and Nance Oldfield, appeared in a dream-vision to rouse Hughes from despondency following an unsuccessful debut performance as Desdemona. Some reviewers felt that Christopher St. John was a careless historian in claiming Hughes as a contender for the title of first actress on an English Restoration stage.[1] Suffragists often made audacious plunders into the past, appropriating as proto-suffragists anyone from the ancient Egyptians to Shakespeare. St. John claims a similar role for Hughes. Suffering from a lack of role models and subjected to the manipulations of powerful men, Hughes is the first to enter this male-dominated profession. She is explicitly aligned with a tradition of female performers and activists in the suffrage movement working for equality in employment. From the outset, the Pioneer Players were committed to the politics of firsts. They had a revisionist attitude to history and identified the female performer as a political activist.

Cicely Hamilton said that the women's suffrage movement marked a new departure in the political function of cultural practices:

> There were two respects in which the Woman Suffrage Movement differed from the general run of political strife. It was not a class movement; every rank and grade took part in it. And it was the first political agitation to organize the arts in its aid – how drab was the ordinary procession of protest before suffragists took to the march!...On decorative art, as aid to propaganda, followed the arts of entertainment — music and the drama.   (Hamilton 1948: 7)

68 *Women and Theatre in the Age of Suffrage*

It was the actresses who particularly embraced the cultural battle of the movement. Their performance of plays to raise funds and to raise awareness of the arguments for women's suffrage were crucial. The organisation by the Actresses' Franchise League (AFL) in 1908 of women working in the theatre to use their skills for the movement provided opportunities for women new to acting to learn the craft of the public sphere: the strength and clarity of voice in public speaking and how to work an audience. The metaphor of performance, alive in the period 1908–14, has been revived, in a different context in recent years. Lisa Tickner (1987) produced a definitive study, attending to processes of production and consumption of the imagery of the women's suffrage movement; Lesley Ferris (1995) identified the metatheatrical strategy in *The First Actress*; Barbara Green (1997) analysed the performativity of the suffrage movement from a Foucauldian perspective; while Lesley Hill has recently claimed: 'The Suffragettes Invented Performance Art' (2000). This chapter will explore the figure of the female performer as pioneer and the implications of the power she acquired as a political activist. The Pioneer Players developed from the AFL and had connections with other political organisations such as the Women's Freedom League (WFL). A brief analysis of the founding performances of *A Pageant of Great Women* and *How the Vote Was Won* will consider the political significance of the pageant form and performance in women's suffrage culture. Strategies of reversal and mimicry were used in the literature of the movement to challenge anti-suffrage arguments. The naming of the Pioneer Players society situates the pioneer, like the New Woman and the suffragette, in a volatile position, as sites of appropriated or reverse discourses. For this theatre society, the 'pioneer' marks a nexus of feminism, politics and performance.

The Pioneer Players did not explain their choice of name. The 'pioneer' was such a common feature of women's suffrage discourse that it was not the subject of debate. In 1910, a year before the Pioneer Players were launched, the term 'pioneer' featured widely in a feminist context. Christopher St. John used it in her essay in Charlotte Despard's pamphlet *Woman in the New Era*. The WSPU newspaper, *Votes for Women*, published an extract from Olive Schreiner's short story, 'Three Dreams in a Desert', under the title 'The Pioneers', and also a poem by V. H. Friedlander[2] entitled 'The Master Joy', which used the term.

Charlotte Despard claimed for suffragist 'pioneers' a significant function in the evolution of humankind. Such ideas were influenced by the Theosophical Society, founded in 1875 by Madame Helena Blavatsky, which expounded an unconventional, subsequently derided but very popular, synthesis of religious and scientific ideas. It was particularly attractive to women such as Despard, who were seeking a belief system flexible enough to endorse women's rights to citizenship and to spiritual salvation. As Lucy Bland explains, theosophy argued for a 'universal brotherhood of humanity' without any distinction. It valued women and men equally since both female and male principles were required for evolution of the harmonious whole or 'Absolute' (Bland 1995: 167). The 'pioneer', unmarked with respect to sex, drew its strength from such ideas. In the context of theosophy, 'spirituality' signified women's rights to a conscience and to consciousness: to think and to choose. Apparently transparent terms – such as pioneer – acquired an opaque quality in the discourses which produced women's suffrage writing. An awareness of the need to make explicit the power of language to shape thought was expressed by Christopher St. John in her biographical portrait of Charlotte Despard in *Woman and the New Era*:

> Always in sympathy with what we call 'the Woman's Question' (object, briefly, Woman to be a noun herself, not an article relating to a noun eternally), she begins now to see its absolute importance.
> (St. John 1910: 19)

The deliberate renaming by Christopher St. John of what was known as 'the Woman Question' claims the women's movement and the campaigns for women's suffrage as belonging to women. A similar awareness of the political inflections of language would have informed the choice of the name 'Pioneer Players'. While *Woman in the New Era* may not have been a manifesto for the society, the ideas it embodies are reflected in both the Pioneer Players' choice of plays and in their stated aims and objectives.

The 'pioneer' appears as a martyr in 'The Master Joy', a Whitmanesque poem by V. H. Friedlander, published by the WSPU in *Votes for Women*, 19 August 1910:

> 'The Master Joy'
> We shall not travel the road that we have made;
> Ere day by day the sound of many feet
> Is heard where we have toiled and fought and prayed,
> We shall be come to where the Cross-roads meet.
>
> For us the heat by day, the cold by night,
> The inch-slow progress and the heavy load,

> And Death at last to close the long, grim fight
> With man and beast and stone: for them – the Road.
>
> For them the shade of trees that now we plant,
> The safe, smooth journey and the ultimate goal –
> Yea, birthright in the Land of Covenant –
> For us day-labour, travail of the soul.
>
> And yet – the Road is ours, as never theirs;
> Is not one joy on us alone bestowed?
> For us the Master-Joy, O Pioneers!
> We shall not travel, but we have made the Road.

The suffragist-pioneer is aligned audaciously with Moses. The wandering in the wilderness towards the 'Land of Covenant' in the Book of Exodus finds Moses leading the Israelites out of slavery in Egypt into the desert where salvation appears through the Ten Commandments. The authority of Christianity was widely used in the women's suffrage movement to endorse the self-sacrifice which political commitment necessitated. Religious and political journeys, such as the one indicated by Friedlander, draw on the literary conventions of Romanticism and the project of colonialism. Caravans, crusades and pilgrimages were common terms for mass meetings and marches. Both the NUWSS and the WFL took suffrage 'caravans' all over the country to spread their political message.

Women taking up space to travel in the public sphere, the open road and the street draw strength from the authority of religious discourse. Street sellers of the *Vote* were described as front-line workers, like pioneers in the army preparing new ground for the ensuing forces advancing in battle:

> So much ground seems unbroken, despite all our efforts. If anyone is over confident about the progress of the movement, let her try VOTE selling. If anyone is despondent, let her try the same remedy, for though at one moment one is struck by the ignorance still existing with regard to 'Votes for Women,' at another time, in unlooked for quarters, one finds much sympathetic insight. Just before deserting our pitch two ladies came towards us, bought papers, and exclaimed, 'You call us "lady" Suffragists, but we are all travelling the same road, and a number of us are very near you'.
>
> (Fenton 1910: 286)

A review of the Pioneer Players' first production deploys similar expressions:

> So I, a woman journalist, heartened and encouraged by the work and personality and pluck of the women all around me, left the theatre jauntily to take tea with another pioneer, herself an actress and writer of plays. We shall arrive; and when we join hands with our brothers we shall see things happen – the real right things.

The pioneer is a product of allegorical and utopian forms which were particularly effective in exploring the possibilities for the future rather than the realist mode usually associated with women's suffrage writings. A tradition of feminist utopian writing has been constructed from such texts as Margaret Cavendish's *The Description of a New World, Called the Blazing World* (1668), Sarah Scott's *Millenium Hall* (1762), Elizabeth Gaskell's *Cranford* (1851–3) and Charlotte Perkins Gilman's *Herland* (1915). The setting and the manipulation of time are significant features of texts where the suffragist-pioneer occurs. As Donawerth and Kolmerten have suggested:

> Feminist utopian writing can be interpreted using Anne Cranny Francis' concept of a 'literature of estrangement...a literature concerned primarily with the alienation experienced by individual subjects, realized textually by a setting displaced in time and/or place'.
> (Donawerth and Kolmerten 1994: 2)

Suffragists were thus able to rethink dominant ideologies because, 'In utopian writing this displacement means that gender roles can be more easily revised when the reader is estranged form her ordinary world' (Donawerth and Kolmerten 1994: 2). The revolutionary potential of the allegorical mode is illustrated by Olive Schreiner's symbolist short story, 'Three Dreams in a Desert'. Published in Schreiner's collection *Dreams* (1890), it became an influential text in the women's suffrage movement.[3]

Schreiner, like Cicely Hamilton, was a member of the Women Writers' Suffrage League. Although her pacifism made her critical of the WSPU's militancy, her short story was appropriated by them and published in *Votes for Women* under the heading 'The Pioneers':

> He [Freedom] said: 'They are the feet of those that shall follow you. Lead on and make a track to the water's edge. The ground where you stand now will be beaten flat by ten thousand times ten thousand feet. Have you seen the locusts, how they cross a stream? First one

comes down to the water's edge and is swept away, and then another, and at last with their bodies a bridge is built and the rest pass over.'

She said: 'And of those that come first – some are swept away and are heard of no more; their bodies even do not build the bridge.'

And are swept way and are heard of no more. And what of that?' he said... 'They make a track to the water's edge.'

They make a track to the water's edge.' And she said: 'Over that bridge which shall be built by our bodies who will pass?'

He said: 'The whole human race'.

('The Pioneer', *Votes for Women*, 11 March 1910: 373)

This endorsement of self-sacrifice became effective for the WSPU when their militant tactics began to incur greater risks. Schreiner's short story became so well known that it was possible for Mrs Pethick Lawrence to commit it to memory. In February 1909 in Holloway Prison, she recited it to the other inmates. Lady Constance Lytton remembered this occasion. Lytton had been imprisoned for one month for refusing to keep the peace after being arrested for her part in the deputation to the House of Commons organised by the WSPU. She had been a member for just one month. During this imprisonment she noted her changed reaction to Schreiner's story which had been a family favourite (Lytton 1988: 156). When she heard it recited in Holloway she also changed her view of literature, regarding the story as realistic rather than allegorical:

> Olive Schreiner, more than any one other author, has rightly interested the woman's movement and symbolised and immortalised it by her writings. Now after even so short an experience of the movement as I had known, this 'Dream' seemed scarcely an allegory. The words hit out a bare literal description of the pilgrimage of women. It fell on our ears more like an ABC railway guide to our journey than a figurative parable, though its poetic strength was all the greater for that.... We dispersed and went back to our hard beds, to the thought of our homes, to the depressing surroundings of fellow prisoners, to the groans and cries of agonised women – content. As I laid my head on the rattling pillow I surrendered my normal attitude towards literature, and thought 'There is some point, some purpose in it after all.'
> (Lytton 1988: 157–8)

The potential of literature for empowerment was considerable. For this reason, perhaps, H. G. Wells depicts Ann Veronica as the spontaneous author of bad poetry in Holloway prison. Utopian writing provided spaces for new female subjectivities because the estrangement of time and place allowed consideration of position rather than essence to challenge gender ideology. Of course, the role of the pioneer was open to men also. One problem facing the women's suffrage movement apparent in this short story concerns the implications of women appropriating power. An asymmetry of power is maintained if a simple inversion of positions leaves the structure intact. Thus, man as the Cupid-like child at Woman's breast is infantilised by Woman, positioned as mother superior. The category 'Woman' often tacitly supported white supremacy. Woman in Schreiner's African desert, like the pioneer, was moving into occupied territory, however empty or strange the terrain might appear.[4] This movement was variously celebrated for its novelty and deplored as invasion. Shortly after Schreiner's *Dreams* were published, the Pioneer Club claimed that the women who took part in their debates were

> learning to separate personal friendships from matters of principle; and so making great strides along the broad new pathway they are hewing for themselves out of the rocks of prejudice before and around them, the growths of past ages. These Pioneers have resolved to destroy the distinctions of sex and class.
> (*Shafts* II.10. December 1893: 183)

However much the 'pioneer' might try to transcend differences of sex and class these troubling positions would surface.

The opacity of the term 'pioneer' demonstrates the difficulty with which these writers were struggling to find an appropriate mode of self-representation. The kinds of subjectivity available to women during the women's suffrage movement in Britain were fraught with tensions and contradictions. As Chris Weedon explains:

> subjectivity is of key importance in the social processes and practices through which forms of class, race and gender power are exercised. We have to assume subjectivity in order to make sense of society and ourselves. The question is what modes of subjectivity are open to us and what they imply in political terms
> (Weedon 1987: 173)

Schreiner's 'Three Dreams in a Desert' exemplifies the risks associated with appropriating the pioneer as an active female subjectivity precisely because it drew its strength from the discourses of colonialism and religion. The ultimate risk was, as Weedon indicates, self-defeat:

> Different discourses provide for a range of modes of subjectivity and the ways in which particular discourses constitute subjectivity have implications for the process of reproducing or contesting power relations.
>
> (Weedon 1987: 92)

The naming of the Pioneer Players was, therefore, an instance of a careful attention to language typical of the women's suffrage movement.

The specificity of feminist subjectivities has been blurred by comparisons made between the ends of the nineteenth and twentieth centuries. New Woman, 'femmes de siècle', pioneer, suffragette and flapper are not interchangeable terms occupying different points on a historical line from the 1890s to the 1920s. This history of the Pioneer Players exposes the conflicts between some of these positions and their function for women. The New Woman and the suffragette were not simply positive or negative images of women, but available positions of potential empowerment for women. Feminist critics have engaged with the complexities of the New Woman but have yet to explore the points of transition and overlap with the pioneer and the suffragette. The significance of these terms is not discernible from the known political position of the author of the text in which they feature. The instability in relationships of power rendered such positions open to appropriation. During the lifetime of the Pioneer Players both the New Woman and the suffragette were sites of reverse discourse. The New Woman had become obsolete, superseded by the pioneer. The density of resonance apparent for these terms is discernible given an appreciation of the arguments for and against women's enfranchisement.

The common anti-suffrage arguments were based on a biological essentialism, such that women and men were regarded as essentially different from each other. Women's feminine nature was taken to be biologically determined. These natural differences between women and men led to different occupations and social roles which were complementary and occupied separate spheres, women operating in the private sphere and men occupying the public sphere. Since women were thought to be physically weaker than men and a citizen's duty was to defend the country at time of war, women were disqualified from citizenship. This argument was based on the dependence of government on physical force, to defend itself from outside threats. Women's physiological instability and limited capacity for intellectual activity were scientific 'facts' used to argue for women's unsuitability to have the responsibility for voting. Women's enfranchisement would lead to social and moral disorder.

The arguments for women's enfranchisement tended to emphasise either sameness or difference with respect to women's attributes, compared with those of men. It was claimed, for instance, that women were the same as men in all important respects and should therefore be given equal rights and opportunities in government. Enfranchisement was effectively a demand for the inclusion of women in the democratic structure. Alternatively, it was argued that women's unique perspective, particularly the experience of motherhood and child-rearing, would contribute a moral dimension to politics. A suffrage argument which had feminist potential was that enfranchisement was symbolic, a gateway to widespread reforms and social changes to improve the position of women and men.

Lisa Tickner's study of the visual imagery of the women's suffrage movement, its banners, posters and processions, emphasises the dynamic relationship between these images and those used by anti-suffragists. The suffrage artists made use of available imagery. The artwork, drama and writings did not evolve autonomously, and the appropriation of literary, professional or high art modes were not without their problems. Language and representation generally became politically charged. Disguise, mimicry, reverse discourses, ambiguity, were strategies used at every level and in every form of the suffrage movement's cultural practices, even in dress. Feminine hats were adopted by the most militant of activists, members of the WSPU, otherwise stereotyped as masculine by anti-suffragists. Barbara Green has analysed the 'ornamental body as civic body' in the relationship between activism and fashionable femininity. Strategies of self-representation were adopted both in street demonstrations and processions and in the writings of the movement. Three key members of the Pioneer Players – Christopher St. John, Cicely Hamilton and Edith Craig – can now be identified in the photograph showing women carrying the Women's Writers' Suffrage League banner in a street procession. Many suffragists assumed the costume of public display and, to a certain extent, took on the mantle of femininity in strategic fashion. This is elucidated not just in terms of visibility and the body, but by the broader strategy of reverse discourse operating in other cultural forms. Christopher St. John, author of *The First Actress* which had associated the pioneer with the suffrage activist, published a short story in *Votes for Women* which identifies just such a strategy. 'A Defence of the Fighting Spirit', shows Diana and Gertrude discussing strategies in the suffrage movement. Diana argues for militant action, but Gertrude disagrees, rejecting the word 'suffragette' on aesthetic grounds: 'The word offends my literary taste.' Diana's reply concludes the dialogue:

> You must emancipate your literary taste from its conventions. We didn't invent the word, but ungrammatical, half-contemptuous as it is, there is not one of us who would exchange it now for a more refined and literary title. They say that a man has never achieved greatness until he is called by some nickname. Perhaps the same thing applies to movements!
> (St. John 1909: 808–9)

Literary value is here positioned as oppressive. Diana argues that culture and language are crucial sites for women's struggle for emancipation:

> 'The Philistine upholds and supports the blind mechanical forces of society and doesn't recognise dynamic force when he meets it, either in a man or a movement.' David, or the child of light, marches against the Philistines, armed with the truth that life is changeful, fluid, active, and to allow it to be stereotyped into any form is death. The Suffragette is the modern David. (ibid.)

St. John distinguishes between a prehistoric aesthetics and a revolutionary art in which all forms and images are available for political ends. The organisations which, as Hamilton said, were uniquely using the arts to support the movement took differing, sometimes ambivalent positions, regarding aesthetic value. The Suffrage Atelier and the Pioneer Players, for instance, were encouraging of amateurs whereas the Artists' Suffrage League would admit only professionals.[5] Aesthetic value was used by suffrage artists and writers to demonstrate their achievement and to prove their worth against the charges that there had been no female Platos or Shakespeares. For some women, including Cicely Hamilton, copyright was an important issue. Others rejected or reassessed the whole notion of aesthetic value, the criteria for evaluation and the relationships of power supporting the distinction between amateur and professional.

The Pioneer Players were launched in May 1911 at a time when the women's suffrage movement appeared to be on the verge of victory. The Conciliation Bill had been redrafted, passed for a second reading and referred to parliament for consideration. During the summer of 1911 the NUWSS and WSPU worked together, expecting imminent enfranchisement. In November that year a new piece of legislative reform was announced which effectively diverted attention from women's enfranchisement. Uproar ensued, and militant violence escalated through 1912 and 1913. Mrs Pankhurst provocatively declared: 'The argument of the broken pane is the most valuable argument in modern politics' (Tickner 1987: 132). Her incitement to violence led to militant attacks on property in 1913. These were proudly listed by type and cost of damage caused in *the Suffragette*'s 'A Year's Record'. The early years of the Pioneer Players' activity therefore coincided with the most violent period of the suffrage movement when militants were strategically choosing increasingly destructive actions rather than the non-violent cultural interventions favoured by the WFL and NUWSS.

When the Pioneer Players were launched, many organisations, such as the Artists' Suffrage League, the Suffrage Atelier, the Women Writers' Suffrage League and the AFL, had already been formed to support the women's suffrage campaign culturally. They were largely independent but supportive of the political suffrage organisations. The Pioneer Players shared members with several of these organisations. The women's suffrage movement gave rise to some new forms of organisation and new ways of working, in some cases in women-only spaces. Lisa Tickner has shown that the suffrage artists were the first to organise themselves into a separate suffrage society around a particular profession and that they worked on a principle of co-operation. This 'sisterhood based on diversity' (Tickner 1987: 66) applied also to the working practices of the suffrage-affiliated theatre, which would appropriate social events and informal spaces in order to take suffrage arguments to a wider audience. The notion of co-operation between professionals and amateurs challenged the idea of the artist as a unique individual; on many occasions the identity of the artist was suppressed so that attention would not be diverted from the political campaign. The use of informal networks amongst women broke down divisions between private and public spaces. This was articulated formally in the cultural products of the women's suffrage movement which were contesting the separate-spheres ideology underpinning the anti-suffrage arguments.

The suffragists sought representation for women in parliament and some were determined to represent the diversity of women in their organisations. The initiative of the suffrage street processions in representing different groups of women was emulated by suffrage political organisations. Differences between women were not always denied.

They were celebrated and accommodated by the departmentalising of organisations. The Women's Freedom League (WFL) formed a separate propaganda department in July 1910, and the AFL formed a separate play department. The Pioneer Players developed from Edith Craig's work with the AFL and her freelance production of Cicely Hamilton's *A Pageant of Great Women* across the country in 1909–10.[6]

The Pioneer Players' official relationship with the suffrage campaign was non-partisan in that it did not publicly align itself with any single suffrage political organisation such as the WFL, WSPU or NUWSS. The society's commitment to respond to the changing political and social landscape was written into its constitution (*PPAR 1911–12:* 3), but this was never limited to women's suffrage. *The Suffrage Annual and Women's Who's Who* (1913) does not, for instance, list the Pioneer Players under 'suffrage societies', 'clubs' or other 'associations interested in the franchise'. It appears only in a reference to the production of Margaret Wynne Nevinson's *In The Workhouse*, under Nevinson's biographical entry. The society's membership lists reveal that many members were prominent suffragists.[7] These members were drawn from a number of suffrage political organisations which adopted different strategies, but they were all welcomed by the Pioneer Players. It was not unusual for suffragists to belong to several societies: individualism was accommodated and often encouraged where it might benefit the suffrage campaign. Edith Craig's activities exemplify this working practice of co-operation which has not been sufficiently recognised; she is an important focus of various cultural practices which were emerging in the suffrage movement.[8] My investigation of the women's suffrage newspapers has revealed Craig's membership of the WFL, which was an unofficial influence on the Pioneer Players. Craig was a committed activist whose enthusiasm and energy were appreciated and developed by both the WFL and the WSPU. In an interview for *Votes for Women* she said: 'one of her chief joys was organising anything anybody would allow her to organise' (*Votes for Women*, 15 April 1910: 455). She would not admit to being 'chief organiser of the Actresses' Franchise League' (455).

During the period in which the Pioneer Players was forming (1909–10), the WFL's strategy was one of tolerance and multi-party demonstrations to accelerate publicity and support. Co-operation between individual women and suffrage societies was greater than the media and public images of the leaders might suggest, particularly where cultural activities were concerned. The precise relationships between the cultural organisations of the movement have yet to be established. Plays produced for the AFL, for instance, would later be produced by other societies and theatres. Individuals worked within organisations and also on a freelance basis. Edith Craig seems to have directed plays in this way. George Bernard Shaw's *Press Cuttings* which had been directed by Craig, was produced at Miss Horniman's Gaiety Theatre. Cicely Hamilton and Christopher St. John's *How the Vote was Won* and Inez Bensusan's play *The Apple* performed by the AFL were taken up by the Play Actors in its fourth season.[9] On the fifteen-member council of the Play Actors were four women who were also members of the Pioneer Players: Inez Bensusan (also secretary of the AFL play department); Winifred Mayo (member of WSPU and AFL executive); Agnes Imlay; and Ruth Parrott (secretary of the Play Actors).

While co-operation and collaborative work was a significant feature of the movement, there were also situations in which individuals were exploited or worked in ways which seemed to contradict the egalitarian ethos of the movement. Both Beatrice Harraden and Cicely Hamilton were concerned about their plays being performed without permission. In Hamilton's case it provoked a letter to the Society of Authors (Whitelaw 1990: 126). It is likely that the performance in question was of *A Pageant of Great Women* given by the Pioneer Players for the WSPU in Liverpool and directed by Edith Craig. Craig was not oblivious to author's or performance rights since she owned rights of performance to many plays, including some written by Hamilton. However, she did not own rights of performance for *A Pageant of Great Women*. As regards her own work, Craig had been identified in a suffrage newspaper for her generosity and 'self-effacement' (*Vote*, 12 March 1910: 232).

Many members of the Pioneer Players were actively involved in the WFL and in its newspaper, the *Vote*, launched in 1909. This newspaper was edited by member of the Pioneer Players' executive: at first by Cicely Hamilton who resigned due to ill-health in October 1909, and later by Marie Lawson. Margaret Wynne Nevinson was a regular contributor. Leading members of the Pioneer Players were committed to the WFL, producing theatrical pieces, as well as attending and holding office at branch meetings. Edith Craig was elected Literature Secretary of the Mid-London branch (renamed Central London Branch) on 14 February 1911. She was, with Cicely Hamilton, an active member of the Central London branch of the WFL which met at the Bijou Theatre, 3 Bedford Street. This theatre was not used as a venue for the Pioneer Players, which may suggest that the society's executive did not wish to impose their political affiliations on the work of the society.

80 Women and Theatre in the Age of Suffrage

Although Craig and other members of the Pioneer Players belonged to other suffrage organisations, Craig's views were influenced by the WFL which became disenchanted with party politics and was formed in reaction to the increasingly autocratic practices of the WSPU. The WFL drew its membership from a liberal reformist milieu, committed to militancy of symbol and word rather than violent actions. They organised a boycott of the 1911 Census, which Margaret Wynne Nevinson described as 'passive resistance' to a government that failed to represent women (Nevinson 1926: 229). The WFL, more than any other suffrage political organisation, was concerned with cultural intervention. Contributors to the *Vote* frequently published interviews with actresses, writers and photographers in order to debate cultural strategies. Madeleine Lucette Ryley, a prolific writer, was asked whether she had considered writing a suffrage play:

> No. I have thought of doing so several times, but the difficulty is not to miss the broad issues in dwelling on one of the irritations. And that is what one would have to do in taking up a single point in which there is sex disability and writing a play round it. It is because I regard the whole question as so vital and so great, and so cumulative in its possibilities as a whole, that I think it dangerous to dwell on one of the little flies in the ointment – a little fly which in itself it might not be impossible to eliminate. Remedying small disabilities is the insidious method of delaying the great result, and it is the great uplifting, that the responsibilities of full and perfect citizenship will give us, that we are waiting for.
>
> (*Vote*, 26 March 1910: 257)

Just as Mary Wollstonecraft demonised the sentimental novel, the suffragists condemned the distorting effects of the novel and the drama. Margaret Kennedy's article was a rally for women to take up the pen:

> Much of the misrepresentation of women is due to the playwright and the novelist of the past who have depicted women as concentrating on their emotions, and finding in erotic and domestic sensibilities the business of their lives.... Those men who have had the power of speech have declared that they would represent them [women]. But they have not done so, and the misrepresentation has been not so much on the part of the electorate as on that of their representatives.
>
> (*Vote*, 23 January 1911: 161)

Such a critique appeared to posit a 'real' or 'true' woman concealed or distorted by male-authored literature. However, Cicely Hamilton provocatively identified the female author's complicity in gender ideology:

> The woman writer, when describing a 'good woman,' used to endeavour to reproduce a man's point of view, forgetting that in herself she had all that she required – that she was a condensed version of the world. It was not until the New Woman came along that this was ever realised. The Womanly Woman was the most unnatural thing in creation, but whatever the modern woman was at least she was natural.... Women would never be anything until they learned to be themselves, until they paid their debt to themselves and gave up pretending to be what they were not. The fundamental reason why there had been no great women to cap the Platos of the world was because so far the woman had been working to please other people and not to please herself. [...Women] had got to claim more for themselves; it was only when they possessed they would be able to give. Christ had said it was more blessed to give than to receive, but He had never said it was more blessed to have it taken from you. Only those who had something they had made their own could afford to give.... Women were now at the beginning, and the earth was open to them. It was only when they knew their heritage they could perfectly understand.
>
> (*Vote*, 4 June 1910: 621)

Louisa Thompson Price argues that gender ideology was oppressive to women all over the world and that this was subject to historical change. She does, however, attribute its construction to men:

> One is compelled to conclude that this 'womanly' woman is what the male Anti-suffragist wishes woman to be. The man, in fact, has fixed the standard in the various countries of the world, and it, of course, changes with the flight of time. The Mohammedan considers it 'unwomanly' for a person of the female sex to be seen with her face uncovered. The Chinese think it 'unwomanly' for a woman to leave her house or to wish to walk. The Chinese woman is therefore taught to bandage her feet. In our own country we are told that 'womanly' women are contented to let their fathers, husbands, and sons decide what is politically best for them, and that if they desire to advance they must only do so within strict limits.... Surely if in aiming to accomplish these things woman has sometimes to lay aside the

garments of old-time respectable conventions and to adopt the attitude of revolt, she is at least earning for the word 'womanly' a finer and a grander meaning than it has hitherto borne.

(*Vote*, 8 October 1910: 236)

Thompson Price thus establishes the concept of patriarchy by locating such national and religious identities as irretrievably Other. Differences between national identities are effaced in Cicely Hamilton's play, *A Pageant of Great Women*, which brought together great women of the past from many different countries in order to make visible their international achievements.

Edith Craig's performances of *A Pageant of Great Women* and *How the Vote Was Won* with performers named the 'Pioneer Players' mark the beginnings of the society. Craig had already worked on pageants. A form associated with civic ritual, it was to acquire an association with women. Elsewhere such forms were linked to political movements. The Pioneer Players' involvement with the nationwide performances of *A Pageant of Great Women* aligned it with the potentially disruptive mass-produced spectacles of the French popular theatre and the influential Paterson Strike Pageant (1913) in USA. As Karen Blair has demonstrated, women such as Hazel MacKaye made use of the pageant form in the movement for women's suffrage in USA.

The court scene of *A Pageant of Great Women* emphasises the legal dimension of the suffrage campaign. Justice is a female figure, blindfolded to imply objectivity – sight could cloud judgement. The hunger-striking suffragettes who were forcibly fed and those women who were assaulted during public demonstrations were constructed anachronistically as the publicly tortured bodies of an ancient penal system. Michel Foucault has demonstrated that, in the modern penal system, the physical punishment and torture of the body is concealed, replaced by a system of surveillance and the deprivation of freedom of movement. The freakish display and critique of stereotypes in Cicely Hamilton's *Anti-Suffrage Waxworks* acted as a curtain-raiser to the *Pageant*. Power circulated around the visible and vulnerable body. As Foucault observed, the Enlightenment movement for liberty and human rights marked a shift in the penal system, such that 'if one intervenes upon [the body] to imprison it, or to make it work, it is in order to deprive the individual of a liberty that is regarded both as a right and as property' (Foucault 1991: 11). Arguably these women were not citizens, had never enjoyed 'liberty' and were not therefore privileged as modern subjects of the penal system. In representing forcible feeding as torture and rape in posters and cartoons, the suffrage artists were identifying a powerful challenge to the anti-suffrage system. *A Pageant of Great Women*, performed on the notorious day of violence (known as 'Black Friday') on 18 November 1910, emphatically presented women as modern subjects on a day when one or two had been fatally constructed as the tortured bodies of an ancient society.

The great women in the play – with the exception of Nance Oldfield – do not speak. Their silence seems to have been underestimated by recent critics. However, Nina Auerbach has indicated that the tableaux shown at Drury Lane theatre would be available allusions for contemporary audiences. When the *Pageant* was performed to vast audiences (some 2,000 in Sunderland, for instance) of which women were the majority, different relationships of power were possible between the silent actress on stage and the spectator. The making visible and audible of women in the movement were conventions of Enlightenment discourse.

The significance of visibility when female bodies take up space in the public sphere concerned their insistent claim to be regarded as modern subjects. Women were becoming spectators as well as self-consciously presenting themselves as 'objects-to-be-looked-at' (Aston 1995: 43). Association with other women was bringing about change. Acting in the *Pageant* or watching it being performed would, for local activists, allow them to experiment in becoming a different sort of woman. The advertisement for the performance in Kent in September 1910 uses the language of consciousness-raising:

> You believe that women have been great, that they are great. Come to the Public Hall, Beckenham, on Saturday, September 24th and realise your beliefs! As learned women and saintly women, artists, heroines, rulers, and warriors pass before you, as you hear of the work they have accomplished, give rein to your enthusiasm, let your hands proclaim your pride in Womanhood; as these illustrious ones of all nations appear, let every woman present thank god that she belongs to the sex that, in spite of fearful odds, has left such splendid record upon the annals of history.
>
> (*Vote*, 10 September 1910: 231)

Although writers such as Cicely Hamilton and Christopher St. John were concerned with constructing women's history, Hamilton at least identified a different perspective which was gendered and generational:

> behind the Suffrage movement is the new consciousness in woman that she is free to think for herself... Think of the years, of the

generations that women have been told they must not think!... We see things with a view which is entirely different from that which our brothers had; they saw them as their fathers saw them, but we see things very differently from the way our mothers saw them.

(*Vote*, 11 January 1911: 140–1)

The 'mothers' Hamilton envisages are supporters of the Womanly Woman whom the new generation must reject. By contrast, Virginia Woolf was to claim, 'We think back through our mothers, if we are women.' Suffragists often represented a breach between older and younger women. Many writers were attempting to redefine femininity and represented 'woman' in different ways. The category 'woman' and the function of role models or heroines have been criticised by feminist critics. Some of the criticisms which Michèle Barrett levelled at Judy Chicago's 'The Dinner Party' (1974) could be applied to *A Pageant of Great Women*:

> The list of names in the catalogue is studded with epithets like 'pioneer,' 'prizewinning,' 'cultural leader,' and 'eminent intellectual' – all of them terms of evaluation which we have developed a critical stance towards. The search for heroines and role models, for the great women of history, is one which raises a number of difficulties.
>
> (Barrett 1990: 162).

An emphasis on the exceptional women (or men) of the past seems to displace the majority of ordinary women:

> A feminism based on the assumption that there could be a category 'Woman' outside philosophy or male fantasy, or a category 'women' within the social world, untraversed by differences of, among other specificities, class, sexuality, race, nationality, or ethnicity, will be bound to repeat the imperial gesture whatever its intentions.
>
> (Landry and Maclean 1993: 9)

However Some of the destabilising effects of *A Pageant of Great Women* derive from the circumstances of its performance: the representation of Prejudice instead of Man; and the representation of Woman, great women *and* ordinary women in the same space. The parts of the great women were taken by local activists.[10] The *Daily Mirror* took the trouble to devote its front page to photographs of actresses in the debut performance (Plate 5). The captions indicate the women's suffrage context of the play, and yet slyly and emphatically construct these women as beautiful. The suffragette body, when forcibly fed, was constructed as 'sick' by medical discourse and 'tortured' in suffrage iconography. The suffragette was 'mad', 'ugly', not a woman, according to the anti-suffragists. National newspapers such as the *Daily Mirror* represented the suffragette as a new species. The headline in 1914 ran, 'The Suffragette Face: New Type Evolved By Militancy' (*Daily Mirror* 25 November 1914: 5). The photo-journalistic coverage of *A Pageant of Great Women*, when read against this later piece, seems to subvert the political position of the actresses by reproducing them as objects to be seen.

Although *How the Vote Was Won*, a result of collaboration between Cicely Hamilton and Christopher St. John, is ostensibly realist, its title suggests a distortion of time which makes the play hard to locate. The action of the play concerns a strike of women which prompts Horace Cole, a clerk, to rush from the house to campaign for women's enfranchisement to rid him of his burdensome female relatives: 'You may depend on me – all of you – to see justice done. When you want a thing done, get a man to do it! Votes for Women!' Although at the end of the play the vote has not yet been won, the title suggests otherwise. This sets up a comic space, positioning the audience somewhere else. Suffrage writers were providing a new perspective on the world, a new reality which pushed the limits of realism. This play, like *A Pageant of Great Women*, was extremely popular. Its effectiveness derives from the witty parody of separate-spheres ideology whereby many uninvited, striking women occupy the domestic space, and the men leave the home hurriedly to take up political campaigning in the public sphere. Furthermore, the visual image of a group of women filling the acting space generated allusions to the association of women in demonstrations and processions elsewhere. The sign of women gathering together with political purpose was, and is, particularly volatile. The production of this sign in public was an incitement to rebellion. Thus the Pioneer Players aligned the performer with the political activist in a tradition beginning with Margaret Hughes as the 'forgotten pioneer'.

The quotation from Schreiner's utopian story, published under the title 'The Pioneers' only months before the Pioneer Players was formed, envisages a new landscape for which new maps will be required. The actress is endowed with the privileged role of radical cartographer of the separate spheres allocated in dominant discourse to women and men. Christopher St. John had applied her expertise as an historian to the task of women's history in her one-act play, *The First Actress*. Since female roles were conventionally played by boys, Hughes faced resistance. The play argues that Hughes ironically owes her début to the machinations of a male aristocrat, Sir Charles Sedley, in whose feud she was implicated. She has been set up to fail. However, at this crucial moment of failure her disillusionment is checked by the appearance in her dream of actresses of the future. Hughes is to found the tradition for her modern counterparts. The closing lines focus on Hughes as an actress and a pioneer:

> I see an old map where the world is divided into two by a straight line. The man who ruled that line across the world said: 'All territory discovered to the right of the line in future to belong to Spain; all to the left to Portugal.' To my age such a division of the world will seem comical indeed; yet that is how I see them still dividing the world of humanity – 'This half for men,' 'That half for women.' If in my day that archaic map is superseded, we shall not forget that it was first made to look foolish when women mounted the stage. Brave Hughes – forgotten pioneer – your comrades offer you a crown!

This conflates the role of the female performer with that of the pioneer/feminist; it emphasises the importance of women's history in challenging patriarchy by exposing the undervaluing of women's work. Significantly, St. John does not, as one reviewer remarked, consider Hughes' affair with Prince Rupert, cousin of Charles II (Gilder 1931: 168). *The First Actress* demonstrates the effects on women of a male-dominated commercial theatre. Hughes' first role as Desdemona (killed because of man's jealousy and deception) refers us ironically to the similarly destructive effects on Hughes' self-image. How vital it was then for women to organise their own theatrical space.

The First Actress is of interest beyond its persuasive argument. The play manipulates the dream vision, indebted to a long literary tradition of utopian and religious writing, such as *Pilgrim's Progress* and *A Dream of John Ball*, which was a common feature of women's suffrage culture. Margaret Wynne Nevinson's short story, 'A Night Out', for instance, depicts a suffragist petitioning parliament. In her weary sleep at the gates of parliament she dreams of Steven Langton's rebellion against the 'robber barons' and imagines Langton speaking for the suffrage cause (*Vote*, 7 October 1909: 14). The materialisation of women of the past was influenced by *A Pageant of Great Women*. However, the scene in which actresses of the future emanate from Hughes' dreaming consciousness could be paralleled with the expressionist technique where the Self is dramatised as Others(s), its different elements embodied by different actors on stage. The transgression of the unities of time and place by these actresses is presented as a revolutionary act and bears comparison with more recent preoccupations of women writers.[11]

The Actress of Today, played in the Pioneer Players' production by Lena Ashwell, hails Hughes as a pioneer, destined to challenge the 'archaic map' of separate spheres. As the manager of the Kingsway Theatre, Ashwell has fulfilled this destiny as radical cartographer, negotiating forbidden ideological as well as geographical space. As Christine Dymkowski puts it, 'with the colonialist reference, the fight against male supremacism is viewed not in isolation but as part of a wider context of political imperialism reinforced by religious power' (Dymkowski 1992: 230). Yet the power acquired by the feminist pioneer is made available from the appropriation of colonialist discourse. Such a dangerous journey is, for Hughes, secured by the promise of the support of other women. The play ends with Hughes crowned by her 'comrades'. Their project is given a socialist context, underwriting the spiritual project with a materialist revision of the social, legal and economic conditions that determine women's oppression. The metaphor of matrilineal coronation implied at the end of *A Pageant of Great Women* is revived. While women are here constructed as supporting and valuing one another, the metaphor of the coronation is problematic in its emphasis on the exceptional woman, implying that the hierarchical social structure will remain unchanged. While women's suffrage is not explicitly mentioned in many of the plays discussed in the next two chapters, they prove to be drawing on prevailing arguments concerning women, work and marriage.

5
Working Women

Although the women's suffrage movement in Britain has been regarded as a largely middle-class movement, working-class women were also involved and women's economic oppression was a significant issue in the suffrage debate. The economic arguments for women's suffrage were based on the fact of many women's economic independence, their status as workers and their contributions to income tax. The Tax Resistance League, founded by Pioneer Players member Clemence Housman,[1] resumed the ancient strategy of non-payment of taxes in order to put pressure on the government to secure women's enfranchisement. The vote signified citizenship, the right to work and for that work to be valued. These rights were denied by the anti-suffragists. They insisted that women and men occupied different spheres of activity, women operating in the private sphere of home while men operated in the public sphere of work and politics. Women operating in the public sphere risked being associated with prostitutes. As Lisa Tickner notes, the anti-suffragists played on the anxieties which the organisation of women as workers posed to the male labour force. Inevitably, the types of work pursued by women varied across social class and were visible to different degrees. Moreover, the situation had changed remarkably during the lifetime of the Pioneer Players. Research into poverty and employment in the early years of the twentieth century demonstrated that between 1869 and 1911 there was a 300 per cent increase in women working as teachers, nurses, clerks and civil servants, and a 400 per cent increase in women working as shop assistants, the field of work dramatised by Cicely Hamilton's *Diana of Dobson's*.[2] Women involved in sweated labour, in domestic labour for their own or other families, and women working jointly in business with their husbands were often not recognised as workers (Tickner 1987: 180). The making visible of these women workers therefore constituted a challenge to the separate-spheres ideology. Lisa Tickner has argued that, while the women's suffrage banners used in street processions represented the professions of middle-class women, they failed to represent the labour of working-class women. It was, arguably, in dramatic forms that such complex relationships could be more adequately represented. The Pioneer Players' pre-war productions include some remarkable plays which represent women working as a central theme and which, in this context, can be regarded as implicitly supporting women's suffrage, through the representation of working-class women in the Pioneer Players' drama differed from that usual in women's suffrage iconography.

The separate-spheres ideology assumed that women did *not* work. Martha Vicinus has demonstrated that middle-class women were involved in teaching, nursing and philanthropy. Suffragists campaigned for women's right to access to middle-class occupations, the professions and higher education. Some middle-class suffragists criticised employment legislation as restrictive; others, such as Mary MacArthur and Beatrice Webb, defended those laws that protected working-class women and children from exploitation (Tickner 1987: 176–7). However, there were many working women in Britain at all economic and social levels. Women were setting up their own businesses and the Pioneer Players' membership supported and was supported by these ventures. Their play programmes advertised occupations in the clothing industry, such as millinery and weaving, and others, such as Mrs Wood Smith's dispensing chemists and the Hon. Gabrielle Borthwick's Automobile Garage, which saw women moving into new fields of work. For working-class women, work did not attain the metaphoric significance it had for middle-class women, for whom it was often a choice rather than a necessity. The Pioneer Players' drama might be expected to reflect the interests of their membership and therefore to present the work of middle-class women, but this is not always the case. Two of their plays represented women working at home and in sweated labour, making an important contribution to the diverse images of women to be found in suffrage culture. The image of the working woman in the art of the suffrage movement was problematic, as Tickner states: 'the suffrage artists, who were predominantly middle-class, were engaged in their own particular and well-meaning form of exploitation: that of the image of the oppressed and sweated worker to further their own campaign' (Tickner 1987: 181). The plays discussed in this chapter expose: the undervaluing of women as workers; the difficulties for women in reconciling work with commitments to family; the competition between women as a result of the capitalist system; and the psychological costs of capitalism for both women and men. In addition, this chapter will examine several plays which expose the economic determinants of prostitution, and one play which represents prostitution as work.

Many socialists regarded women's suffrage as a diversion from the proper cause of adult suffrage. The issue of affiliation to particular political parties, indeed, split the WSPU. Restrictions on membership of the Independent Labour Party (ILP) and affiliation to political parties led to the founding in 1907 of the rival WFL. Socialist newspapers, such as the *Clarion* and the *Daily Herald,* reviewed the Pioneer Players' work, taking an interest in the plays which promoted a socialist perspective, such as Herman Heijermans' *The Good Hope* and Edith Lyttelton's *The Thumbscrew*. Some of these plays concerned issues pertinent not only to the women's suffrage campaign but also to the later socialist political theatre movement in Britain.[3]

The inequalities of the double standard were represented in a particularly effective way in one of the first plays produced by the Pioneer Players which dramatised the effects of a strike of women. *How the Vote Was Won* by Christopher St. John and Cicely Hamilton demonstrates the economic contributions of women to society denied by the anti-suffrage lobby. This one-act comedy shows the numerous female relatives of one man giving up their jobs and, taking the anti-suffrage argument to its logical conclusion, expecting him to support them all financially. This play exemplifies an understanding, common amongst suffragists, of the economically subordinate position of women. A play like this seems to suggest that a close association between suffragists and socialists was possible.

However, there was frequent conflict between the Labour Party and the women's suffrage movement. Women were campaigning for the vote on the same terms as enfranchised men: on the basis of property. Many critics have noted the middle-class suffragists' patronising attitude to working-class women, which was apparent in the cultural practices of suffragists. The WFL, usually more attentive to diversity than the other organisations, held a 'Hard-Up Social' where middle-class suffragists put on fancy dress to represent the poor (*Vote*, 26 March 1910). Political activities brought many suffragists into contact for the first time with the circumstances of working people. This can be seen in Evelyn Sharp's short story 'Patrolling the Gutter', in which suffrage activism takes on the function of class tourism. The AFL apparently attempted to take drama to the East End of London but many plays seem to have been performed by and for middle-class suffragists. For instance, Evelyn Glover's *A Chat With Mrs Chicky* represents a working-class woman converting her female employer to campaign for the vote. Although she serves an important function in the play, the working-class woman is nevertheless represented as subordinate throughout. This narrative dynamic conforms to the promise that property-owning women would represent working-class women.

In the Pioneer Players' drama, working-class women are sometimes represented as individuated central characters. The Pioneer Players' concern to represent women as workers with real economic value possibly reflected the influence of the WFL, which organised a regular vigil at the law courts to publicise cases of sexual abuse and assault against women. The abuse and exploitation of women engaged in sweated labour were cited by suffragists as arguments for women's enfranchisement. The first plays produced by the Pioneer Players discussed forms of oppression which most directly affected the society's membership of middle-class educated women working in professions, such as acting, writing and teaching. Although women were in some cases able to take control of their own working environment in the short term, it was assumed optimistically that, after enfranchisement, new ways of working would ensue. Women's lives would be improved and the problem of prejudiced critical judgment and restricted opportunities would be solved. In male-dominated institutions women's work was undervalued and marginalised. This theme appears in two plays in the Pioneer Players' inaugural production: Margaret Hughes in Christopher St. John's *The First Actress*, like the protagonist in Cicely Hamilton's *Jack and Jill and a Friend*, is a woman whose working life is subject to sexual discrimination.

Hamilton began her own career as a dramatist by concealing her female identity. This strategy was unnecessary when her successful play, *Diana of Dobson's*, was produced at Lena Ashwell's Kingsway Theatre in 1908. With the Pioneer Players, in contrast, Hamilton was even free to direct *Jack and Jill and a Friend* herself. This play dramatises the problems women face as writers in the male-dominated publishing industry. A comedy of two scenes, it presents the changing relationship of an impecunious couple. When Jill, unknown to Jack, enters – and wins – a writing competition, Jack cannot accept Jill as his equal, as a writer or as a partner. The Women Writers' Suffrage League and the Independent Theatre had both offered prizes for new plays. The Pioneer Players did not emulate this practice. The tension in the play centres on the results of the novel writing prize, and then on the effects of this prize on the couple's relationship. *Jack and Jill* insists on economic equality and mutual respect within marriage. Class and gender are examined as the emotional relationship between Jack and Jill changes with the fluctuations in their relative economic positions and social status. Winning the prize radically alters the woman's life and this crucially transforms the lives of the men in the play. For Jill it means financial independence and public recognition. She regards work as essential for her self-esteem and expects Jack both to accept her financial support for the marriage and to recognise the worth of her writing. He is reluctant to do either: 'You wanted me to be your wife; but also, being your wife, you wanted to be able to look down on me. Now that you can't look down on me – now that you know I'm as good a man as you are – you don't want me any more' (Hamilton 1911: 19).

The title of the play promises a more prominent role for the 'Friend' than seems to be delivered. Roger, a financially independent artist, acts both as confidant to the couple and as unofficial patron. The play, set in Roger's studio which he shares with Jack, begins with the revelation that Jack is being financially supported by Roger. This ironically reveals Jack's double standard when later he refuses to accept financial support from Jill. Roger is marginal to the plot, serving as a contrast to Jack and emphasising Jack's unreasonable and unrealistic expectations of Jill. The intimacy between the two men introduces an alternative emotional relationship that remains unresolved. Eve Kosofsky Sedgwick's concept of the 'homosocial triangle' may explain the significance of the 'surplus' friend in this play which otherwise seems to be concerned with the couple's marriage (Sedgwick 1985). In this perspective, the relationship between Roger and Jack can be seen as disrupted by Jill. Jack cries when he learns that he has been unsuccessful in the competition. Jill arrives, awkwardly interrupting Roger's attempts to comfort Jack. Roger is generous and understanding; the friend that Jack has to learn to be with Jill. Similarly, in Schreiner's 'Three Dreams in A Desert' Woman regrets that 'man' only speaks of passion: 'I have dreamed he might learn to say "Friendship" in that land [of Freedom].' Woman must break away from man, who is the child at her breast, in order to achieve her own freedom. The resolution of Hamilton's play similarly infantilises the man, implying that any relationship between the sexes will be fraught until that utopian moment of equality. Hamilton's play ends rather abruptly, undermining confidence in its mimetic function. As in many women's suffrage texts the power-relation is reversed, and there is a momentary allusion to Madonna and child when, at the end of the play, Jack kneels symbolically next to Jill.

Although the characters are, as their names suggest, on one level merely types, it is significant that a male character fulfils the function of the 'friend'. Such a representation of masculinity suggests a more complex treatment of gender than this one-act play has space to develop. Hamilton had disturbed an essentialist approach to gender in *A Pageant of Great Women* where the only male character is 'Prejudice' rather than, as one might expect, 'Man'. The relationship between Roger and the couple unsettles the binary female/male opposition. Similar rhetorically memorable, destabilising triads are at work in Gertrude Colmore's *Suffragette Sally* (1911) and 'The Nun' (1912), Charlotte Perkins Gilman's *Three Women* (1911), and Olive Schreiner's 'Three Dreams in a Desert' (1890). The subversion of power is mediated through adult–child relationships or through the conflation of literary and other modes. The oral form of the nursery rhyme is used by many suffrage poets, notably in *Holloway Jingles* (1913), to represent the direct communication characteristic of propaganda. Forms associated with children's literature were appropriated by Laurence Housman in *Alice in Ganderland* and *Suffragette Alphabet*, both of which were extremely popular. In *Jack and Jill and a Friend*, the nursery rhyme also alludes to the dominant notions of conflict and struggle between women and men.

Hamilton resists here, as in her other writings, a simple essentialist or 'sex antagonist' line. The different economic situations of all three characters are shown to affect the work they produce. Roger's financial independence allows him creative freedom, whereas the couple have to make compromises in their writing to earn a living. Although Jill's prize money promises creative freedom, this economic independence threatens her relationship with Jack. This conventional expectation that a middle-class woman must choose between work and marriage is the theme of Charlotte Perkins Gilman's *Three Women* performed by the Pioneer Players in November 1912.[4] The central character of Gilman's play is an independent woman who runs a crèche, and whose success is called into question when she is asked by her fiancé to choose between marriage and her career. She seeks advice from two other women. One has married and given up the chance of a singing career while the other has pursued a career and never married. Both women urge her not to follow their example. Following their advice, she chooses both marriage *and* a career, and convinces her fiancé that this is possible. Unusually, in this play a middle-class woman insists on the compatibility of both roles, avoiding the rejection of marriage so characteristic of the New Woman plays. Significantly, also, the woman's choice is accepted by her fiancé. This is a little too convenient and implausible. It is relevant here that, although there was no marriage restriction on female teachers in Britain until the 1920s, before the First World War, only 12 per cent of women elementary school teachers were married (Oram 1983: 138). However, Gilman acknowledged the importance of child care to the lives of working mothers. Sylvia Pankhurst, similarly, had taken this issue seriously, establishing in 1915 the Mother's Arms, a crèche for the children of working mothers in the East End of London. After training with Maria Montessori in Barcelona, Pioneer Players' member, Muriel Matters joined the Mother's Arms as a teacher (Taylor 1993: 30). Two plays produced by the Pioneer Players concerned the position of the working-class woman exploited through sweated labour and additionally burdened with child care. In Edith Lyttelton's *The Thumbscrew* her role is central while in *The Coronation* by Christopher St. John and Charles Thursby it is minor but nevertheless pivotal.

Edith Lyttelton went to some lengths to ensure a realistic depiction of women outworkers in her one-act play, *The Thumbscrew* in 1912, corresponding with J. J. Mallon, secretary of the Anti-Sweating League.[5] The play is set in one room of a house where two families live supported by Bernice, her mother and the children working all hours, sewing hooks and eyes onto cards. The retail clothing industry relied on such sweated home working. The plot centres on Bernice's rejection of Joe's marriage proposal and plan to emigrate to Canada.[6] The tension surrounding Bernice's decision is complicated by a change in the women's working conditions. Mrs Muggle, a Jewish middlewoman,[7] intends to pay the workers less for transporting their work to the factory, which promises to increase their workload. Bernice's opportunity for personal happiness would entail abandoning her family to even greater poverty. She decides to stay with her mother.

Joe represents a Marxist critique of capitalism, exposing the problems faced by women workers not represented by a trade union in the sweated trades. His angry words ('You 'aven't got a bit of spunk in you, any of you women! You don't deserve the vote, nor nothin' else' (p. 959) are lines deleted in the prompt copy of the Pioneer Players' production. This production was to leave implicit the hostility of traditional class politics towards the plight of women. Yet, if this was the thinking behind the Pioneer Players' adaptation, it was too subtle for some socialists, unsympathetic to the specific conditions of women. Joe's speech is one with which Derek Ross, reviewer for the *Daily Herald*, would have concurred. Ross was scathing, particularly regarding the perceived lack of action in the play, 'a presentation of hopeless, aimless suffering and social misery, gradually increasing in volume and intensity as the action goes on' (*Daily Herald* 17 December 1912: 5). Ross's description of the characters is significant:

> There is absolutely no relief to the gloom, all the characters are without any energy except that of the slave; no one seems to have any knowledge whatever of the necessity of combination and political education in order to better conditions; there is not enough collective spirit to strike one blow in anger.
> (*Daily Herald*, 17 December 1912: 5)

While the play fails to identify unionisation as a promising response to sweated labour, Ross fails to understand Lyttelton's attempts to dramatise the limitations of the Marxist perspective for women in its prioritisation of class over gender. The emphatic action in the play is Bernice's decision to remain with her mother rather than to marry Joe. Here there is no shortage of 'energy': 'I can't do it, Joe – to think of me on that rolling ship, and them all here starvin'' perhaps. Supposing mother falls ill, or anything happens – my heart's going to crack – it's going to crack – I can't go and leave them' (Lyttelton 1911: 958). Bernice's decision cannot be dismissed as a failure to act simply because she does not identify the collective action of unionisation as a solution to her problems. While Joe becomes the imperialist pioneer, for Bernice the pioneering space must be with other women, specifically with her mother.

The plot presents painfully the ways in which women may be doubly oppressed, by poorly paid outwork and domestic work, and then forced to compete with each other for subsistence wages. *The Thumbscrew* shows that women, more likely than men to be bound by the institution of the family, are subject both to patriarchal and capitalist oppression. It offers no easy solution.

The characterisation of the Jewish middlewoman is a racial stereotype which deserves critical judgement. It is comparable with another Western perspective endorsed, but problematically gendered, in one of Lyttelton's other plays.[8] Although Lyttelton was sympathetic to the issue of sweated labour and had written on the subject before,[9] it is above all an *issue*, of which she has no immediate experience. The middle-class constituency of the audience, if not the dramatist, was the focus of Ross's indignation and disgust. One member of the audience exemplified for Ross the damaging effect of this play:

> The play harrows up one's feelings in approved melodramatic style. A beautiful and well-gowned girl came out saying to a friend on the way

as she wiped away a tear, 'I'm just heartbroken.' Transient emotional outbursts like that won't help much: there are too many luxuries and luxurious persons on top of underpaid and sweated Labour, and it is very easy to feel moved for a moment and then just let things go on.
(*Daily Herald*, 17 December 1912: 5)

Ross's criticism recalls Madeleine Lucette Ryley's view that women's suffrage drama risked trivialising complex political arguments. It also anticipates Brecht's attacks on sentimental bourgeois drama. Yet Ross seems to expect the play to offer solutions in the manner of the conventional propaganda play. The play demonstrates a moral dilemma in which a woman ultimately sacrifices her own happiness in order to support her family. The function of the play is didactic, aimed at educating a middle-rather than a working-class audience, about the problems of sweated labour. It refuses to promote the single message of propaganda though the central place given to female self-sacrifice may be accused of supporting dominant gender ideology.

The second play dealing with this issue is very different in style: symbolic and idealistic rather than grimly naturalistic. In this play, the woman involved in sweated labour is shown – however implausibly – to transform an entire society. *The Coronation*,[10] by Christopher St. John and Charles Thursby,[11] is set in the capital of Omnisterre (Everyland) on the day of the coronation of Henricus XVI.[12] This is delayed when a woman in the crowd hands the king a petition indicting the government for its treatment of the working class. The first scene establishes that the heads of the army, navy and court are indifferent to the state of the country. When the woman is given an audience with the king she reveals that since the repeal of the Anti-Sweating Bill she has been working 18 hours a day, her child has died of starvation and she has vowed to kill the king. He is converted by her petition and refuses the crown until his conditions, including universal suffrage, are met. He looks

> forward to the creation of a society in which there shall be comfort and science and beauty for all! – A society that shall at least be better than the present one for our sons and daughters! Forward... to the steps of the Cathedral... where the poorest of my brothers and sisters in humanity may see me crowned! (51–2).

The woman is given the last words of the play, 'I believe in God!' (52). This declaration could allude to the spiritual nature of dissent in the women's suffrage context: a belief in 'God' would depend on a transformation of women's position in society, effected by a radical change in social institutions.

The Coronation presents an individual woman, whom the king calls a 'brave soldier' and a 'great heart' (45), reminiscent of the peasant warrior Joan of Arc and possibly the second part of *Pilgrim's Progress*. She has sufficient strength of spirit to transform society. Indeed, her petition wins universal, not just women's suffrage. The unnamed woman, representative of all oppressed working women, successfully convinces the king with her words, not through a violent deed. This dramatises the WFL's argument that a single non-violent act by a courageous individual could transform society. The meeting of the king and the woman is revelatory in more than the sense that the king is informed of the appalling social conditions of the country. When the two meet, they become aware of their preconceptions about their respective social roles. This moment reveals the characters as types which are then transformed into individuals. The woman is deterred from regicide when he treats her with respect and ceases to act the king. Transformed from an unknown woman to a representative or symbolic figure, she is instrumental in the conversion of the king to social reform.

Both Cecil Fisher's *The Great Day* and Herman Heijermans' *The Good Hope* emphasise the costs of a capitalist system for the individual and the extent to which compliance with that system is necessary for its continuation. These plays give priority to a critique of the social system with an implicit reference to gender. Cecil Fisher's play *The Great Day*,[13] performed in 1913, is set in an insurance office, and examines conflict between employer and employed. The clerks find out that their annual pay rise, 'the great day' to which they look forward, does not include payment for the long hours of overtime worked that year. There are references to the 'new Act' (Lloyd George's Insurance Act) which has caused the increased workload in the office. When Armstrong, one of the clerks, questions this he discovers that shareholders in the company have been given an increased dividend. One clerk, on intimate terms with the management, has received twice as much as the others. Armstrong is condemned as a socialist and the play concludes with his observation that this system continues because of the individual's fears of losing their job: 'The great thing is to keep your job at all costs. That's what makes this office life so contemptible – this fear and respect for men you ought to despise' (28).

This analysis of the issue with its emphasis on the need for collective action incurred a dismissive review from *The Times*, which described it as 'one of the not uncommon examples of the pamphlet drama.... the drama does not enter, one way or another, into the question' (*The Times*, 19 May 1913: 10). The issue is given some breadth with the inclusion of a minor character who acts as a warning to those who submit to such oppression. Hemming, an older clerk, has just returned to work after a leave of absence following a nervous breakdown. The psychological costs of working such long hours for the benefit of shareholders have been considerable. Hemming is an interesting pre-war representation of the male psyche under pressure, dramatising the alienation of men through capitalist competition. One reviewer noticed that, unusually for the Pioneer Players, there were 'no female parts' (*The Times*, 19 May 1913: 10). The society was therefore not confined to examining the monstrosity of femininity. The play is more than a mere 'pamphlet drama'. The *Pall Mall Gazette* found it 'decidedly interesting, and, acted with due discretion, it enjoyed, and on the whole deserved, a favourable reception' (*Pall Mall Gazette*, 19 May 1913: 7).

With its revival of Heijermans' *The Good Hope* in 1912,[14] the Pioneer Players challenged the bourgeois audience vilified by Derek Ross. St. John summarised Heijermans' attitude, explaining the Pioneer Players' interest in his plays: 'As in all Heijermans's plays, our sympathies are roused for those who suffer and fail, for the victims of poverty and of all the evil and distress it involves' (St. John 1929: vii). Although said to be the greatest Dutch dramatist, in his lifetime his 'Socialistic views were distasteful to a thoroughly comfortable and powerful bourgeoisie' (St. John 1929: v). Heijermans' four-act naturalist play drew on his experience of living in a fishing village for two years and witnessing oppressive working conditions. The 'Good Hope' of the title is an unseaworthy vessel which is heavily insured and put to sea in spite of the risk to the sailors on board. The ship sinks and many lives are lost.

Claimed by one reviewer as 'a Suffragist play by accident' (*Votes for Women*, 8 November 1912), the play dramatises the villagers' responses to the dangerous work on which they depend and the effects which it has on their relationships. The play centres on Kniertje, the mother of two sailors, Barend and Geert, who rebels against the social system. Barend's refusal to sail in the unseaworthy vessel incurs accusations of cowardice, while Geert has returned after serving a naval prison sentence for insubordination. Although Kniertje, like many of the other characters, is conformist, she is the focus of several scenes that emphasise the strength of the collective life of the villagers. During Kniertje's birthday celebrations, the guests sing the *Marseillaise* which, not incidentally, was used as a suffrage poem and its tune used for a suffrage song. The important third act of the play shows women gathering at Kniertje's house, talking about their lives. The sharing of experiences amongst women is presented as a means of transforming lives also in plays such as *In The Workhouse* and *The Surprise of His Life*. In Heijermans' play no simple solution is offered. Its strength, as with Lyttelton's *The Thumbscrew*, lies in the exposure of an oppressive social system and the sympathetic treatment of the experiences of those oppressed. *The Good Hope* was regarded as a 'suffrage play' because it emphasised the need to change the entire social system,

> the condition of things that the Suffragist is out to revolutionise. It is, in fact, a Suffragist play by accident, simply because it is a sincere picture of the sufferings of humanity under a regime that is being attacked root and branch by the Suffrage movement.
> (*Votes for Women*, 18 December 1912)

The play itself was successful in bringing about social change. After it was written, protective legislation was introduced to the Dutch fishing industry. The WSPU's reviewer readily compared the objectification and alienation of the individual in the capitalist system, which Heijermans highlighted, with the situation of women. Suffragists were concerned not merely with the vote, but the transformation of society which enfranchisement promised. The WSPU regarded the vote as a 'gateway' to other changes.

Some of the most challenging plays produced by the Pioneer Players were those which dealt with prostitution. Those middle-class women who transgressed separate-spheres ideology and claimed the right to work, always risked the conventional association that the working woman had with the prostitute. Equally, in some cases, the suffragists' use of the image of the working woman to emphasise the association between low pay and exploitative working conditions with prostitution also risked stereotyping all working women as unchaste (Tickner 1987: 181–2). They exposed the trade in women that depended on their objectification and commodification. One of the most disturbing plays produced by the society, *Honour Thy Father*, made explicit the role of the prostitute as a working woman. The following analysis of the plays produced on this theme will investigate both the unconventional treatment of prostitution in some plays and, in others, the problematic representation of the religious conversion of the prostitute. The appropriation of religious discourse by suffragists will be discussed further in Chapter 6.

The challenge to the institution of prostitution has a long connection with the history of feminism and the women's suffrage movement. Susan Kingsley Kent argues that the campaign in the late nineteenth century to repeal the Contagious Diseases (CD) Acts, which Josephine Butler described as 'the State Regulation of vice', gave rise to the argument that 'Prostitution served as a metaphor for the predicament of women under patriarchy, carried only to a more extreme degree' (Kent 1990: 76). The CD Acts placed women suspected of being prostitutes under surveillance and liable to forcible examination and confinement in hospital if found to be infected. Women such as Butler were acknowledging that this constituted a 'battle for our bodies' (Kent 1990: 120). Those feminists, who together with Butler, fought against the CD Acts, strongly identified themselves with the vulnerability of the prostitute. However, some were concerned to distance themselves from prostitutes, complaining that the CD Acts were not sufficiently specific, and should be removed because applicable to all women. There was also a risk that middle-class women were claiming the moral high ground, associating all working-class women with prostitution. This is demonstrated by the postcard, 'The Scylla and Charybdis of the Working Woman', the equally threatening obstacles being sweated labour and 'social evil' (Tickner 1987: 182). Kent argued that the CD Acts, like the separate-spheres ideology, effectively constructed two classes of women:

> Pure women remained within the private sphere of home and family, where sexual relations between men and women assumed the existence of love, companionship, and above all, procreation all consistent with the ideology of a woman as the angel in the house. The impure woman operated in the public sphere, where she sold sex for material gain. The one realm had no relation to or connection with the other, the argument went.
>
> (Kent 1990: 65–6)

This conventional construction of the prostitute in separate-spheres ideology is challenged in several of the plays produced by the Pioneer Players which sustain the impetus of Butler's campaign. They insist on the economic determinants of prostitution, emphasised by the individuated characterisation which gives a voice to the prostitute. The conventions of naturalism situate the prostitute in the home, where she charges the family with complicity in her oppression.

The Pioneer Players' production of George Bernard Shaw's *Mrs Warren's Profession* in 1912 was one of its least innovative incursions into the debate about prostitution. However, Vivie Warren was still an influential role model in 1909 and it is therefore credible that H. G. Wells' Ann Veronica sees the play performed and this becomes one of several decisive moments leading to her involvement with the suffrage movement. *Mrs Warren's Profession* was not the Pioneer Players' first unlicensed play, neither was it their first play about prostitution.[15] However, this production incurred a loss of members,[16] and was publicly debated by Christopher St. John in a suffrage newspaper:

> Why all this fuss and commotion about this particular play? Why have some members of the Pioneer Players' Society resigned as a protest against its being performed? Is it because Mrs Warren belongs to the 'underworld,' and frankly gives her reasons for having adopted her ghastly trade? There have been many plays before 'Mrs Warren's Profession' with heroines of her type, but they have always been treated romantically. Efforts have been made by dramatists to render them attractive and sympathetic. And from this point of view they may be counted far more subversive of morality than poor, truthful Mrs Warren, accepting standards of society as they are, blurting out the awful knowledge of human nature at its worst that her life and position enabled her to gain. . . . 'Mrs Warren's Profession' is a highly moral play!
>
> (St. John 1912)

The hostility may have arisen from the play's representation of the independent woman, which differs drastically from Jess Dorynne's *The Surprise of His Life*, or plays by Hamilton and St. John discussed earlier in this chapter. Jill Davis argues that Vivie Warren is Shaw's 'theatrical parody of the New Woman' (Davis 1992: 25) and that Shaw's representations of women are 'deeply ambiguous and . . . are not representations of women, but cyphers for a strategy to achieve and protect masculinity' (Davis 1992: 31). Nevertheless, in the Pioneer Players' production, Vivie and Mrs Warren were played by actors familiar to the society's audience in roles which inscribed femininity with an active and necessary rebellion. Mrs Warren was played by Gertrude Kingston, formerly Queen Caroline in Laurence Housman's *Pains and Penalties*, while Ellen O'Malley played Vivie, she had also played the revolutionary nun, Macrena (in St. John's play of the same name). Long-standing members of the society may have associated a particular kind of role with such well-seasoned acting members. The 'actor as sign' thus contributed to the available interpretations for this audience (Aston and Savona 1991: 103).

A more topical and similarly unlicensed play about prostitution was *The Daughters of Ishmael*.[17] This was adapted by A. D'Este Scott from a novel of the same name by Reginald Wright Kauffman,[18] which exposed the 'white slave trade', a term which problematically denounces the traffic in women on the grounds of white supremacy. The performance of this play was nevertheless a significant political statement for the Pioneer Players.[19] It was deliberately performed at the King's Hall to avoid what Craig called the 'fuss' of censorship. The novel had been banned by Boots lending libraries (*Vote*, 29 June 1912: 177), and the performance therefore challenged censorship of the novel rather than drama. The issue of prostitution was acutely topical. In the summer of 1913 a brothel in Piccadilly run by Queenie Gerald was raided, exposing many MPs as clients (Kent 1990: 155). Gerald's sentence was reduced, and the identity of the (distinguished) clients concealed. The treatment of the case was regarded by many suffragists as typifying the hypocrisy of politicians. The AFL had held a public meeting on the subject (*Vote*, 13 July 1912: 216), and Christabel Pankhurst wrote about the case in the *Suffragette*. Pankhurst's writings, later collected and published, have been described by Kent as 'part of a discourse of resistance designed to reverse the stereotype of women as "the Sex" by accusing men of sexual perversion and of using the law to further and protect their perverted behavior' (Kent 1990: 155). Pankhurst's *The Great Scourge and How To End It* and *The Daughters of Ishmael* were both advertised in a Pioneer Players' play programme which invites an assessment of this performance in the light of this topical and scandalous case. *The Daughters of Ishmael* emphasises the complicity of the police, magistrates and politicians in prostitution, and one suffragist reviewer was alert to the current scandal: 'Is there not an echo of the Queenie Gerald case in this episode?' (*Common Cause*, 6 March 1914). The Pioneer Players' performance was therefore situated in a campaign by suffragists to expose the prostitution industry and those who supported it. As early as 1885 W. T. Stead had publicly exposed the traffic in child prostitutes in the *Pall Mall Gazette* but the suffragists were politicising this issue.

One of the society's most effective critiques of prostitution had been H. M. Harwood's *Honour Thy Father*, performed in 1912, which argues that the limited education of women restricted the employment open to them. *Honour Thy Father* returns the prostitute to her family. This is no melodrama and differs significantly from *Mrs Warren's Profession*. The prostitute does not function as the scapegoat, exposed and exiled from the family, but is instead given an opportunity to denounce her family for its responsibility for her means of subsistence:

'I had to find something to do. And I knew nothing – I was utterly ignorant – and utterly useless... I made up my mind that if I had to sell myself I would do it frankly – and get the best price I could. Besides, if one's looks are the only things one has that are worth anything it's silly to waste them – and I was getting pale and ugly'. (48–50)

In *Mrs Warren's Profession* and *Ann Veronica* the younger independent woman is seen not only to thrive on the economic rewards of others' prostitution but also to condemn it. Thus Ann Veronica discovers that her education has not provided her with the means of supporting herself and yet is revolted by the prostitutes she encounters: 'It did not occur to her that they at least had found a way of earning a living, and had that much economic superiority to herself. It did not occur to her that save for some accidents of education and character they had souls like her own' (Wells 1993: 78). Where the Pioneer Players' drama diverges from such representations of prostitution is in presenting the point of view of the prostitute herself and setting up a confrontation between the middle-class woman and the prostitute.

Reviewers of *The Daughters of Ishmael* indignantly identified the 'white slave trade' as a foreign phenomenon, located at a safe distance in America. As one reviewer put it, 'some of the suggestions contained in the play scarcely apply to England' (*Justice*, 12 March 1914). Another claimed that the brothel in the play 'winked at for valuable consideration by the police, and, worse, still supported by the magistrates, and, even more startlingly, encouraged by "politicians," is unthinkable in London' (*Westminster Gazette*, 3 March 1914). Although *Honour Thy Father* is set in Belgium, where the Morgan family are exiled after bankruptcy, Claire Morgan's work as a prostitute takes place in London. The precarious financial situation of the Morgan family is established from the first scene where Mr Morgan is seen gambling the housekeeping money, and asserting his principles that 'Debts of honour, however small, should be paid at once' (p. 30). This statement foreshadows the action of the play but may also allude to the suffragists' charge that the government had reneged on its promises of enfranchisement. Ironically, Morgan owes his debt to Mr Stearn, a travelling tradesman. When Claire returns from London to visit her family, she unexpectedly encounters Stearn, one of her London clients. When she refuses to entertain him that evening, he exposes her real occupation to her family.

Claire's response is persuasive and salutary. She explains her reasons for prostitution, demystifying the notion that every prostitute is a victim of romantic love and betrayal. She presents her own entry into prostitution as a practical and self-determined solution to the economic problems of her life. She had worked at several shops, living in, and had thus been exposed to sexual harassment from employers, a subject that had been dramatised by Cicely Hamilton in *Diana of Dobson's*. Like Ann Veronica and many other rebel women, she blames her father for the limited education which prevented her from finding alternative employment:

> I wanted to be independent, because I was afraid of the future. I saw that we were gradually getting poorer – gradually having to do without things – first one thing – then another. I asked mother how things really were – she didn't know – she daren't ask. 'It wasn't a woman's business to pry into money matters,' you said. Then I asked you myself – I asked whether I oughtn't to learn to do something – I suggested several things – and you were furious. 'No daughter of yours should do such a thing.' Nothing I suggested was fit for 'your daughter' to do. 'My place was at home.' 'I was to leave matters to you.' Like a fool – I did. I gave up asking questions – I settled down to do all the silly useless things that girls 'of your class' do in the country.
>
> (p. 47–8)

The father's debts to Claire are long overdue.

The play concludes uneasily, emphasising the financially beneficial results of Claire's chosen occupation. Her money supports the family and enables her younger sister, Madge, to train as a gymnastics instructor. Claire says that no one wants to improve their minds any more: it is the body that counts. The anti-suffrage argument that women were physically inferior to men was answered on a different level by a flourishing interest among women in physical culture. Mrs Garrud led the Athletic Section of the WFL, giving displays of ju-jitsu as effective self-defence. Similar training helped Ann Veronica fight off the predatory Ramage. In *The Surprise of His Life*, there is a similar scene where a woman effectively fights off a male attacker. Claire's strength in *Honour Thy Father* is mediated through both the physical and the economic. This is sufficiently disruptive to provoke banishment. Morgan threatens to prevent Claire from seeing Madge again. However, the force of this is somewhat deflected by the landlady's interruption for the overdue rent. Claire pays the debt, and the play ends with Claire and Madge leaving for the *Café Riche*. Although the relationship between the two sisters is underdeveloped, Claire's support of her younger sister compares with a similar scenario in Edward Knoblock's play *Mouse*, where a governess works to sponsor the education of her niece. In women's suffrage literature this is a common motif. The self-sacrifice of the older generation of (female) pioneers is necessary for the sake of the younger (female) generation.

Honour Thy Father is a challenging play which returns the prostitute to the family. It was praised by Derek Ross in the *Daily Herald*. This play alone in the triple bill was 'terse, vivid, and powerful' and the author 'deserves to be congratulated upon dealing with a much-discussed subject, namely, prostitution, with a commendable absence of the usual sloppy and statistically inaccurate gush' (*Daily Herald*, 17 December 1912: 5). A similarly unconventional treatment, emphasising the economic determinants of prostitution, is presented in Antonia Williams' *The Street*.

In *The Street*, as in *Honour Thy Father*, the exploration of the domestic situation of the prostitute challenges the stereotype of the prostitute perpetuated by the separate-spheres ideology. The play links prostitution with poor housing. *The Street* rejects the conventions of the melodrama or society play in which the prostitute is exposed and banished. The two female characters, Violet and Margaret, adopt a distinctly different discourse from that of their prospective husbands, Owen Ford an impoverished writer and Mr Castleton a wealthy man, working temporarily as a rent collector to gain experience of poverty. Like many nineteenth-century social reformers, Castleton was exploring the world of poverty as if it were a 'foreign' country. Such class tourists were also to be found in the suffrage movement. In Evelyn Sharp's short story 'Patrolling the Gutter' a 'sentimental' member of the suffragist party taking to the streets to sell newspapers was convinced after only a few hours 'that a human link existed between her and all sandwich-men' (Norquay 1995: 226). In *The Street*, the men speak a confident, optimistic language, whereas the women exchange oblique references to their experiences of sexual harassment. Although Ford and Castleton occupy different social positions, Castleton is inspired by Ford. Both men have confidence in the strength of the spirit, but in the play the material hardships they have to bear are minimal compared with the dangers faced by the women. Castleton romanticises Margaret's situation as a spiritual victory: Margaret sacrifices herself for her mother and sister by selling herself to the landlord in lieu of rent.

The women have a different perspective on their predicament. The play focuses on this and the fact that it is determined by their relatively powerless position. Violet, concerned about communicating with Owen, attempts to describe this to Margaret, 'I shouldn't like – I shouldn't like – I don't quite know how to explain it – but I shouldn't like, for instance, to be offering him pale blue when he was asking me for pale green – and I couldn't see it. Do you know what I mean?' (104). Their widowed mother, Mrs Martin, shows a distinct preference for Violet, encouraging her children to use their femininity to secure their future in marriage to wealthy men. She rejects Margaret's plea for affection: 'Come, get up. You know I can't abide them foreign ways. I hate family play-acting too. It worries me. Don't do it, there's a good girl' (79). Mrs Martin, a less financially successful version of Mrs Warren, colludes with the sexual harassment of and trade in women. The *Stage* described the play as 'sentimental', dismissing the men as 'crudely and unconvincingly drawn' and suggesting that the play had 'something of the Ibsen touch' (*Stage*, 4 December 1913: 29). However, the complicity of the mother in her daughter's fate as a prostitute was a challenging concept that this play refuses to sentimentalise. The use of lighting in the play as a naively conventional metaphor for the human spirit may also have contributed to the perceived 'sentimental' tone. At the end of the play, Ford observes that the light in the room is stronger than outside; it remains inviolate. Yet the room is owned by the landlord who is significantly never seen on stage, and as such is rendered more menacing; he features only in the dialogues of the characters whom he is exploiting. The landlord's name was changed to Murphy in the Pioneer Players' prompt copy, possibly another instance of the racial stereotype seen in Mrs Muggle, the exploitative Jewish middlewoman in *The Thumbscrew*.

Elaine Aston has analysed an earlier production of this play at the Gaiety Theatre, Manchester, focusing on the romantic relationship between Margaret and Castleton. Aston says the play:

> returns to the somewhat dated question of the definition of a 'pure' woman.... The central argument of the drama is that a woman who has been wronged may in fact find love and happiness with a man who has full knowledge of that wrong.
>
> (Aston 1992: 209)

The Pioneer Players' production of this play yields other possible interpretations. It was performed in November 1913 placing it in a series of plays about prostitution engaging with the suffragists' campaign in the aftermath of the Piccadilly Flat Case. The production at the Gaiety

Theatre may have emphasised the romantic possibilities, only faintly raised, in my view, by Castleton's appraisal of Margaret's predicament. The play ends with Castleton's approbation of Margaret's self-sacrifice; he is aware of Margaret's predicament but still declares his love, believing that she has 'proved that the body is nothing where the spirit is all' (128). However, as the rest of the play has emphasised, through the subtle exchanges between the two sisters, the women have a different perspective. While *The Street* rehabilitates the prostitute as a woman with a consciousness, it provides little hope for transforming her economic situation. *The Times* pondered the pessimistic ending of the play (*The Times*, 2 December 1913: 12). The distinction between the spirit and the body which Castleton espouses is one which supports rather than challenges the separate-spheres ideology. Castleton is only able to celebrate Margaret's prostitution because he regards it as a spiritual victory rather than as a business transaction. In this respect, Castleton regards Margaret as the fallen woman whom he may save. Conventional representations of the prostitute are determined to control her: fixed either as a victim or as depraved; banished and punished in order to preserve the double standard.

In spite of these problems, the play makes the important connection between housing and prostitution, exposing women's sexual harassment by landlords and presenting the very different experiences of women and men in poverty. The need to argue against the home as the only sphere for women did not preclude the need to argue for the specific needs of women for shelter, an argument to which the WFL in particular attempted to do justice.[20]

It is somewhat ironic that one of the most historically significant of the Pioneer Players' productions should reinforce the image of the prostitute as deadly, redeemed only through bodily privation, religious conversion and death. The Pioneer Players' production in January 1914 of *Paphnutius* by the tenth-century Benedictine nun Hrotsvit was an historic event. This first production of a play by the first female playwright attracted much publicity. Reviewers noted that while the Woman's Theatre had produced no plays by women, the Pioneer Players 'have gone one better than the promoters of the recently highly successful "petticoat theatre" season at the Coronet Theatre in the cult of the feminist drama' (*Daily Despatch*, 2 January 1914). The assumed competition between the two organisations may have been expressed through a different attitude toward experimentation with staging techniques. Cicely Hamilton, for instance, had distanced herself from this attention to the aesthetic in her contribution to the pamphlet issued by the Woman's Theatre:

In order to avoid disappointment it will be better to state at once that we have no unusual views on the presentment or production of plays. We have been influenced neither by the Russian Ballet nor by Reinhardt: we make our exits into the wings instead of into the stalls and I have not heard of any particular struggles to attain that ideal of nobody acting better than anybody else which is frequently admired as 'ensemble' .... We feel these admissions may be damaging; but we plead, in excuse for our deficiencies, that we are only beginning our enterprise. Later on, perhaps we shall put out the footlights and tinker with the building and go in for Really High Art.

(Holledge 1981: 94)

The Pioneer Players' staging of plays was occasionally compared with that of the Russian Ballet. The production of *Paphnutius* had been especially praised for its economical use of opulent, coloured fabrics to create an atmospheric setting.

Paphnutius the hermit has heard a voice calling him to save Thais the courtesan from her wicked life. The first scene shows Paphnutius talking to his disciples about harmony between the soul and the body, between the planets and the music of the spheres, which is unheard:

Some think it is not heard because it is so continuous that men have grown accustomed to it. Others say it is because of the density of the air. Some assert that so enormous a sound could not pass into the mortal ear. Others that the music of the spheres is so pleasant and sweet that if it were heard all men would come together, and, forgetting themselves and all their pursuits, would follow the sounds from east to west. (99)

The discussion turns to ignorance and knowledge. Since Thais is a Christian, her sin is committed through an act of will rather than ignorance, which (in Paphnutius' opinion) increases its gravity and therefore her penance: she must be enclosed in a small cell for three years. Paphnutius's disciples and the Abbess of the monastery where Thais is secluded question the severity of the punishment:

All I have done is to gather up the many sins on my conscience into a mighty bundle and keep them always in mind. All day I have sat gazing towards the East, saying only this one prayer: 'O God Who made me, pity me!' If my bodily senses have always been conscious of the offensiveness of this place, my heart's eyes have never been blind to the dreadfulness of hell. (126)

However, Paphnutius's mission is successful. When they visit Thais she is about to die but her soul has been saved by extreme privation; the cell in which she has been enclosed has not been cleaned, contributing to her punishment. Thais's instant conversion is convincing only if Paphnutius is taken to be God's instrument. The context of Hrotsvit's play in tenth-century Catholicism explains the function of sin, sacrifice and conversion. The Pioneer Players' production, following *Mrs Warren's Profession*, *Honour Thy Father* and *The Street*, highlight the absence of an economic explanation for prostitution in Hrotsvit's medieval perspective. The emphasis falls on Thais' wilfulness and the destructive effects she has on men and society. The necessity of bodily privation for Thais's salvation indicates the ways in which women have been denied body and soul.[21] The prostitute functions as a scapegoat for the ills of society and her destruction is necessary for the restoration of order (Kent 1990: 65).

Yet, while *Paphnutius* may be an unappealing play for a twentieth-century reader in its condemnation of the prostitute, the play is formally unusual. Its unconventionally episodic thirteen short scenes led the *Stage* to conclude that in this play there was 'little real drama' (*Stage*, 15 January 1914: 25).[22] In spite of this, Christopher St. John identifies Hrotsvit with innovation:

> This dramatist, who was a nun consecrated to the service of God, did not write for money or for fame. She did not consider the box-office or the actor-manager; and her message was not clouded by speculations as to what the public wants.... I venture to say that many plays written in the year 1913 are already more old-fashioned than 'Paphnutius'.
>
> (Play programme; ECD)

However, the representation of the prostitute in *Paphnutius* is, as one would expect, highly conventional and directly contradicts the sympathetic treatment of the prostitute in the Pioneer Players' other plays.[23] Although these contradictory positions are not directly acknowledged, one annual report asserted that the 'play of ideas' was characteristically antagonistic, accommodating all points of view (*PPAR 1913–14*: 9). The Pioneer Players could see *Paphnutius* both in terms of modernism and women's suffrage. In some respects Hrotsvit's drama exhibited characteristics, such as the appropriation and manipulation of dramatic forms and the emphasis on virginity, which were unusually relevant for St. John and some of her contemporaries. Indeed, the imprisonment of Thais, the necessity of her suffering and the punishment of the body could be seen as providing a religious endorsement of the hunger strikes of the political prisoners of the women's suffrage movement. Hrotsvit appropriated pagan drama for Christian ends:

> There are many Catholics, and we cannot entirely acquit ourselves of the charge, who, attracted by the polished elegance of the style of pagan writers, prefer their works to the holy scriptures. ... Wherefore I, the strong voice of Gandersheim, have not hesitated to imitate in my writings a poet whose works are so widely read, my object being to glorify, within the limits of my poor talent, the laudable chastity of Christian virgins in that self-same form of composition which has been used to describe the shameless acts of licentious women.
> (St. John 1923: xxvi)

The deliberate manipulation of existing forms to produce an entirely different ideological perspective can be seen in Cicely Hamilton's treatment of the romantic comedy and the pageant, and in the work of other suffrage artists. Hrotsvit was identified by St. John as a female – rather than a religious – writer. The recovery of her work by St. John and the Pioneer Players was an important part of women's history. This production, and St. John's translation of the play, have received little attention from Hrotsvit scholars,[24] who are concerned rather with the place of her drama in the medieval visionary tradition in which the female authority derives authority from her celibacy (Petroff 1986: 5). According to Elizabeth Petroff, Hrotsvit is distinguished not merely as the first female dramatist, but as 'the earliest poet known in Germany and the first dramatist since classical times' (Petroff 1986: 89). Hrotsvit's plays predate the *Quem Quaeritis* dialogue conventionally ascribed the status of first Church drama (Wilson 1984). Significantly, it was in a religious community of women that the earliest female dramatists, Hrotsvit and Sor Juana Ines de la Cruz, were produced. The women's suffrage movement similarly brought women together in a productive way and through their association made possible new ways of thinking.

The most challenging of the Pioneer Players' productions were those which dramatised the perspective of dissenting women resisting separate-spheres ideology by working, as seen in this chapter, or by resisting marriage, to be discussed in Chapter 6. Most of the plays discussed here were produced by the Pioneer Players in the first few years of its existence when the society had established an interest in recovering women's history, in exposing the double standard and in demanding equality for women in work and in (or out of) marriage. A recurrent feature of these plays is the different perspectives of women and men which dramatically shape the dialogue and plot, often providing a conflict or crisis which is not easily resolved. The dramatisation of such a different point of view requires the manipulation of existing forms. In this chapter the Pioneer Players' treatment of women as workers and of the prostitute's situation as economically determined, has shown an engagement with issues which not only relate to contemporary women's suffrage debates but also lend themselves to descriptions of the society as 'feminist'.

6
Outside Marriage

If, as Cicely Hamilton contended in her incisive critique, *Marriage as a Trade* (1909), that marriage was practically a 'compulsory trade' for women, then economic independence promised an alternative existence. Many writers supportive of the women's suffrage movement identified marriage as a problem and argued for its reform. Some even rejected marriage and, specifically, the sexual relationship with a man that marriage represented. This was identified as a political decision and could take the form of a 'silent strike of women' (Bland 1995: 247) with ancient precedent. Aristophanes' sex war was appropriated when, in 1910, Emmeline Pethick Lawrence cited Lysistrata as 'a suffragette of 2000 years ago'. In November 1911, while he was a member of the Pioneer Players' executive committee, Laurence Housman provided comic allusions to the suffrage movement which were incorporated into the script for a performance of *Lysistrata* (Joannou and Purvis 1998: 152). In dominant discourse the Suffragette's opposite was the Womanly Woman, elided with (potential if not actual) Wife and Mother. The suffragette wife and mother was assumed to disrupt the home and family life. A memorable anti-suffrage postcard depicted a crying baby whose mother was a suffragette. However, as Susan Kingsley Kent states, the majority of '[suffragists] did not mean by the elimination of separate spheres that women should no longer marry and bear children or abandon the home, nor did they suggest that men should participate equally in child-rearing and other domestic chores' (Kent 1990: 59). Even Laurence Housman's poem 'Woman This and Woman That' reinforced the conventional role of woman as mother: 'For the soldier bears the rifle, but the woman bears the race' and reinforces her occupation of the domestic sphere: 'Give us the vote, that we may make the home a happier place!' The principle of complementarity could therefore be used to argue for an extension of available opportunities for women, for access to both public and private spheres, and for the reform of women's role in marriage and in the domestic sphere.

Debates about marriage inevitably concern sexuality, whether in relation to reproduction or sexual desire. Suffragists united in their desire for the vote and the transformation of society which this promised, disagreed about tactics and as Sheila Jeffreys has shown, it was the issue of sexuality over which there was the most disagreement. One view 'advocated the joys and necessity of heterosexual intercourse in or out of marriage' and another 'launched a major critique of the form of male sexuality, and advocated non-cooperation with the sexual desires of men' (Jeffreys 1985: 100). A common metaphor for political commitment to the suffrage movement was 'marriage' to the 'Cause'. In J. S. Stainton's novel, *The Home Breakers* (1913), Elinor Gifford forcefully states, in rejecting a marriage proposal,

> 'I have told you. I will never marry. I am one of the women who has only room in her life for one thing. I have given myself to it absolutely. Ted's word "obsessed" is the right one. There is no room in my life for you or for any man.'
>
> (Norquay 1995: 301)

A rejected marriage proposal could also be interpreted as a sign of political activism, as demonstrated by Mrs Honeychurch's reaction to Lucy's revelation in E. M. Forster's *A Room With A View* (1908) that, not only would she not marry Cecil Vyse but that she might even share a flat in London:

> 'And mess with typewriters and latch-keys,' exploded Mrs Honeychurch. 'And agitate and scream, and be carried off kicking by the police. And call it a Mission – when no one wants you! And call it Duty – when it means that you can't stand your own home! And call it Work – when thousands of men are starving with the competition as it is! And then to prepare yourself, find two doddering old ladies, and go abroad with them.'
>
> (Forster 1908: 285)

The desire for the vote was presented as all-consuming and displaced. One anti-suffrage music hall turn provided the snide revelation that 'Mrs Pancake' really wanted 'blokes for women'.[1] A lack of self-knowledge regarding their 'true' sexual identity was a significant element of the spinster-suffragette stereotype. And for some suffrage activists, of course, celibacy or same-sex desire were realities. An inchoate lesbian identity was emerging in the iconography of the nun and the martyr of religious discourse. This chapter therefore explores the diverse representations of marriage in the Pioneer Players' drama and considers the appropriation of religious discourse in some of the plays in this context.

Many of the conservative representations of marriage are to be found in the society's later plays. In 1915, for instance, the society staged Edward Knoblock's *Mouse* which concludes with the promise of marriage, resolving the earlier disruption caused by the adulterous relationship of two other characters. A different condemnation of adultery occurs in Claudel's *Exchange*, performed by the society in the same year. Claudel depicts characters for whom marriage is a business transaction, but this critique is shaped by a Catholic perspective. Rather than offering a critique of the institution of marriage, the play merely condemns those for whom marriage is not sanctified by religious belief. Claudel's *Exchange* presents marriage as a necessary part of a woman's life and the role of wife as subordinate to that of her husband. The three plays by Chekhov produced by the society in 1920, are similarly conventional in their representation of gender. In *The Bear*, a widow is visited by her dead husband's boorish creditor. His insults provoke an aggressive response from the widow, yet the play concludes, incredibly, with a passionate embrace.[2] In these plays, relationships between women and men are portrayed as founded on inequality and aggression. In Chekhov's *On the High Road*, the responsibility for Bortsov's tragic decline into alcoholism and poverty is attributed to his ex-wife.[3] His story so moves the company at the roadside inn that, when his wife appears, she is attacked and given no opportunity to challenge his version of their life together. In *The Wedding*, Chekhov exposes the cynical attitude to marriage of both the bridegroom, obsessed with the dowry, and the bride's parents, preoccupied with procuring prestigious wedding guests. This play, like others produced by the society discussed below, exposes marriage as an economic transaction.

In Sholom Alecheim's monologue 'Gymnasie', performed for the society in 1917 by Michael Sherbrooke, the protagonist

> describes with a wealth of humorous detail the difficulty experienced by a Jewish parent in Russian Poland under the old regime in getting his son into a Government school.
>
> (*PPAR 1916–17*: 8)

In the course of the story, the man's misogynistic attitude to his wife is revealed by his repeated warning that marriage to a clever woman is a tragic fate. The effectiveness of this piece relies on the irony set up by the absence of any other – particularly female – characters.

Violence as a means of reorganising unsatisfactory relationships features in several plays: Torahiko Kori's *Kanawa* and Jose Echegeray's *The Cleansing Stain*, both produced in 1917; Susan Glaspell's *Trifles* and Christopher St. John's *On the East Side*, both produced for the Pioneer Players in 1919.[4] Breaking the bonds of marriage is seen to be both inevitable and destructive. The means of negotiating changing relationships could even entail murder, sometimes with cathartic effect.

However, as Jane Lewis and Susan Kingsley Kent point out, it is the critique of the institution of marriage (dramatised in many plays produced by the Pioneer Players before 1915) which posed an unusual challenge to separate-spheres ideology and prevailing attitudes amongst suffragists. Lewis has said that while feminists pressed for women's right to move into the public sphere, 'they *ignored* the implications of their demand to enter the public sphere for the role of women in the private sphere of home and family' (Kent 1990: 58). The drama produced by the Pioneer Players was often concerned with exploring the possibilities of women's desires. A number of the prime movers in the society were indeed already living the 'new life'. The headquarters of the society was the flat at 31 Bedford Street which Edith Craig shared with her partner Christopher St. John and, after 1916, Tony Atwood. Members of the Pioneer Players such as Cicely Hamilton, Edith Craig, Christopher St. John and Laurence Housman were demanding a 'single sphere for men and women' (Kent 1990: 219) and that choice should be extended to women in the matter of marriage.

The critique of marriage in these plays took different forms. It presented the destructive effects of marriage for women. It exposed the economic determinants and the ideological basis of marriage so that it was seen as a choice rather than a necessity. The rejection of marriage is represented as possible through the support of other women. This is made explicit in Margaret Wynne Nevinson's *In the Workhouse,* Jess Dorynne's *The Surprise of His Life* and Gerolamo Rovetta's *The Month of Mary,* concerning the topical issue of the unmarried mother. In 1911 the *Vote* had reported the case of Daisy Turner who had been raped by a married man and subsequently killed her baby (*Vote*, 19 August 1911: 206). Charlotte Despard wrote an article about this case and the general position of 'The Unmarried Mother' (*Vote*, 7 October 1911: 294).

In The Workhouse was written by Margaret Wynne Nevinson whose regular column in the *Vote*, 'Woman: the Spoilt Child of Law', exposed current examples of the double standard (*Vote*, 2 April 1910: 273). Edith Craig commissioned the play as a dramatisation of Nevinson's article 'Detained by Marital Authority', one of a series in the *Westminster Gazette*, called 'Workhouse Characters'. Nevinson criticised the current state of marriage rather than marriage as an institution, but the ambiguity of the play's ending lent itself to either interpretation. Although she publicly denied it, *In The Workhouse* seems to argue for a woman's right to be an unmarried mother. The reviews significantly confuse the setting of the play as 'obstetric' when in fact it was not set in a hospital or a maternity ward, but a women's ward in a workhouse (Nevinson 1926: 227). This exemplifies what Foucault named the 'hysterisation' of women. Arguments about women's independence invariably led to a discussion of motherhood. In medical discourse and the writings of sexology women were defined in terms of physiology, namely their reproductive function. Sheila Jeffreys identified some problematic aspects of Havelock Ellis's ideas. He argued that: there were innate biological differences between women and men; relationships between women and men should be ones of dominance and submission; and that the ideal woman was distinguished by motherhood (Jeffreys 1985: 129). Nevinson's play argues against innate biological differences, emphasising the social, specifically legal and economic, determinants of women's lives. As one would expect, reviewers were anxious about female characters who discussed what could be regarded as indecent matters of motherhood and marriage.

Although Mary Watson, like many of the play's contemporary reviewers, dismissed this play as a 'fervent tract, naive, and crude in both its characterization and its moral theory' (Watson 1970: 121), its propaganda function was effective. The law of coverture which the play criticised was indeed reformed a year after the play was produced (Nevinson 1926: 225). Under this law a woman had no legal existence separate from her nearest male relative, a state of affairs which had been satirised in one of the Pioneer Players' first productions, that of Cicely Hamilton and Christopher St. John's *How the Vote Was Won*. In that play a group of economically independent women are brought together and occupy the stage.[5] Similarly, *In the Workhouse* shows a group of women talking to each other. However, in this case, men are completely absent from the stage, only featuring in the women's stories about their lives. These stories show that, once married, women have no legal control over their lives or their children. The conclusion is, in Lily's words, 'Vice triumphant'. Decisions which affect these women's lives are made elsewhere but one way of retaining some power is to refuse marriage. Lily decides not to marry Augustus, the father of her baby. The women's discussion shows that their experiences are common and it is this shared knowledge which transforms their lives. The emphasis is on speech, not action. The only movement on stage is Mrs Cleaver's arrival from the committee. Her husband has refused to give permission for her to leave the workhouse as he has the right to do, since she is legally his property. She reflects on her experiences, and concludes that if she had the choice again she would not marry. The play emphasises the need for legal reform and shows that women of all social classes are capable of identifying political arguments, and promoting change in their lives through sharing their experiences.

In the Workhouse refuses to victimise the unmarried mother and in this respect it compares with Jess Dorynne's *The Surprise of His Life*. That play begins with the Jenkins household in crisis. Emily Jenkins is pregnant and Alfred Williams, the father of the child, has abandoned her in favour of her friend, Sally. Joseph Jenkins, Emily's father and a very ambitious, class-conscious greengrocer, plans to bribe Alfred to marry his daughter and consequently preserve his reputation and his business. These ingredients, suitable for a conventional problem play or even a melodrama, are given a disturbing reorganisation. Emily's Aunt Eliza, like Mrs Cleaver in *In the Workhouse*, compares her own experience with that of Emily. Like the older women in Charlotte Perkins Gilman's *Three Women*, she advises Emily not to follow her example. Eliza reveals that when she became pregnant, she had married the father of her child and has lived to regret it. The climax of the play is reached when Emily refuses to marry Alfred. She argues that since he is not respectable, marriage to him could not make her respectable. She leaves with Eliza, to lead an independent life supported by Mrs Wilson and her society which helps independent women.

Dorynne's play, bearing some resemblance to her own history as the mother of Edward Gordon Craig's child, argues that it is not essential for a pregnant woman to marry and that a marriage of convenience could risk loss of self-respect. Emily, Eliza and Sally are all transformed in the play. Joseph seems devastated by the news that there are points of view radically different from his own. It may be felt as a weakness of the play that Emily's transformation has been effected off stage, significantly as a result of attending suffrage meetings and associating with Mrs Wilson, who is never seen on stage. Emily declares that she knows nothing of politics, but that these meetings have taught her to respect herself as a woman. This importantly demystifies politics, and aligns marriage, the home and a woman's body with political and moral choices.

When Emily repulses Alfred's attempt to kiss her with a 'scientific jerk', an allusion is made to the self-defence taught to suffragists as a necessary means of dealing with the brutal manifestations of anti-suffragists' hostility.[6] The literature of the women's suffrage movement found it difficult to represent such moments of violent encounter despite the fact that they were features of the daily experience of street propagandising.[7] The precise details of the brutal violence of 'Black Friday' on 18 November 1910, which led to the death of several women and the indecent assault of many others, were unrepresentable within the conventions of the day. It shattered the illusory equilibrium of male chivalry and female deference. The suffragists subsequently armed themselves and took a 'scientific' approach to self-defence. The monitoring of court cases was used to expose systematic violence against women and children. The suffragette characters following the court case of 'fallen children' in Edith Zangwill's *The Call* (1924) are not allowed to hear the child's statement regarding the abuse, as all women are asked to leave the court:

> The child burst into tears and clung to the woman beside her. 'Mother, don't let him take me! I don't want to tell them.' The magistrate was again conferring with the clerk. 'All women to leave the Court,' came the peremptory order.
> (Norquay 1995: 50)

The lenient treatment of such offences in the courts indicated the double standard of sexual morality and the assumption that women are the property of men.

In *The Surprise of His Life*, Alfred's behaviour, like that of Emily's father, is presented as selfish and destructive, and some attempt is made to relate this to men's privileged economic position. Joseph is obsessed with his business, and regards his wife and children as his property. Alfred finds amusement in taunting Emily with the notion that Lloyd George's Insurance Act, in providing financial support for unmarried mothers, would leave men such as Alfred free from responsibility. Similarly, Emily's attitude is shown to have been affected by her involvement in women's suffrage. Even before Emily reveals this, her father associates Emily's dissent with the suffrage campaign. Jenkins registers the threat symbolised by the prospect of a community of women: he regards the women's departure from his house as exemplifying magic or madness.

1 Photograph in *Daily Graphic*, January 1914, showing Ellen Terry, Harcourt Williams and Miriam Lewes rehearsing at the King's Hall for the Pioneer Players' production of Hrotsvit's *Paphnutius*.

2 Photograph of printed envelope for Evreinov's *The Theatre of the Soul*.

3 Photograph of actors in the Pioneer Players' production of Delphine Gray's *The Conference*.

4 Photographs in the *Tatler*, 25 March 1914, of participants in the Pioneer Players' second Mi-Carême Ball.

5 Photographs in the *Daily Mirror* of participants in the Scala Theatre production of Cicely Hamilton's *A Pageant of Great Women*; ETMM.

6 Photograph of actors in the Pioneer Players' production of Marjorie Patterson's *Pan in Ambush*; Raymond Mason.

7 Photograph of actors in the Pioneer Players' production of Marjorie Patterson's *Pan in Ambush*; Raymond Mason.

8 Photograph of Pamela Colman Smith's design of the programme for Lady Randolph Churchill's charity matinee.

The representation of Emily's father's dismay at his daughter's behaviour is nicely comic, and the reduction of the patriarchal figure, necessary to the argument, provides a humorous ending to a play which promised to be tragic.[8]

While *In the Workhouse* and *The Surprise of His Life* offered single parenthood as an alternative to marriage, later plays (Mrs Herbert Cohen's *The Level Crossing* and Salvatore di Giacomo's *The Month of Mary*)[9] emphasise the inevitability of marriage for a pregnant woman. *The Month of Mary* like Nevinson's play, is set in a workhouse and concerns motherhood, illegitimacy and bureaucracy in southern Italy, providing a swingeing critique of the treatment of individual women at the hands of institutions. When Carmella visits her illegitimate son in the workhouse it transpires that he has died the previous night. The officials at the workhouse (more from cowardice than compassion) do not inform her of this news. Her son was, it seems, the product of a rape, from which Carmella's father did little to protect her. Her husband rejected the child: 'The boy is not mine, he is another's and I don't want to have him around. Either you pack him off, or – I do not know what I may do, I do not know, but we shall not live in peace' (17). The tragedy of this play, described by one reviewer as 'one of the most pathetic short plays in the contemporary Italian Theatre' (*Pall Mall Gazette*, 19 May 1913: 7), is the depiction of an isolated and neglected woman, who is treated deplorably by the workhouse officials. Even the nun does not tell her about her son's death; the representatives of both religion and social work are presented as unfeeling and negligent.

Di Giacomo's play is limited to the exposition of Carmella's situation rather than suggesting any means of changing it and in this respect it differs greatly from the plays by Nevinson and Dorynne. A similarity in the circumstances of Carmella's motherhood and the Daisy Turner case can be seen in the woman's experience of rape and a consequent pregnancy. This allusion is not acknowledged in the society's annual reports, which instead proudly announces that it was 'the first occasion on which one of the author's works has been presented to an English audience' (*PPAR 1912–13:* 8–9). Reviewers similarly made no association between the play and the court case two years earlier.[10] This, together with the society's emphasis on the novelty of producing a play by Salvatore di Giacomo, rather than on the contentious representation of the female protagonist perhaps indicate the society's first steps towards the 'art theatre' it attempted to establish in 1915.

The dilemma of a mother who has been forced to continue in an unhappy marriage rather than lose her child is dramatised in Mrs

Herbert Cohen's *The Level Crossing*. The Lord Chamberlain's reader found this 'strained but morbidly effective' (ADD LCP 1914/18; BL). It was subtitled 'A Village Tragedy' and significantly set in *c.*1880, before the law allowed divorced women custody of their children. In Cohen's play, Rizpah's investment in an unhappy marriage proves to be misguided. The play begins four months after the death of the child on a level crossing, an accident for which her husband, John Gibbs, is indirectly responsible. Rizpah has been in hospital since but is due to return home. The first scene shows Gibbs, comforted by his friend George Wright, preparing for the reunion. When Gibbs maintains that his wife is unlike other women his friend remarks, 'Women be such queer cattle.' Gibbs' fears about her return prove to be well grounded. Rizpah has suffered mental ill health as a result of her bereavement. The child's father died in an accident, some years ago, also on the same level crossing. She admits that her five-year marriage to Gibbs had been a convenience; she married him to ensure the child's financial security. In spite of this, she argues that while Gibbs has had the use of her body, she has withheld her spirit as the only means of survival. Gibbs' confession prompts the tragic dénouement of the play. Although he injured his arm when he tried to save the child, the accident had happened because he was drunk and the child was free to wander. Rizpah leaves, apparently to commit suicide on the level crossing. The play reveals the community's fear and ignorance about mental illness. Rizpah needs to talk about her grief, but the hospital and her husband impose silence on her. The sick woman may have her own ideas about dealing with her health but she is constrained by the institutions of marriage and hospital which deprive her of any choice in coming to terms with her bereavement. As in *The Month of Mary*, the mother's isolation in the loss of a child is shown to be exacerbated by the alienating effects of institutions. The rest cure invented by Silas Weir Mitchell served to increase the woman's sense of isolation and has destructive effects, as Charlotte Perkins Gilman's short story 'The Yellow Wallpaper' had eloquently demonstrated. Showalter has indicated that the isolation of the patient tended to render her dependent and more likely to conform to a conventionally feminine role (Showalter 1987: 139–40).

The reviews were favourable but significantly overlooked Rizpah's attitude to marriage as a means of keeping her child by entering into a contract with a husband for whom she had little feeling. The *Stage* commended Elaine Sleddall as Rizpah: 'her fierce, motherly love recalling that shown by the mother in Tennyson's masterly poem of the same name' and J. Fisher White for 'a pathetic picture of the bereaved John

Gibbs, wounded in his tenderest affection' (*Stage*, 25 June 1914: 22).[11] Rizpah's deception of Gibbs is foregrounded in the play, and in the light of the earlier plays produced by the society, it is likely that Rizpah represents those women for whom marriage is a trade. The representation of the bereaved mother conveniently obscured this argument for the *Stage*.

Some of the society's plays explored the constraints on women in marriage without explicitly offering any solution. An early and important example of such a play is Laurence Housman's *Pains and Penalties*[12] which shows that all women, no matter how privileged, face discrimination in a patriarchal society. In Housman's play a heroine emerges temporarily triumphant in Queen Caroline whose life is recovered and celebrated in this controversial and unlicensed performance (*World*, 5 December 1911: 866).

The trial of Queen Caroline in 1820 is used by Housman to emphasise the sexual double standard and the means by which the law is used to oppress women, including in Caroline's case, a queen. Caroline of Brunswick separated from her husband soon after their daughter Charlotte was born. Before his coronation George IV instigated extraordinary legal proceedings in the House of Lords to dissolve their marriage.[13] The bill of 'pains and penalties' was 'a special procedure in the House of Lords... which provided a way of punishing a person without legal trial' (Davidoff and Hall 1988: 50). Although George openly conducted relationships with other women during his separation from Caroline, it was her sexual conduct that was put on trial.

The play in some ways conforms to the conventional interpretation of this episode 'as an important moment in radical politics with the royal divorce proceedings symbolising the corruption of the political system' (Davidoff and Hall 1988: 151). Caroline's rights as a woman and as heir to the throne are subordinated to political intrigues at court. The dramatic scene in which Caroline attends the trial in the House of Lords recalls the powerful, silent, great women in the court of Justice in *A Pageant of Great Women*; her silence exposes the emptiness of the men's words. The political manoeuvring of the politicians who use her case to threaten the government recalls the ways in which women, such as Margaret Hughes in *The First Actress*, fared at the hands of male-dominated institutions.

In this respect the play offers a critique of British institutions of government at the time of George IV and also, more topically, of the recent Conciliation Bill. When Caroline attempts to enter Westminster Abbey, like so many suffragists, she is turned away. The points are made that the law is used for political ends, that a woman knocking at the door of Westminster has been shut out, and that a great turning point for reforms, including those of the rights and status of women, has been reached and lost. This play served as an example of the ways in which even a queen is subject to the whims of her husband. Set in the English court of the early nineteenth century, Housman's play suggests that the legal position of women in marriage has changed very little.

In appropriating Caroline for the women's suffrage movement, Housman was concerned with emphasising the ways in which even the prospective queen was subject to discriminatory laws.[14] Davidoff and Hall note that Caroline was subsequently used to reinforce the ideal of domesticity, a standard to be set by the royal family:

> The moral issues raised, the defence of the virtuous female victim, the defence of marriage, the refusal of divorce meant that, for a precarious and short-lived moment, a moral majority was produced, too powerful for the king and his government. John Bull had triumphed in his insistence that the king must be a husband too.
> (Davidoff and Hall 1988: 154)

Housman's play did not challenge the 'ideal of womanhood' which Caroline subsequently came to represent.

Cicely Hamilton's play *A Matter of Money* dramatises the constraints on women caused by the economic determinants of marriage which Hamilton had explored in her feminist study *Marriage as a Trade* (1909). Sheila Stowell has linked the arguments of this remarkable work with that of Michel Foucault:

> The book launches an attack upon the hysterisation of the female body as Michel Foucault would come to characterise it, condemning the artificial reduction of women to sex, and celebrating celibacy and spinsterhood as alternatives to the subjugation and dependency that marriage and motherhood entailed.
> (Stowell 1992: 178)

However, rather than offering any of the solutions which Hamilton discusses in *Marriage as a Trade*, *A Matter of Money* confines itself to exposing the problems which marriage causes, as Lis Whitelaw indicates: 'The theme of the play is the difficulty of ending unhappy marriages when those involved have no money of their own and also the complexity of human relationships – the idea that passions are rarely clear-cut' (Whitelaw 1990: 129).[15] The relationship between Dr Channing and his patient Lucia Coventry is complicated because they are both married. Divorce is presented as impossible because both parties are economically dependent on their respective marriages. The tragic response to this predicament is provided through a melodramatic convention: Lucia's suicide on a level crossing.

The Pioneer Players' production of the play cast a real husband and wife – Ben Webster and May Whitty – as the ill-fated Channings,[16] and reviews of this production reveal complexities to the play not examined by Whitelaw. Channing is devoted to his wife and his invalid daughter which suggests divided loyalties. In addition, Channing's ethical status as a doctor is compromised when he falls in love with his patient. Although a divorce would mean 'professional ruin' for Channing (Whitelaw 1990: 129), in some respects his professional role has already been questioned and this concerned some reviewers of the Pioneer Players' production.

Whitelaw remarks on the alarmed response of the *Stage* to the unsympathetic representation of the male characters in the play (Whitelaw 1990: 130). However, as Sheila Stowell has noted, the reviewer seemed unduly concerned with Dr Channing's breach of professional decorum (Stowell 1992: 87), asserting that the doctor was seduced by Lucia; in this way the doctor's credentials are protected. Stowell suggests that these critics regarded 'Hamilton's portrayal of the play's doctor... as a maligning of male professionalism' (Stowell 1992: 87). Furthermore, their sensitivity to Hamilton's depiction of the medical profession may be explained by the high profile of doctors at this time in the debates about the forcible feeding of hunger-striking suffragists. The play was performed by the Pioneer Players in the same month which saw Mrs Pankhurst imprisoned in connection with the arson committed on Lloyd George's country house, resulting in the new law – the 'Cat and Mouse' (Prisoners' Temporary Discharge for Ill Health) Act – which attempted to end the use of the hunger-strike (Kent 1990: 202). In addition, the status of doctors had been analysed in the *Vote* which ran a report on 'The Moral of the Crippen Case', emphasising the part played by Mrs Crippen's female friends in the capture of Dr Crippen for the murder of his wife (*Vote*, 6 August 1910: 178). Three women provided Scotland Yard with a dossier of information, exemplifying (so the article argues) the intellect of women. In this respect it bears comparison with the plot of Susan Glaspell's *Trifles*. The article also implied that the reticence of the police in the investigation was partly because a woman was murdered and the suspect was a male doctor. The anxieties regarding *A*

Matter of Money felt by the *Stage* and the *Sketch*, concerned the scenario, which was judged incredible, since the doctor 'would have succeeded in resisting temptation, particularly seeing that the sin in the case of a doctor is peculiarly heinous'.[17]

The ending of this, as with many of Hamilton's plays, however, is problematic. The self-destruction of the dissenting woman conforms to the conventional options of marriage or death available to women and it neatly obviates the need for the divorce. Norquay has noted that the 'creaky' or 'shaky' plots of some suffrage narratives sometimes end conventionally with death, as in *Suffragette Sally* (1911) or marriage, as in *A Fair Suffragette* (1909) (Norquay 1995: 29). The revelatory function of literature is demonstrated by narrative ruptures exposing the limitations of the ideological forces which hold the text in tension. Thus in *A Matter of Money* the manner of Lucia's suicide is significant. It is at the level crossing, the place where Lucia and Dr Channing held their secret meetings, that she commits suicide.[18] As in Cohen's *The Level Crossing*, the pioneering woman places herself in a dangerous position when she transgresses femininity.

The Pioneer Players' production of *A Matter of Money*[19] engaged, like many of the plays about prostitution discussed in Chapter 5, with a topical issue, in this case the recent Divorce Commission (*The Times*, 10 February 1913: 10). If divorce was financially inaccessible to Dr Channing and Lucia Coventry it was even more difficult for working-class women. Two years after Hamilton's treatment of divorce, the Pioneer Players produced Constance Campbell's play *A Dilemma* (*The Times*, 9 March 1915: 11). This play has not been located, but it is important that the dramatist may have regarded it as a play which would interest suffragists. Campbell wrote to Craig offering her a play (possibly *A Dilemma*) to be performed for suffrage societies:

> If you do get a chance of recommending the enclosed play to Suffrage Societies – it is the one you were so very kind to get licensed for me – I should be so awfully obliged. The copy is yours if you will honour me by accepting it!
> (Unpublished letter from Constance Campbell to Edith Craig, 24 July 1914; 3.117, ECCF)

The *Stage* dismissed *A Dilemma* as 'designed apparently for propaganda purposes, and of no particular importance' (*Stage*, 11 March 1915: 21). However, by 1915 the production of 'propaganda' plays was no longer a priority for the society. None the less, Campbell's play was not the last play on the issue of divorce to be produced by the Pioneer Players. In 1920 the society produced M. E. M. Young's *The Higher Court*.

Although Young's play is assumed by at least one reviewer to be arguing for divorce reform, like Nevinson's *In the Workhouse* the play offers an ambiguous ending which subverts the formal conventions of propaganda. In some respects Young's play compares with *A Matter of Money* in that a relationship ends because divorce is considered to be impossible. But in *The Higher Court* divorce is impossible because it is not permissible for Catholics. The play shows obstacles to marriage on financial and religious grounds, but while financial circumstances may change, religious ones should not.

The relationship between McManus, the divorced millionaire owner of *The Meteor* newspaper, and Idalia, a devout Catholic, develops as a result of an accident. Idalia's family take in a man suffering from amnesia having been injured in a road accident outside their house. It is during McManus's period of amnesia when he is named 'The Stowaway' by the family that Idalia falls in love with him. However, when he regains his memory their relationship changes as a result of their different economic and religious positions. Although McManus is willing to convert to Catholicism in order to marry Idalia, she is not prepared to give up her religious principles when he reveals that he is divorced. This moment is poignantly dramatised: he tears up the catechism she has given him and she tears up the cheque he has given her as a contribution to the school where she works. This unambiguous breaking of the bonds of their relationship is then called into question by the closing scene of the play in which Idalia's brother and sister comment on her situation. While her sister expresses her fears for Idalia, her brother asserts that Idalia is by no means afraid.

Idalia's courage could thus be interpreted as a resistance to temptation, and therefore supportive of the Catholic stance on divorce. However, her response to McManus could equally be regarded as a tragic sacrifice in that her faith deprives her of happiness. Virginia Woolf observed that the audience when she attended the play seemed to hope that love would win out over Roman Catholicism (Woolf 1988: 207). The title of the play, and Young's other published writings, suggest that Catholicism was not the target for criticism in the play. Idalia looks to 'the higher court' for judgement, rather than that of the law. In this sense, the play takes a very different approach to divorce reform from the other plays produced by the Pioneer Players. Agravaine in the *Referee*, nevertheless, assumed that *The Higher Court* was a play about divorce reform, and 'discloses an attack upon . . . the still rigid attitude of the Roman Catholic Church towards divorce'.[20] The motion to reform the Divorce Law had just been defeated in the House of Commons.[21] The society acknowledged some hostile responses to the play which 'provoked a great deal of controversy owing to its subject, and was otherwise remarkable for the brilliant acting of the two leading parts by Miss Mary Jerrold and Mr. Randal Ayrton' (*PPAR 1919–20:* 6). Mary Jerrold's appreciative letter to Craig about her experiences in this play further suggests that there had been doubts about the society performing the play:

> I appreciate what you say so much indeed. I am so glad we really did the play after all & I loved all the work connected with it, in spite of the rush & the terror about [illegible]! But you were all so lovely to work with & for. Thank you so much for the cheque enclosed in your letter.
> (Unpublished letter from Mary Jerrold to Edith Craig, 15 April [?]; 3.385, ECCF)

Since the play was produced at a time when divorce reform was the subject of parliamentary debate, it may have provoked controversy merely by dramatising a situation in which divorce was a possibility. The submission to Catholic authority at the end of the play baffled and irritated Virginia Woolf.

While Young's play features sacrifice, Catholicism and marriage rejection, it does not challenge the institution of marriage. In the plays to be discussed next, the themes of sacrifice, Catholicism and marriage rejection, and their relationship to the religious discourse of the women's suffrage movement, constitute a more radical challenge to the institution of marriage. The Pioneer Players' production of religious plays, such as those of Hrotsvit and Paul Claudel, demonstrated the society's interest in poetic drama and, in the case of Hrotsvit, in plays written by women. The representation of the female martyr in these performances yields some unusual interpretative possibilities. In Claudel's *The Tidings Brought to Mary* Violaine is transformed by leprosy.[22] Her self-sacrifice unites Pierre and her sister Mara, absolving Mara's jealousy and enabling Violaine to resurrect her sister's child. For Claudel, the self-destruction of the female protagonist signifies an act of faith, a renunciation of sexual desire for the love of God which has a healing effect on others. It is, however, significant that the play features a female martyr whose virginity is central to the plot. During the period of the Pioneer Players' activity, the virgin martyr and the nun featured in women's suffrage culture as a developing sign of resistance to marriage; the celibacy of the nun is endowed with a political significance. This may explain the society's interest in Claudel's plays which otherwise seem merely to offer the stereotypes of virgin/whore that obsessed, *fin-de-siècle* writers.[23]

Suffrage activism was frequently represented in terms of religious commitment. New recruits were subject to 'conversion', deployed on a 'mission' for 'the Cause'. The suffragists' appropriation of religious discourse, with its emphasis on martyrdom, sacrifice and comradeship, endorsed an oppositional political position, lending it authority by the allusion to a religious precedent. The religious iconography of the suffrage movement has been widely acknowledged, although it has been particularly associated with the WSPU's appropriation of Joan of Arc.[24] Further examination is required to assess the extent to which religious discourse endorsed or subverted dominant ideas of femininity and the function of sexuality in the construction of a possible feminist subjectivity through the nun/martyr.

Religious allusions were a common feature in the suffrage movement. In the WFL, there were proposals to form a 'Corps of Suffrage Missionaries' (*Vote*, 12 November 1910: 26). Hirschfield maintains that in the drama of the suffrage movement the sacrificial act was rarely embodied in a feminist version of the Christ figure,[25] but in some respects Joan of Arc served a similar function. Thus Gertrude Vaughan's play *The Woman With The Pack*, produced by the AFL, on 8 December 1911, showed 'a symbolic female saviour ultimately materializing on stage in the guise of Joan of Arc, to the accompaniment of heavenly voices' (Hirschfield 1985: 136). While Lisa Tickner has commented on sado-masochistic elements of some of the women's suffrage posters (Tickner 1987: 38), she regarded the figure of Joan of Arc as the most disturbing and effective image of women in the militant suffrage iconography:

> She defied order, division and convention in all the aspects of her marginality and strange, militant sanctity. In her virginity, transvestism and military vigilance she subverted the order of femininity.
> (Tickner 1987: 211)

As Tickner suggests, as the patron saint of the militant suffragists, representing the persecution of women by the English government, Joan of Arc resisted categorisation. It is therefore significant that when the Pioneer Players produced Paul Claudel's *The Tidings Brought to Mary*, the *Stage* remarked on its many references to Joan of Arc (*Stage*, 14 June 1917: 7).

I would argue that the figure of Joan of Arc was particularly effective because it combined heroic activity with sexual independence where desire is not oriented towards men. Gilbert and Gubar have interpreted the women's suffrage movement as engaging in a 'battle of the sexes', manifesting a claim for matriarchal power (Gilbert and Gubar 1988: 12). While 'sex antagonism' and theories of matriarchy and female moral superiority were available at this time, gender was deeply troubling, linked essentially to sex *and* becoming radically dislodged by the politicisation of cross-dressing and traversing of boundaries. Joan of Arc was characterised by militancy, virginity, cross-dressing and divine inspiration. She, and other female religious figures, represented suffrage militancy in something more than a reversal of the active/passive role, in a struggle to replace patriarchy with a matriarchy. Gilbert's and Gubar's interpretation of the 'battle' over gender does not take into account the virginity of the militant nun. The oppositional role of the militant nun depends not on the power of the maternal but on the rejection of heterosexuality.

Truly committed suffragettes were married to the movement and renounced relationships with men. Thus Elinor Gifford told her suitor in J. S. Stainton's *The Home-Breakers* (1913), '"There is no room in my life for you or for any man"' (Norquay 1995: 299). Conventionally, political activism has been constructed for women in rational discourse as a field opposed to marriage, desire or emotion. Thus, Gertrude Marvell remarks in *Delia Blanchflower* (1915) when Delia falls in love with Mark Winnington, '"What shall we ever get out of her as a married woman? What would Mark Winnington – to whom she will give herself, body and soul – allow us to get out of her?"' (Norquay 1995: 279). The opposition between politics and desire contributed to the criticism of marriage in women's suffrage writings. There were difficulties for suffragists in representing female sexual desire. H. G. Wells achieved this in *Ann Veronica* but the plot requires the conventional displacement of political activism by romance. The stereotype of the spinster-suffragette is characterised as masculine and, as Mark Sheridan put it, ultimately in need of 'blokes' rather than votes. The joke concerns a displacement which reveals the 'truth' about the suffragette's sexuality. Her lack of self-awareness means that she does not know what she really wants. As Foucault has argued of the nineteenth century, 'Not only did it speak of sex and compel everyone to do so; it also set out to formulate the uniform truth of sex. As if it suspected sex of harboring a fundamental secret' (Foucault 1990: 69). Sexuality became a means of defining and categorising the whole person. The anti-suffragists demonised the suffragettes as a threat to heterosexuality.

In the women's suffrage movement, representations of celibacy or virginity sometimes provided a space in which same-sex desire could be envisaged as something other than immature or defective, other than the exceptional, freakish, pathologised 'invert' or 'intermediate sex' of the sexologists. As Chris Weedon notes: 'Modes of subjectivity, like theories of society or versions of history, are temporary fixings in the on-going process in which any absolute meaning or truth is constantly deferred' (Weedon 1987: 173). Gertrude Colmore's short story, 'The Nun' published in the WFL newspaper the *Vote* (29 June 1912: 175), makes explicit the spiritual/political mission of the suffragist. The figure of the saint or nun was frequently used in women's suffrage culture, exploiting the few positions open to women in institutionalised religion. 'The Nun' shows three women discussing the future of the youngest woman. The unattributed direct speech of the narrative obscures the identities of the different women and the setting for much of the story. The women discuss commitment to the suffrage movement in terms of a nun's renunciation, penance and fasting and the ritualistic marriage to Christ in 'taking the veil'. One character asks:

> 'You will say, next, that like the nuns you are the brides of Christ, I suppose?'
> 'No, for we aspire only to be His servants, serving Him in that we seek to serve the most oppressed, the most degraded, the least of His brethren.'
>
> (Colmore 1912: 175)

The story concludes with the girl's decision:

> The girl was still looking out into the park with eyes that had grown a trifle dim, a little wistful. Then, all at once, they shone.
> 'I take the veil,' she said.
>
> (Colmore 1912: 175)

It is significant that Colmore's story places the girl making her commitment to militant suffragism in the presence of other women and that her conversion is described in visceral terms. Her eyes, formerly 'wistful', after commitment to the cause 'shone'.

The image of the militant nun, willing to risk her life for her beliefs, draws on images available from Romanticism and symbolism. The Romantic poetry of Percy Bysshe Shelley, particularly *Prometheus Unbound*, was a common feature of Charlotte Despard's political speeches for the WFL. The metaphors of sacrifice and revolt and the individualism of the Romantic hero, influenced the figure of the female pioneer of the suffrage movement. Gilbert and Gubar have suggested that the desiring female subject was signified through the conflation of already existing images such as Romantic hero and *femme fatale* in Djuna Barnes' *The Ladies Almanac* (1928) where the (lesbian) character of Evangeline Musset alludes to the Romantic writer Alfred de Musset (Gilbert and Gubar 1988: 187).[26] In the writings of the women's suffrage movement, the militant nun appropriated the role of the Romantic hero (conventionally male) and the challenging sexuality of the *femme fatale* (conventionally heterosexual, objectified and destroyed). Two months before Colmore's short story was published in the *Vote*, the Pioneer Players produced Christopher St. John's play *Macrena*. St. John's nuns are militant, politicised and woman-identified, resisting oppression which is maintained through the government, religion and the control of sexuality. The model of the militant martyr clearly owes much to Romanticism and dissenting traditions but in the context of an emerging lesbian identity in association with Catholicism, it is the resistance to marriage which needs to be examined further.

In *Macrena* it is important that it is a community of women, rather than an individual, which effectively challenges the State. The significance of the conventual life was identified in *Marriage as a Trade* by Cicely Hamilton, who

> attributed the institution of chivalry to the fact that there had been a socially approved alternative lifestyle open to women in the middle ages which offered a choice instead of compulsory marriage. This was the conventual life. She connected the end of chivalry at the reformation with the downfall of the conventual life.
>
> (Jeffreys 1985: 92)

The Edwardian obsession with the medieval (as with the pageant form) is therefore appropriated by Hamilton for feminist purposes. Her emphasis on the community of women in the convent as signifying a challenge to the institution of marriage explains Christopher St. John's interest in Hrotsvit, the 'strong voice of Gandersheim' as both the first female dramatist and a nun. In this sense the nun is reclaimed as a pioneer, an active, militant force, embodied in St. John's *Macrena*. Irena Macrena was a Polish nun who in 1840 defied the imposition of Russian Orthodoxy. Even the (male) former head of the rebel clergy who had been the nuns' confessor gives way to apostasy, but, in spite of the threat of rape, Macrena and her sisters resist.

The nuns' resistance in *Macrena* may be compared with the resistance of medieval holy women by fasting. According to Frank, 'Between religious discourse and the discourses of marriage and feminine submission, an oppositional space was opened up, which it was the genius of these women to exploit strategically' (Frank 1991: 58). The effectiveness of such individual acts of resistance is, however, limited. Macrena finds, as Frank says, 'the body is formed not just of corporeality, but this together with discourses and institutions' (Frank 1991: 59). Macrena is determined to save her soul. By controlling her body, and ultimately willing to sacrifice it entirely, she attempts to exempt herself from the discourses and institutions which have produced her. Without her body she will have no means of resistance; she may become only a symbol of dissent for others.

Religion is manipulated for political ends; the nuns are imprisoned in the convent of the Black Daughters. Two communities of women are contrasted, the apostate Black Daughters and the followers of Macrena, showing that some women contribute to the oppression of others. Macrena and her nuns should be safe in a convent, but it is here that many of them meet their death, are tortured, and are threatened with rape. The plot turns on the threat of rape as a means of controlling women, anticipating Andrea Dworkin's argument by several decades. The celibacy of the nuns is the ultimate challenge to the male clerics. Although an unsuccessful appeal is made to Macrena's desire for power (she is offered jewels), it is significant that the means of subjugating the women is the threat of sexual abuse. The soldiers have been drinking vodka for some time and many references are made to the danger which this represents for the nuns. Colonel Fedor Uszakoff, military governor of Polock, warns Macrena, 'I know what the beast is like when ignorant half-savage men are drunk. It is a foul, filthy thing... those poor women. They must be saved from it!' (18). In Hrotsvit's plays institutionalised chastity is presented as a challenge, and in the context of the women's suffrage culture, celibacy is politicised as it was in Colmore's 'The Nun'.

Macrena attracted the attention of the Catholic Women's Suffrage Society (CWSS) whose patron saint was Joan of Arc, the symbolic spiritual warrior. Christopher St. John lectured for the society and was invited to produce her play.[27] *Macrena* was performed twice by the Pioneer Players, although it is not certain that the second performance was connected with the CWSS.[28]

Joanne Glasgow's study of the interface of Catholicism and lesbianism in this period may elucidate this play. This is not to ignore the differences between celibacy and lesbianism, but to suggest that in *Macrena*, and in other representations in the women's suffrage movement, celibacy signifies a resistance to patriarchy. In this respect Christopher St. John was engaging with available discourses to explore different desires. The orthodox Catholic view of sexuality is misogynistic, recognising the sexuality of men while for women 'sexuality only exists in so far as it elicits sexual responses from men' (Glasgow 1990: 249).[29] As Glasgow shows, while the Church's prohibition of homosexuality was emphatic, lesbianism was erased: 'Lesbian sexuality did not exist as a Catholic reality' (251). Since lesbianism was neither recognised nor condemned by it, Catholicism offered a space which did not position the lesbian as outlaw but offered rather a sense of community. As Glasgow notes:

> The ultimate irony, therefore, is that in its phallocentric blindness it made asexual beings of lesbians, and created for some of them a refuge from the virulent homophobia and misogyny of the secular world.
>
> (Glasgow 1990: 252)

Furthermore, the dominant inversion model of lesbianism was capable of different interpretations. The congenital abnormality imposed on the lesbian through sexological discourse could be interpreted as signifying innocence; since lesbianism was perceived to be an innate condition no guilt could be attributed to her. In addition, the 'difference' of homosexuality could be interpreted as a sign of superiority; the lesbian could therefore be regarded as one of the chosen, the elect. Such idealising of the lesbian is a common image in literature of this period (Griffin 1993).

All available discourses, including the sexologists' theories, constructed same-sex desire in terms of deviation or illness. If Radclyffe Hall and Christopher St. John could reconcile their sexual identity through Catholicism it was by accepting the hierarchical structure of society; for Hall at least this involved accepting the lesbian invert's subordinate position in this hierarchy. In this chapter my analysis of the militant martyr questions the conventional descriptions of religious discourse in the suffrage movement as *necessarily* suggesting the 'moral superiority' of women. This has often obscured the feminists' recourse to religious discourse in order to support an oppositional perspective and the significance of the militant martyr in the context of inversion as constructed by the sexologists and internalised by writers such as Radclyffe Hall and Christopher St. John.

The argument about moral superiority has been discussed by Susan Kingsley Kent who seeks to qualify Olive Banks' assessment of two distinct intellectual traditions in feminist thinking during this time: that of the 'innate moral superiority of women, derived from evangelical Christianity'; and that of the 'Enlightenment belief in reason [which saw] differences between men and women as products of the environment' (Kent 1990: 205). Kent argues that these tendencies were not so clearly defined and that feminists 'demanded simultaneously equal rights and moral reform' (Kent 1990: 206). This is borne out by the Pioneer Players' repertoire. Some of the plays, although written by middle-class suffragists, show concern for equal pay and equality for women in work, while others articulate, in a metaphysical language, women's different desires grounded in an egalitarian transformation of society.

The separate-spheres ideology depended on the definition of women as 'the sex', the hysterisation of women and the construction of women as pure (Foucault 1990). This was perpetuated by emphasising the differences between women and men, maintaining the boundaries between the 'natural' sphere of men in the public world and that of women in the home as producers of children, providers of sexual gratification for men, and guardians of morality. The resistance to this dominant discourse, Kent says, involved 'the elevation of women to human status' (Kent 1990: 13). The argument that women are not (just) bodies but have minds (or souls) was challenging, although the case of the Pioneer Players shows that it was not just a matter of what Olive Banks refers to as the 'invasion of the masculine world... by womanly values' (90).

The denial of separate spheres was an important suffrage argument. When this was reversed, showing women in the public sphere, the emphasis could fall on the separateness of spheres of activity rather than on the binary nature of such a concept; this could reproduce the colonising strategies of patriarchal structures. The emphasis on equality sometimes merely inserted women into existing patriarchal structures. However, the denial of the binary opposition of separate spheres made possible the questioning of gender identity, positing it as socially constructed, as unstable, and therefore open to change.

The appropriations by some suffragists of the domestic and the spiritual may now be regarded as – to an extent, at least – deconstructing, not propagating, separate-spheres ideology. What was regarded as 'moral superiority' was sometimes a proto-type of radical feminism, the forceful articulation of a different system of values from that of the dominant discourses, a radical notion of women's spirituality through a rejection of marriage. This was often expressed in the vocabulary of evangelism, but as Kent says, 'Feminists spoke the language of their time, even as they sought to alter the meaning of some of its terms' (Kent 1990: 58–9).

7
The Luck of War

The 'Luck of War' could be devastating, as Gwen John's play, produced by the Pioneer Players in May 1917, demonstrated. Repressed by other theatre societies, the anxieties of wartime Britain – fear of the 'foreigner,' disrupted families and unprotected women-were scrutinised in painful detail by the Pioneer Players. In some ways, the Pioneer Players benefited from the changes brought about by the war. At the outbreak of war the society had been in operation for three years with a fluctuating membership of some 250. Unexpectedly, the years 1914–18 were the most successful, if financially precarious, for them. The Pioneer Players were one of only two theatre societies to survive the war. The other survivor, the Stage Society, had four times the membership and funds. How did the Pioneer Players respond to the outbreak of war? The society's official statements in the annual reports will be compared with an assessment of the attitudes to the war of key members of the society's executive. How did the Pioneer Players' wartime activities compare with those of organisations such as the Actresses' Franchise League (AFL) and the Stage Society? Some of the Pioneer Players' plays were explicitly supportive of the war; others were translated plays produced in the spirit of supporting Britain's allies. Of especial interest are the plays which explored the effects of war on non-combatants, particularly working-class families, and plays in which anxieties about the effects of the war were signified through representations of the female performer.

The Pioneer Players weathered the wartime pressures to change. Their determination to continue producing challenging plays was unorthodox. Hugh Hunt's pessimistic survey of the constraints imposed on British theatre in this period is applicable generally, but not to the Pioneer Players:

E. A. Baugham writing in the *Stage Year Book* in 1915 joyfully asserted that one effect of the war would be to 'sweep the boards of finicking problem plays'. It was not only problem plays that were swept off the boards, but nearly all plays of quality. The dramatists who had provided the new drama of the early twentieth century could neither ignore the war nor deal with it adequately. The great forward movement of British drama was halted, and the stage suffered a blow almost as severe as the closing of the theatres in 1642. The art theatres closed down; many of the repertory theatres disappeared; the national-theatre movement was halted; Craig and Granville-Barker withdrew from the theatre; the actor-managers were driven out of business and the London theatres lost their distinctive characteristics.

(Hunt 1978: 30–1)

This bleak picture does not acknowledge the remarkable resistance of the Pioneer Players to such restrictions. The Pioneer Players did not close down,[1] and its repertoire included some 'finicking problem plays' which explored the effects of the war on non-combatants.

The outbreak of war changed people's priorities. The women's suffrage movement, which had been a significant influence on the Pioneer Players, was transformed. As Johanna Alberti maintains, the suffragists' response to the war was diverse but decisive:

The immediate reaction of very many suffragists was to deny responsibility for the war, and of many more to deny their own power. The calls for national unity in face of an outside enemy, combined with the almost unbearable sense of powerlessness, splintered the suffrage movement, although not irrevocably. Close cooperation between suffragists was eroded by the many different shades of attitude and commitment which the war revealed.

(Alberti 1989: 38)

The Pioneer Players' initial response to the war was one of denial and distance. Subsequent productions reflect the diversity of the society's response to the war. The first season during the war was delayed because the society, unsure whether it could continue, was determined to conduct its activities on a sound financial footing:

Literature, art, music, and the drama all appeared to be submerged by the high tide of that most violent of human activities which men call war. Apart from the moral discouragement which all artistic enterprise must suffer at such a time, there are economic grounds for its reluctance to assert itself. When your Committee decided to postpone the opening of the season until the spring of 1915, it was in the hope that by then they would know not only whether there was room for the Society's activities in a khaki-clad and khaki-minded world, but whether the general financial situation would permit of their members renewing their subscriptions.

(*PPAR 1914–15:* 8–9)

This statement distances the society in the strongest terms from 'that most violent of human activities which *men* call war'. Did the Pioneer Players take a pacifist stance in the new 'khaki-clad and khaki-minded world'? The society's subsequent productions suggest a determination to offer generally stimulating drama and social critique at a time when elsewhere much was invested in containing and controlling thought and activity. For this reason, Desmond McCarthy praised the Pioneer Players for their contribution to 'the liveableness of life in London' during wartime (*PPAR 1916–17:* 10).

The Pioneer Players' emphasis on the economic problems incurred as a result of the war was dogged but realistic. The need to increase funds was addressed by a membership recruitment drive.[2] The aristocratic members, including Lady Randolph Churchill for whom Christopher St. John worked as a secretary, were particularly useful.[3] In 1915–16 the increase in costs and the unavailability of actors committed to military service posed severe problems.[4] The society's dependence on members for subscriptions was problematic. Many people, understandably, made an immediate assessment of their expenditure and were persuaded to economise as a contribution to the 'war effort':

The response from former subscribers was not altogether encouraging. Many wrote to say that they could no longer afford the luxury of belonging to the Pioneers: either they had not the shillings or they felt obliged to spend them on other things. A few urged patriotic scruples.

(*PPAR 1914–15:* 9)

While the financial reasons for some members' failure to maintain their membership are explained, the reference to 'patriotic scruples' is not elucidated, but seems to suggest reasons that were not economically determined. It seems likely that some members were dissatisfied with the society's apparent attempt to distance itself from the war. In 1912 the Pioneer Players' performance of *The Coronation* by Christopher St. John and Charles Thursby had been advertised as an 'anti-armaments play' (*Freewoman*, 18 January 1912: 176); some members may have recalled this anti-militarist stance.

Although theatre-going was considered to be a 'luxury' by some, the commercial theatres responded by producing revues and comedies. Other types of plays, including those performed by the Pioneer Players, were often described as gloomy. A defeatist perspective seemed unpatriotic. A restricted budget affected the number of plays the Pioneer Players could produce[5] and limited the number of translated plays, some of which demanded expensive productions.[6] The versatile lighting system at the Little Theatre was lost to the society when it became a YMCA hostel. The Pioneer Players reduced the number of plays performed in a season and cancelled productions of plays which had already been announced. In spite of these limitations, the Pioneer Players were praised by Desmond McCarthy in 1916 for providing a type of drama which was rare in London during the war:

> It has been a most interesting season – a real contribution to the liveableness of life in London. In their choice of plays they (the Pioneers) have been enterprising and judicious. The acting has been excellent.
> (*PPAR 1916–17*: 10)

With its production of Jose Echegeray's *The Cleansing Stain* in 1917, McCarthy said that the Pioneer Players had 'scored a triumph', and that 'It is not easy to stir people in the theatre at the present time' (McCarthy 1917: 131). The continued praise for innovation which the Pioneer Players received during the war was all the more remarkable because of the financial constraints, which in 1918 caused problems for the society in securing a venue on Sundays.[7] The 1919 production of Herman Heijermans' *The Rising Sun* was praised by Acton Abbas:

> I lived the happy Heyermans' [sic] days all over again. It was a bold adventure & it was rightly crowned with a huge success.... With renewed thanks for an afternoon of *rare* & *refreshing* theatrical fruit.
> (Unpublished letter from Acton Abbas to Edith Craig and Christopher St. John, 3 June 1919; 3.000, ECCF)

The Pioneer Players' productions were rare. They were at a premium in London during the war precisely because the society was taking risks where others were not.

Although the society took the risk of producing unfamiliar plays during the war, several of its productions were explicitly supportive of the government's position, and the earlier, openly oppositional, stance towards the government regarding censorship of the stage became less clearly defined during the war. The society continued to produce unlicensed plays on some occasions and plays which dealt with uncomfortable issues, in contrast to the escapist revues and jingoistic plays of the commercial theatre. A range of views and political positions were represented within the society's executive which must have given rise to considerable tensions concerning the society's position on the war and also the types of plays to be produced.

The society lost significant members during the war.[8] Cicely Hamilton was one. She spent the war years in France, having taken the position of clerk for the Scottish Women's Hospitals run by Dr Elsie Inglis. As a result membership lapsed for two years at the end of 1915, and her active involvement in the society was severely curtailed. (Whitelaw 1990: 138). Hamilton, like Laurence Housman, recalled that the advent of war had changed their attitude to the social value of writing. The war had brought about writers' block. Some military men were listed in the society's membership,[9] 28 being recorded in the membership lists during the war years. A public expression of regret was made in the Pioneer Players' annual report to the effect that the country was being deprived of many capable individuals, threatening the standard of their work:

> Those of our Members who have its future at heart, who hope to see it do better work when the violent activity of war has ceased to absorb all the best energies of this country, will no doubt stand by it, if it is forced as a temporary measure to adopt a system of rations.... The wiser course would seem to be to keep the venture honourably alive by giving one or two performances of high quality.
>
> (*PPAR 1917–18:* 10)

It is likely that Christopher St. John played a major role in writing the society's annual reports. In retrospect she argued that the war instigated a fundamentally changed relationship between women and men:

> During the war of 1914–18, Cat and Mouse became allies. Men and women became allies. Not all women were satisfied with their position in the alliance. It was definitely that of inferiors. While the War gave women the chance of manifesting potentialities with which they had not hitherto been credited, it did not raise their status.

Rather it lowered it, by emphasizing a disability. Women could not be soldiers.

(St. John 1935: 58)

St. John's view contrasts with Virginia Woolf's who famously asked: 'When the guns fired in August 1914, did the faces of men and women show so plain in each other's eyes that romance was killed?' (Woolf 1993:16). According to St. John, the First World War initiated a peace between women and men, formerly in conflict over the suffrage. Arguably the war St. John alludes to, that between hunger-striking suffragists (mice) and the government (the cat) engaged in hostile and sometimes brutal conflict, had already produced a significant rift. The Prisoners' Temporary Discharge for Ill Health Act of 1913 sounded like protective legislation, but became widely known as the 'Cat and Mouse Act'. The temporary respite from prison for suffragists weakened by hunger strike and forcible feeding was regarded as a temporary delay before reimprisonment. The 'alliance' between the sexes was unsatisfactory for St. John because women could not fight. Deprived of the warrior role which she and Cicely Hamilton had adopted in *A Pageant of Great Women*, Christopher St. John concluded that the war lowered women's status, depriving them of the potential for heroism. The militaristic iconography of the women's suffrage movement often elided the warrior and the saint or martyr. This countered the physical force argument of the anti-suffragists which claimed that citizenship should be reserved for those able to defend the country in time of war. The exclusion of women from the army was thus perceived as a 'disability'. Supporting the war effort was therefore seen by women such as St. John less in terms of international politics than as part of a continuing debate about women's role in society.

In the light of St. John's views, the Pioneer Players' first wartime annual report may perhaps be interpreted as showing not pacifism, but indignation that women were excluded from warfare (*PPAR 1914– 15:* 8). The military handmaiden of the First World War had supplanted the heroic role of the militant suffragette fighting the women's suffrage war, martyred in hunger strike. In her biography of Dr Christine Murrell,[10] St. John describes Murrell's work in caring for hunger-striking suffragists temporarily released from prison. St. John emphasises their heroic status:

> Some of these poor broken mice, the victims of their own heroic obduracy, were nursed back to health in her own home. A restoration

which had only one sequel for the most obdurate of the martyrs. The Cat pounced on them again. Back to Holloway and the horrors of forcible feeding.

(St. John 1935: 57)

The heroic role formerly available to suffragists through religious discourse, exemplified by St. John's play *Macrena*, was to be confined to men during the war. St. John regarded this exclusion from battle as a 'disability' for women which served to limit women's aspirations, particularly after the war:

It is possible that the consciousness of this disability had something to do with the stagnation of the woman's movement after the War came to an end. Women had played second fiddle in wartime, and well as they had played it, so well that they might have aspired to play first, they seemed content to leave that to men. Men had gone up in their opinion, we must remember. The whole male sex were living in the odour of heroism in which a goodly number of them had died. Women were not at all disposed to consolidate any advantage which they had gained during the War, at the expense of men. They meekly submitted to the restoration of pre-War restrictions on their activities, and made little use of the weapon the concession of the parliamentary vote had put into their hands to fight for equality of opportunity.

(St. John 1935: 58)

The increased opportunities for women in proving their capacities was to be seen in voluntary work, and from 1915 onwards, in industries which saw a tremendous increase in women in the workforce. During the war the number of women in the industrial labour force increased by 1.5 million (Braybon and Summerfield 1987: 39). According to Johanna Alberti, many suffragists, including Helena Swanwick who was opposed to the war, became involved in relief work, particularly for other women (Alberti 1989: 41). It was therefore possible to rationalise relief work during wartime as dealing with the effects of war rather than supportive of the war itself. This response was shared by many members of the Pioneer Players. Lady Maud Warrender, for instance, worked for the Red Cross Hospital library founded by Mrs Gaskell (Warrender 1933: 125). Edith Craig was involved in charity work during the war to raise funds for organisations which supported soldiers returning on leave. She organised theatre productions at the Shakespeare Hut, built on the site in Gower

Street proposed for the National Theatre (leased by the YMCA), and used to entertain troops home on leave (programme; ECD).[11] She produced plays in aid of Prisoners of War of the Scottish Regiment, Anglo-Russian Hospital Funds, and Women War Workers. However, Craig seems generally to have supported the war. In 1917 she worked as floor manager on the 'National Film', made to show the effects of a German invasion.

Many individual members of the Pioneer Players were involved in charity work. As a society, the Pioneer Players was itself involved in several charity productions. In 1915–16 two of its productions of Nikolai Evreinov's *The Theatre of the Soul* were included in fund-raising matinées. In 1920 the society's production of Saint Georges de Bouhelier's *The Children's Carnival* raised funds for Serbian Children. This was taken on at short notice with little help from the Serbian organisation, but attracted a distinguished audience. The Pioneer Players were also involved in raising funds in 1915 for church building in Kent. The society's fund-raising function was therefore sustained but redirected from women's suffrage to war relief charities. Priorities had changed.

Some members of the Pioneer Players, however, *were* actively opposed to the war, in particular Irene Cooper Willis who held the post of treasurer through the war years and was described in the annual reports as someone 'who has done much more than fulfill the paper obligations of an honorary office. The finance of the society owes much to her personal direction' *(PPAR 1918–19*: 9). Willis was a friend of both Mary Sheepshanks[12] and Helena Swanwick (Alberti 1989: 47). She was a member of the No Conscription Fellowship, secretary of the Women's International League committed to opposing the war (Alberti 1989: 55) and later the author of *England's Holy War* (1928), a critique of coverage of the war by liberal newspapers. Miles Malleson too was an acting member of the Pioneer Players for most of the war years. Author of 'The Artist', an adaptation of a story by Chekhov, which the society produced in 1919, he was invalided out of the army and became a war resister. In 1916 he wrote pacifist plays such as *'D' Company* and *Black 'Ell* published by the radical bookseller Hendersons and apparently seized by the police (Samuel *et al.* 1985: 25). In April 1916 the society promoted the *Woman's Dreadnought*, the journal of Sylvia Pankhurst's Workers' Suffrage Federation only days before that organisation held an anti-war rally in Trafalgar Square.[13] It is significant, then, that the Pioneer Players did not exclude from membership those who were taking such an openly pacifist position on the war. This was consistent with the society's earlier non-partisan attitude to its members' affiliations to a diverse number of suffrage organisations which had radically different tactics.

The Pioneer Players' attitude to the war can be measured by comparing its activities with those of other organisations, such as the AFL and the Stage Society. The Stage Society responded differently to the war. In the early years of the war it produced Restoration comedies and a very few plays in translation (Watson 1970: 107). It produced new plays rather than plays by new authors, and chose comedies by well-known playwrights, or revivals (*SSAR 1916–17*).[14] This is an important difference between the war-time productions of the Pioneer Players and the Stage Society. In spite of – or perhaps, because of – the Stage Society's relatively secure financial footing provided by its considerably larger membership than the Pioneer Players, it took fewer risks with the types of plays it produced during the war.

Although the Pioneer Players' subscription rates remained stable, the Stage Society increased its subscriptions. The Entertainments Act devastated the theatre. Both societies introduced an entrance fee to offset the new tax.[15] But spite of fewer members and reduced funds, the Pioneer Players survived. The Stage Society's report of 1915–16 refers to prejudices against certain plays during the war. The Pioneer Players' refusal to accommodate such prejudices distinguished them from the Stage Society. The Pioneer Players' annual report of 1916–17 proudly compares its longevity with that of the much larger and, it seems, less innovatory Stage Society:

> of the many play-producing organisations existing in London before the war this Society, and the Incorporated Stage Society, are the only two which have managed to survive. While the older Society had resources and reputation accumulated during a period extending over a generation to meet the changed conditions, the Pioneer Players, still in their infancy, were equipped for the struggle with a record richer in promise than in fulfilment, and with a capital consisting almost entirely of the enthusiasm of its founders. Yet the Society has come successfully through three war seasons, and finds itself to-day in a position which justifies great hopes for the future.
> (*PPAR 1916–17*: 7)

The rivalry between the two societies, suggested by Mary Watson, is supported by a review in the *Sketch*, which shows that the Pioneer Players and the Stage Society scheduled performances on the same day (*Sketch*, 26 December 1917: xiv). The Pioneer Players must have expected to draw a different audience from that of the Stage Society. In addition, the reviewer remarked that the Stage Society production 'seemed rather out of date'. The Stage Society may have viewed a response to contemporary social and political changes as outside its remit which focused on plays of 'artistic merit' rather than 'plays of an immature or propagandist nature' (SSAR 1916–17: 10).

Rebecca West had aligned the Pioneer Players with the Actresses' Franchise League (AFL) in the production of propagandist drama in her review of 1912. The AFL had responded to the war by establishing a means of entertaining troops in the Women's Theatre Camps Entertainment. Drama was thought to have a morally improving effect on soldiers. In *Modern Troubadours* Lena Ashwell describes offering to help the government with theatrical propaganda, resulting in her work with concert parties for English troops in France. In reassessing the representations of the AFL by critics such as Holledge and Gardner, Katherine Kelly has investigated the war-time work of the AFL, finding 'no evidence of pacifism among AFL members' (Kelly 1994: 129). The changing political profile of the AFL may also be measured by comparison with that of the Pioneer Players. The two organisations took a different stance to the war, indicated by their relationships with the National Food Reform Association (NFRA). The NFRA seems to have made use of theatrical productions for fund-raising efforts on only two occasions. In 1912 the Pioneer Players produced Florence Edgar Hobson's *A Modern Crusader* for the NFRA as part of its contribution to the First National Health Week. (This was the play that Rebecca West had judged a 'degradation' of dramatic art.) On 27 June 1916, the NFRA (renamed and reorganised as the Food Education Society) enlisted the AFL to organise a theatrical production. Once the war began, food became a critical political issue. The words 'national' and 'reform' were omitted from its name and the old National Food Reform Association became the new Food Education Society (FES), contributing enthusiastically to patriotic war work, and declaring in its annual report that its new title 'indicates more precisely the nature, scope and, in particular, the *undogmatic* [my emphasis] character of the work' (*NFRA Annual Report 1914–18:* 4). The FES enlisted the help of the AFL in June 1916 to organise fund-raising entertainments at the Duchess of Marlborough's home, Sunderland House (*NFRA Annual Report 1914–18:* 9). Since the Duchess of Marlborough was a member of the Pioneer Players from 1916 to 1919, the FES had the opportunity of enlisting the help of the Pioneer Players. While there is no evidence to suggest that the FES deliberately overlooked the Pioneer Players in

1916, its sponsorship of the AFL rather than the Pioneer Players may be significant.

It is likely that while the Pioneer Players were prepared to support the NFRA in 1912, it did not share the concerns of the FES in 1916. The Pioneer Players produced many plays for charities during the war. These were mostly organisations offering relief to those affected by the food blockade and so may have been regarded by the society as politically neutral bodies. Before the war, food had been used as a weapon against the hunger-striking suffragettes; during the war it became an international political issue. After the war the Women's International League, to which Irene Cooper Willis belonged, became involved in a political campaign to end the hunger blockade (Alberti 1989: 85). The NFRA had begun with a radical agenda, intending to lobby the government on reforms in institutional catering in prisons and other organisations. Its publications included *Economical Dishes for Workers* and it attracted individuals such as Charlotte Despard and Beatrice Webb. However, the FES had a completely different list of committee members,[16] profile and agenda. During the war the FES took part in relief work,[17] and co-operated with other philanthropic organisations,[18] but it had become a government agency[19] with affiliations to the eugenics movement.[20]

The Pioneer Players' insistence on the difficulty of the circumstances and complexities of war-time existence distinguishes its productions. In May 1917 the Pioneer Players produced Gwen John's *Luck of War* and Sewell Collins' *The Quitter*, described by the *Sketch* as 'two of the ablest war-plays that have been seen' (23 May 1917: xii). Both plays show the effects of war on personal relationships and the devastating effects for an individual, attempting to sustain an emotional relationship in spite of the vicissitudes of war.

Gwen John's *Luck of War* is a one-act play,[21] set in a 'Northern Midlands' town. This is a conventional 'homecoming play' in respect of the plot: the returned solider suffers in the need to adjust to changed circumstances brought about by war (Counts 1988). It may, however, be unorthodox in that it is written during, instead of after, the war. The plot is reminiscent of Tennyson's *Enoch Arden* (1864): it concerns the accidental bigamy of Ann Hemingway. Believing her first husband, George, to have been killed in action – the army had declared George missing, presumed dead – she has recently married Amos. A second devastating letter arrives, this time announcing the imminent return of George. Incredibly, and deviating from the convention of the homecoming play, the estranged couple are reunited. Both Ann and

Amos stoically accept the news, in spite of the fact that they are expecting a child, and Ann returns to her marriage with George.

When George returns, his boorish attitude promises a less than happy future for Ann and her children. He has unrealistic expectations. He is surprised to find any changes at home and quick to suspect Ann of adultery. He refuses, for instance, to believe that he is the father of the youngest child Doris, born after he enlisted. The play engages with a common war-time fear of women's sexuality which was perceived to threaten disruption of the family in the absence of the patriarch. Ann's predicament is treated sympathetically in the play. The *Sketch* refers to this as a 'new species of Enoch Arden – a species which, I fear, will be numerous' (23 May 1917: xii).

Although George has idealised his family while at war, his descriptions of combat emphasise the brutality of army life. Unusually, the play pays equal attention to Ann's experience of war. Her description of her isolation as a single parent subject to the whim of the War Office, inefficient both in paying maintenance to the wives of soldiers and in ensuring accurate information about combatants, is convincing. Both non-combatants, Amos and Ann, are shown to be bewildered, subject to the arbitrary turn of events. George is portrayed as cynical and alienated. These characterisations do not subscribe to a sympathetic view of the war. The 'luck' of war has great costs for the family.

The ending of the play finds the two men reconciled and, as it were, exchanging their wife. Clearly problematic from a feminist perspective, the play does, nevertheless, expose the crude and brutal effects of war on women. The emotional centre of gravity of the play lies with the woman rather than with the homecoming soldier. For Ann, marriage is for life and she accepts George rather than Amos as her legal husband. She rebukes George for failing to write to her, but this seems to be the only transgression of femininity which she is able to muster. The experience of war has reinstated the boundaries of separate spheres. The distance between George and Ann is reinforced by George's experiences as a combatant which are beyond Ann's comprehension. However, the non-combatants' experience is not confined in this play to a female character. The gentle figure of Amos unsettles the conventional gendering of war.

Gwen John's plays often engaged with the problems of class and gender. She was not the artist Gwen(dolen Mary) John (1876–1939) but a dramatist born in Chesterfield,[22] whose plays were later to become popular with the Workers' Theatre Movement (Samuel *et al.* 1985: 80).

When the Pioneer Players performed *Luck of War*, her work was well known. The *Stage* described her as a dramatist 'who has gained a certain reputation for herself as a writer with views forcibly expressed' (17 May 1917: 15), which may allude to her play *Edge O'Dark*. Refused a licence for public performance, the play was performed privately at the Clavier Hall on 18 July 1912. A controversial scene concerns a drunken miner encouraging his colleagues to 'approach' his wife, possibly in sexual assault (Knowles 1934: 107).

The exploration of the non-combatant's position in the war was continued in the Pioneer Players' production of Sewell Collins' one-act play *The Quitter*, produced in May 1917, one month after the Americans entered the war.[23] Unusually, the dramatist rather than Edith Craig directed the play.[24] *The Quitter* addresses the possibility of desertion and the American involvement in the war. Ames, an American enlisted as a hospital steward with the British RAMC, has taken a one-day pass on leave from France and has decided to desert in order to return home to marry his girlfriend but, above all, to get away from the grinding physical deprivation: 'it's not the danger, ... it's just the plain discomfort of it all, it's the never being your own master never feeling clean, never being warm.' Helped by his friend Enright, an American music-hall artist, Ames waits in a hotel room until the ship sails for America. After hearing of Ames' experiences at the front line, Enright's two American journalist friends attempt to persuade him to return to France. The Lord Chamberlain censored some of the stage directions during an emotional speech when Ames was to throw his waterlogged uniform into a corner. The Lord Chamberlain substituted 'reputation' for 'medals', when Ames was to say, 'To Hell with the medals', they can take the medals and hang them on Christmas trees.' Questions of national identity are debated. Ames feels that, as an American, the war is not his. Yet he feels that he has done more for the British army than many Englishmen. Bill Tucker of the *Chicago Tribune* and Appleby of the *New York Sun* emphasise Ames' duty as an American to return. The morality of representing the war surfaces when Ames announces his plans to write and lecture about his war-time experiences. Appleby argues that desertion would discredit anything he might say. Ames' descriptions of life on the front line are forceful, and dramatically effected by the display of his blood-stained uniform.

The finale is grim. Ames leaves the room for the boat, back to France rather than America, but without enthusiasm or renewed ideological commitment. Instead of thanking the men for changing his mind, he tells them to go to hell. Ultimately, the question of honour overrides objections to war. This pleased the Lord Chamberlain's reader:

> This is a moving and dramatic little play, reading like a piece of real life and indifferent to the conventions of sentiment. All the characters are Americans... The language is strong, but I see nothing whatever to object to. It is a fine little play.
> (Licence No. 960, ADD LCP 1917/11; BL)

While the play was 'indifferent to the conventions of sentiment' in exploring current anxieties about the depth of the Americans' commitment to the war, it resolved the moral dilemma of desertion by sending Ames back to France. The play drew critical acclaim for its effective treatment of the horrific experiences of war, and for introducing a new actor, George Elton, to the stage who played Ames.[25] *The Times* praised the play for rendering the experiences of the front-line more effectively than any government report: 'the horror of war is more clearly brought home by Mr George Elton's brilliant playing than even by such documents as the Bryce report or the book of Mr Philip Gibbs' (14 May 1917: 5). In this respect a play like *The Quitter* was regarded as informing an audience about the experiences of combat from which it was distanced. In addition, it was entertaining. It provided information, but at a safe distance. The *Sketch* described it as 'An ably written play, really sending some of the thrills and horrors of war across the footlights, and showing finely the soul of the unfortunate man.'[26]

In December 1917 the Pioneer Players produced two plays concerning different aspects of war which did not elicit such favourable responses even though both were topical. *The Inca of Perusalem* was the third of George Bernard Shaw's plays to be produced by the society but the only one they performed during the war.[27] The Pioneer Players withheld the identity of the dramatist, which drew considerable interest. Since the play had already been performed twice elsewhere and George Bernard Shaw was conspicuously in the audience for this performance, this is likely to have been merely a publicity stunt.[28] On the other hand, the society may have wished the audience to judge the play without any preconceptions. One reviewer remarked that Shaw's unpopular views on the war had 'apparently lost him the support of the patriotic press' (*Saturday Review*, 22 December 1917: 501–02). The annual reports admitted that it was written under 'pseudonym, which thinly disguises the personality of a dramatist whose work the Pioneers will always be proud to produce' (*PPAR 1917–18*: 7).

Although *The Inca of Perusalem* satirises abuses of power in general, it explicitly satirised the Kaiser and was therefore endorsed, albert with some reservations,[29] by the Lord Chamberlain's reader:

> There is much satire of his [the Kaiser's] megalomania & artistic ambitions... Such an elaborate presentment of the Emperor is on a different footing from a mere comic introduction in a pantomime. I think that since it is agreed that he need no longer be treated with respect this more intimate & searching picture can be allowed – but it needed consideration. The Princess is left vague & need not be taken for an English royalty.[30]

As far as the Lord Chamberlain was concerned, Shaw's irreverent portrayal of the Kaiser was permissible since 'he need no longer be treated with respect' during the war. This exemplifies the shifting ground of the Lord Chamberlain's office. Earlier the Lord Chamberlain had rejected Laurence Housman's *Pains and Penalties* for its portrayal of a monarch, but he became less concerned once the monarch was that of an enemy nation.

The war with Germany was not the only war represented by the Pioneer Players' war-time productions. In 1917 the society performed a play which dealt with the Easter Rising in Dublin. The Lord Chamberlain was not invited to judge it and W. F. Casey's *Insurrection* was produced by the Pioneer Players without a licence. Although criticised in the press for being too topical and non-partisan,[31] the play seemed to present a creditable response. The annual report described it as 'dealing impartially with the Irish rising of 1916' (*PPAR 1917–18* 7). It drew such an unfavourable response that the author, W. F. Casey, claims to have destroyed it:

> I have only today sufficiently emerged from the gloom that descended on me on Sunday night. Most of the acting was good and the production excellent & yet the play never seemed to 'get over'. The second scene, in particular, was hopelessly ineffective. It is only a little play, of course; but I thought it was good. Now I've lost faith in it. I was going to ask Constable's to publish it, but now I think I'll bury it. I only hope that you don't regret producing it. Your part of it was done so admirably & you took such great trouble. I am most grateful & this is just to tell you so.... I wish I didn't go on hearing those sturdy gentlemen who hissed! And those kindly fellows the critics!
> (Unpublished letter from W. F. Casey to Edith Craig, 20 December 1917; 3.131, ECCF)

The *Stage* dismissed this 'loosely-constructed play', which 'ought never to have been staged, and upon which the hand of officialdom would have come down heavily if the performance had not technically been a private one' (20 December 1917: 18). This review gives a valuable impression of the plot:

> 'Does anybody read literature?' is certainly a pregnant phrase, and some painful parallels of recent Irish history are called up by the character of the young poet and enthusiast, Philip Blake, who joins in the Sinn Fein rising against his better judgment, and, after returning home and then going back to his men, is shot at dawn one April morning as a rebel. Philip had been in command at a house whence were fired shots, wounding, mortally it turns out, his brother Captain James Blake, who had come back from France, slightly wounded, and with the D.S.O., to receive his death-blow in the streets of Dublin. Mr Kenneth Kent imparted much zeal and ardour to the role of the young Sinn Feiner, whose brother, bitterly anti-Irish English wife, and doubly-bereaved old mother, received more or less effective treatment from Mr Philip Anthony, Miss Joyce Carey, and Miss Ine Cameron. One must regret, all the same, the most inopportune production of 'Insurrection'.
>
> (*Stage*, 20 December 1917: 18)

The two brothers are divided by politics and by different wars. The wounded homecoming soldier, holder of the DSO, is fatally shot by Sinn Fein. The location of war is questioned here, when the home front becomes more dangerous than the front line. The Pioneer Players' productions of *The Quitter* and *Luck of War* seem to have been appreciated for their humanitarian appeal in exploring different responses to the First World War. However, although Casey's *Insurrection* was similarly attempting to understand, rather than judge, different perspectives of the conflict in Ireland, it received castigation rather than praise.

An interest in other countries during wartime was politically controversial but could be interpreted in different ways. In spite of the Pioneer Players' initial response to the war, three of the society's productions were identified in the society's annual reports as 'patriotic'. The society's first wartime production at the Little Theatre was announced as 'A Compliment to the Allies' (*PPAR 1914–15:* 10), and was reviewed in *The Times* as presenting 'Plays of Four Nations' (*The Times*, 9 March 1915: 11).[32] In 1917, the society presented Jose Echegeray's *The Cleans-*

ing Stain, translated by Captain Christopher Sandeman and Senor Manuel Gonzales. This production served a diplomatic function concerning Spain's neutrality in the war:

> It was generally known that the Pioneers were doing work of national interest in producing a Spanish play at a time when it was of the highest importance to promote friendly feeling between Spain and England.
>
> (*PPAR 1916–17:* 8)

Lady Maud Warrender had contacted the Spanish Embassy for advice on suitable plays by Echegeray for production. She received an encouraging response from Alfonso Merry Del Val: 'You may feel assured that I am always delighted to help in any enterprise friendly to Spain' (unpublished letter from Alfonso Merry Del Val to Lady Maud Warrender, 1 November 1916; 3.589, ECCF).

In 1918 the society produced Gerolamo Rovetta's 'patriotic play' *Romanticismo (PPAR 1917–18:* 8),[33] which explored Mazzini's Young Italy movement. The explanatory note in the play programme emphasised Mazzini's opposition to the domination of Austria, implicitly aligning this nineteenth-century supporter of republicanism and women's rights with the current war against Austria and Germany:

> During the 10 years from 1847 to 1859 the spirit of liberty matured in Italy, inspired by the genius of Giuseppe Mazzini. This apostle of liberty of all peoples, from his exile in England and Switzerland nourished the small spark which was to become the great flame of Italian Revolution in Lombardy and Venice against the yoke of Austria.
>
> (Play programme; ECD)

Mazzini, like Shelley, was a figure who had long influenced women working for emancipation, such as Emmeline Pethick Lawrence and Katherine Price Hughes (Pethick Lawrence 1938: 72). Apart from its explicit political references to Mazzini's movement, the play is significant in its examination of the ideals of revolution in the context of personal relationships. The personal and political are brought together, potentially strengthening each other. A husband and wife are reconciled after the woman rejects the opportunity of betraying her husband's covert political involvement. The romantic resolution prevails over the political action, drawing a favourable response from the Lord Chamberlain's reader. It was 'a fine play in its way, on rather old-fashioned lines of emotion' with 'some fine scenes' (Licence No. 1455, ADD LCP 1918/5).

The Pioneer Players produced *Romanticismo* as a substitute for the more expensive production of Zygmunt Krasinksi's *The Divine Comedy* (*PPAR 1917–18:* 8). The production of *The Girl and the Puppet* by Pierre Louys and Charles Frondaie earlier in the year had taken up too much of the society's budget. The society was able to use *Romanticismo* as a substitute because Edith Craig had already been involved in a production of this play on 19 March 1918 for the Italian Play Society, [34] one of J. T. Grein's London-based theatre ventures aimed at representing the interests of foreign nationals in the metropolis. The Pioneer Players' interest in translated plays was shared, and possibly influenced by Grein. Through Edith Craig's association with J. T. Grein the Pioneer Players became involved in the production of plays for audiences which also included foreign nationals. J. T. Grein was involved in the Italian Play Society (1918) which performed plays in Italian (Schoonderwoerd 1963: 190). Craig was approached by Frederick Whelen at an early stage in the Italian Play Society's life to invite distinguished people to work on a general committee for the matinees.[35] Craig was involved in the administration of the society,[36] and in finding suitable Italian plays for production.[37] The Italian Play Society's productions of *Romanticismo* raised funds for the Italian Hospital in London and the Queen's Hospital, Frognal, Kent.[38] They were a great success, as Whelen reported to Craig: 'I hear that the Ambassador is delighted and so are all the official Italians.' [39] The Pioneer Players' later production of the same play therefore promised to be successful and possibly to attract a similar audience.

Grein's influence on the Pioneer Players was considerable. The Pioneer Players' production in 1919 of Christopher St. John's play *On the East Side*,[40] translated into Italian and performed by a company of Italian Players (*PPAR 1918–19:* 6), may have been inspired by Craig's involvement with Grein's Italian Play Society. In 1917 the Pioneer Players' play programmes carried advertisements for another of J. T. Grein's London-based initiatives, The French Players.[41] Grein's devotion to fostering a national drama in England had met with xenophobic responses in some quarters (Orme 1936: 234). The Pioneer Players' production of translated plays and its association with Grein's war-time theatre ventures suggest that the society was sympathetic to Grein's promotion of other national identities.

Not surprisingly, many reviewers responded anxiously to the Pioneer Players' production of translated plays during the war (Goddard 1918:

104–5). While some suffragists were becoming committed to international feminism, others were not. In 1916, for instance, when Mary Sheepshanks read a congratulatory telegram from German women at a dinner at the Lyceum Club to celebrate the promised enfranchisement of women, she was banned from the Club (Mulvihill 1989: 118). The Pioneer Players became particularly notorious for the increasing number of translated plays produced. One reviewer noted, 'The Pioneer Players have sometimes been criticised for producing foreign work' (Goddard 1918: 104–5). The Pioneer Players' headquarters at Craig's Bedford Street flat had become 'a Munitions Factory' and Craig's practice was 'always going with the simple directness of a torpedo straight to her clearly-seen objective' (Goddard 1918: 104–5). In this context, militaristic metaphors characterise the activities of the Pioneer Players producing plays written by the allies as legitimate war-work. However, the trajectory of the society's drama is less clear than this description implies. Although the society's attitude to the war appeared to be sympathetic rather than pacifist, some of the society's translated plays gave rise to debate about drama and national identity. The production of 'foreign' plays during the war could be interpreted as unpatriotic.

Acton Abbas had praised the Pioneer Players as purveyors of 'rare & *refreshing* theatrical fruit'.[42] In the role of 'a skilful merchant offering exotic wares to the discerning few', the society was concerned to present translated plays to an English audience (Bassnett-McGuire 1991: 71). The Pioneer Players laid exclusive claim to have familiarised an English English audiences with the drama of Herman Heijermans and Paul Claudel (*PPAR 1918–19:* 7). It is therefore surprising that, in 1912, Craig had declared that she wanted the society to perform only English plays. If translated they should be anglicised:

> I detest translations with their Ollendorffian effects. When a play is translated it ought to be adapted afterwards and the characters *made to talk like English people* [my emphasis].
> (*Pall Mall Gazette*, 13 April 1912: 12)

Although the Pioneer Players, unlike its contemporaries, had never emphasised the production of English plays, the alignment with foreign drama acknowledged that theatrical innovation was initiated abroad. At the same time, the society's productions included plays adapted from short stories or novels.[43] Perhaps Craig felt that non-dramatic texts were easier to appropriate and render into English. The extent to which the adaptations differed from the original text is difficult to determine.[44] In the case of Harcourt Williams' adaptation of 'The Duel', a short story by Guy de Maupassant, the differences are considerable. Williams' one-act play concerns the increasing anxieties of a man facing a duel the next day in which he is to defend the honour of an unknown woman insulted in his presence. The play ends with the man apparently choosing to commit suicide rather than endure the duel. The romantic and psychological treatment in the Pioneer Players' dramatisation are absent from Maupassant's story which places the confrontation between two men in the context of militarist and xenophobic anxieties in war-time France.

On many occasions, reviews of the Pioneer Players' productions debated the significance of culturally-specific acting techniques. The translated play was perceived to present difficulties for English actors. William Archer's lecture on Jose Echegeray, delivered at the Pioneer Players' production of *The Cleansing Stain*, discussed Echegeray's part in contributing to a national drama, a preoccupation of the British avant-garde:

> He was beyond all doubt the regenerator of the Spanish drama, resuscitating, in no small measure, the glories of the seventeenth century. He was in every way a true descendant of Lope and Calderon. In him were revived at once their exuberant fertility of invention, and the fiery impetus of their dramatic style. He was a national dramatist if ever there was one.
>
> (Archer, TS 2; BTA).

Archer noted that Echegeray's characters build themselves up into a frenzy, demanding from the actor a very different approach from that of the British method which, he suggested, depended on 'reserved force' (Archer, TS 3; BTA). Translated plays were therefore rarely seen in Britain because of the difficulty of rendering emotion on stage.[45] Archer's description of the disturbing effects of Echegeray's play on a British audience is borne out by the review in the *Sketch*, which asserted that the play

> failed to grip the audience. No doubt the actors were somewhat at fault: they were too English, too anaemic, for the boisterous story, though they worked with some skill.
>
> (*Sketch*, 14 February 1917: x).

The Pioneer Players' introduction of Echegeray's drama to the British stage did not initiate many further productions. When *The Cleansing Stain* was revived by the Birmingham Repertory Theatre in 1920,[46] it was financially disastrous, eliciting a dismissive response from the Lord Chamberlain's reader.[47]

Many of the reviews for the Pioneer Players' productions of both Andreiev's *The Dear Departing* and Evreinov's *A Merry Death* reveal insecurities and prejudices regarding Russian literature. Evreinov's *A Merry Death* was criticised in *The Times* (3 April 1916: 11), the *Stage* (6 April 1916: 16) and the *Morning Post* as 'a pretentious, delirious ineptitude well worthy of the author of "The Theatre of the Soul"' (3 April 1916). The *Pall Mall Gazette* concluded that 'it is Russia's way to be serious. We shall, one fears, hardly get the characters of the old Italian "Commedia" properly staged until people stop trying to explain the obvious' (3 April 1916). It seems that unrealistic expectations were brought to bear on these plays. Many reviewers, including the *Lady's Pictorial*, commented on the Russian dramatists' lack of humour: 'It is a transparent symbolic sermon all along. That is where the Russian genius – with its strange lack of a sense of humour-cannot quite get hold of the old Commedia and its meaning' (8 April 1916). This line was taken up by the *Referee*, which described the play as 'A grim little satire, typically Russian in its complete lack of a sense of humour' (9 April 1916). The *Star* suggested that the production of Russian plays was regarded as supportive of the Russian involvement in the war: 'It is, I know, both philistine and unpatriotic to fail to be enraptured with everything Russian; but I cannot work up any enthusiasm for this particular brand of humour and of philosophy' (3 April 1916). The *Era* seems to have been disturbed, not by the comic effects of the play nor by its treatment of the harlequinade form, but by its immorality: 'M. Evreinof preaches the doctrine of Hedonism' (12 April 1916: 9). The charge of 'Hedonism' indicated the extent to which Evreinov's attempt to liberate theatre from convention was defamiliarising. In some respects the society was sustaining the interest in Russian culture instigated by the notorious visit of the Russian Ballet to London. In others, the war-time involvement with Russian culture signified friendship with Britain's allies.[48]

Some reviewers responded to anything 'foreign' with a closed mind. Even though Torahiko Kori's *Kanawa* was written in English, some reviewers found the performance techniques difficult to understand. When Kori wrote to Craig to commend the society's production of *Kanawa*, he referred to some adverse criticism of Mrs Christopher Lowther's performance in the play:

> I recollect with pleasure what Miss Ellen Terry said to me of Mrs Lowther's interpretation of 'Wife of the Citizen'. That her way of

acting happened to seem of merit to the great actress showed the possibility on [sic] European stage of a sincere effort at the unaffected interpretation of Japanese rhythm (as her personification struck both me and my compatriots among the audience though it may not have appealed to dilettante orient-mongers.)

I cordially wish your society a growing success and appreciation and thank you for the pleasure I have had in working with you.
(Unpublished letter from Torahiko Kori to Edith Craig, 19 December 1917; 3.405, ECCF).

For Kori and his 'compatriots' Lowther's stylised performance technique was appropriate to the play. For some reviewers it was over-acting. The *Sketch* remarked that while the prologue had announced that it was a play for marionettes, 'we rather regretted it was not played by them. With flesh-and-blood players, it was rather heavy and unimpressive' (26 December 1917: xiv). The *Stage* described this as 'a somewhat crudely dramatic Japanese variant of the incantation legend used by Dante Gabriel Rossetti in "Sister Helen" ', but 'Mrs Christopher Lowther seemed to over-act in the part of this shrieking virago and so-called witch' (20 December 1917: 18). These different perceptions signal the extent to which reviewers were ignorant of the conventions of Japanese performance styles since Japanese drama was new to a British stage at this time.[49]

As one might expect, the Pioneer Players' productions of translated plays were received by some reviewers as unwelcome associations with 'foreign' culture. However, in several other productions, the society dealt explicitly with the problems that the war posed although the plays refrained from offering any clear solutions to them. The Pioneer Players took a non-partisan line. They refused the reflex response of either condemnation or approbation which was generally expected by propagandists. Their insistence on the complexity of such problems was perceived to be particularly unacceptable. As Johanna Alberti has said, at the outset the war was represented as justifiable and honourable. As it progressed propaganda demanded an even clearer and more decisive response to the enemy:

Later the press would submerge questions of honour and civilisation in the need to express hatred of the enemy. Many women, as well as men, needed to feel hatred in order to justify the horror of it.
(Alberti 1989: 48)

The Pioneer Players refrained from producing plays that incited hatred. In many cases the plays rather problematised any claim to honourable action. Moral dilemmas were explored, but the emphasis was on the difficulty of arriving at any satisfactory moral decision. The society welcomed the diverse critical responses to its productions, regarding controversy as a preliminary to debate. Its first war-time production, for instance,

> provoked attack as well as appreciation from the critics – the best of proofs that the performance had not been lacking in what some people always find irritating, namely, ideas.
> (*PPAR 1914–15:* 10)

The Pioneer Players refused to peddle simple resolutions to the issues explored in its plays.

One specific element in the Pioneer Players' war-time repertoire which perhaps deserves special attention is the number of plays which feature a female dancer, a figure of profound anxiety. The changing social structure incurred by the absence of many men in the army provoked fears about disorder, symbolised by uncontrollable female sexual desire. Women became the object of regulation. The pressures to introduce a form of Contagious Diseases Act under the guise of a section of the Defence of the Realm Act (DORA)[50] to regulate prostitution were persistent and eventually successful in 1918, in spite of the vigorous campaigning of the WFL and Sylvia Pankhurst's East London Federation of Suffragettes (Garner 1984: 41).[51] The threat of social disruption is symbolised in several of the Pioneer Players' plays by the dancer who represents a claim for freedom, a sign of dissent. As Elaine Showalter has shown, the veiled woman of *fin-de-siècle* literature, such as Salome, symbolised for male writers a threatening female sexuality. Oscar Wilde's *Salome* was written in French with the help of Pierre Louys, the author of *The Girl and the Puppet*, a scandalous play produced by the Pioneer Players on 17 February 1918 (only one day after Pemberton Billing had libelled Maud Allan in *The Vigilante*). The Pioneer Players' production of *The Girl and the Puppet* showed a girl dancing naked, thinly veiled from the audience by gauzes. This was a memorable performance. Cynthia Asquith recorded it in her diary:

> Found Oggie there and she told me *La Femme et le Pantin* was an unspeakably improper book. I remembered it as the name of the book there was such a row about Hugh giving to the Lewis girl. As a matter

of fact, it turned out not at all bad – threatening in tone, but nothing actually very shy-making. The scene where the girl dances naked was very well managed with a screen. She acted extraordinarily well and I enjoyed the play. The clothes were good and the sunny guitar-twanging sort of atmosphere well suggested. The huge theatre was *packed*. It was nearly eight before it was over.

(Asquith 1987: 411)

Asquith was particularly concerned with the representation of nudity. Although this feature was the most striking, the play did, however, deal with the controversy of female sexual desire and male power through strategies which had been common in women's suffrage cultural representations. The title of the play indicates a reversal of power, echoing Ibsen's *A Doll's House*. The dancing girl in Louys' short story disturbs the man whom she has rendered a 'puppet' precisely because she is in control of her performance rather than victimised by it. In this respect, as Desmond McCarthy said in his review, the play is 'a study in physical passion; its merit is that it contains no sentiment' (McCarthy 1940: 136). McCarthy argued that, in its treatment of desire, the play was unconventional for the English who have problems dealing with sexual passion in art (McCarthy 1940: 138). In a broader political context, the play empowers the female performer, parodying the display of woman to a male gaze and appropriating this for a disruptive self-performance. A similar strategy takes place in Gertrude Colmore's short story, "'Ope' in which an alcoholic woman, notorious in the local pub for earning money for her regular turn as a 'suffragette', actually becomes a suffragette. Performance could be effective for women when it was aligned with political agency and yet it always risked appropriation. The political context was banished from the front-page photojournalist coverage by the *Daily Mirror* of beautiful actresses appearing in *A Pageant of Great Women*.

The politically disruptive dimension of the female performer is the public display of the power of choice. When Salome's unveiling was adopted in performance by dancers such as Ida Rubenstein, Loie Fuller and Maud Allan, the symbolists' image of the veiled woman was, according to Elaine Showalter, disturbed 'when women choose to unveil themselves in defiance or seduction' (Showalter 1991: 156). Showalter refers to Jane Marcus's description of 'Salome's dance as the New Woman's art form, parallel to the tarantella danced by Nora in *A Doll's House*' (Showalter 1991: 159). For the Pioneer Players, the female performer had occupied the stage as a political act for women's suffrage. In Cicely

Hamilton's 'Anti-Suffrage Waxworks', the female performer deconstructed stereotypical images of women by means of mimicry. In Christopher St. John's *The First Actress*, the actress is a pioneer promising to redefine the boundaries of gender categories. In 1916 the female performer in Marjorie Patterson's *Pan in Ambush* adopted a sexually ambiguous position as The Faun, peripheral to the scene but central to the action in her mischievous disruption of the hypocrisy she witnesses (Plate 6). The Faun is disruptive by casting a spell on the characters and by taking drugs. The Faun's pan pipes were later to become a well-recognised symbol of drug-taking and an unconventional lifestyle (Kohn 1992: 121). In the same year, the Pioneer Players' production of *Ellen Young* by Gabrielle Enthoven and Edmund Goulding represented the dancer as a challenging and disruptive force.[52] Although this play has not been located, it is clear that this production was concerned with war-time anxieties about women, dancers and drug-taking. It has resonances with the libel case taken in 1918 by Maud Allan (a dancer well known for her performance as Salome) which brought lesbianism within the bounds of legal scrutiny a decade before Radclyffe Hall was to defend *The Well of Loneliness*.

Ellen Young dramatises the story of a working-class girl from Peckham who goes to 'an artists midnight ball in Covent Garden' (*Morning Post*, 3 April 1916), and becomes a star of the music halls as 'The Don't Care Girl'. Although she is suffering from consumption, her rise to fame is facilitated by drug-taking, but when she takes a holiday she finds that her dancing skills have disappeared together with her illness. The *Morning Post* maintained that the second act 'tailed off into a conventional and unconvincing stage-play of the "Dame aux Camélias" type' (3 April 1916). This inappropriate comparison elides dancer with prostitute and misreads the ending of the play. Instead of suicide, *Ellen Young* ends with her unexpected marriage to a wealthy young man. This play retrieves the figure of the dancer from *The Theatre of the Soul* and places her dangerous desires at the centre of the stage, exploring the association of artistic genius with illness. The *Daily Star* provides an insight into the audience's response to *Ellen Young*:

> when I reached the Savoy Theatre punctually I had to wait ever such a time before the fun started. Young ladies in khaki, and with but a vague notion of the geography of the theatre, attempted to tell people what they didn't know themselves. Then another lady appeared on the stage, and told the audience of the troubles of the P.P.s with an *ora pro nobis* sort of air, and then we got on to a play in

the first five minutes of which a bad-tempered girl told her fiancé she hated him like poison, and was, of course, greeted with enthusiastic applause.

(*Daily Star*, 4 April 1916)

The reviewer remarked that, typical of any Pioneer Players production, 'There is always a crowd', which, on this occasion, included Lady Randolph Churchill,[53] Lady Maud Warrender, Princess Eristoff, the Duchess of Rutland and Lady Diana Manners (*Daily Star*, 4 April 1916). Although not members of the society, Radclyffe Hall, Una Troubridge and Ladye (Mabel Batten) were also in the audience (Baker 1985: 134).

The play received mixed reviews, with disagreement as to the nature of the protagonist's disease. Many reviewers agreed with the *Evening Standard* that the 'conventional ending is so unfortunate' (3 April 1916). Although the *Stage* appreciated the problems incurred by the last-minute transfer to a different venue,[54] it was critical:

> any fault must rather be with the *outré* or unpleasant character of the plays chosen.... scrappily episodical and realistic, and in the *dénouement* tamely sentimental, styled *Ellen Young*, from the name of its morbid, hysterical, and indeed 'unnatural' heroine.
>
> (*Stage*, 6 April 1916)

The play therefore gave rise to a debate about the viability of the role of artist for a woman. The *Stage* criticised the ending which detracted from the idea of the play: 'the seeming incompatibility of being at once "a great artist" and "a nice woman, and also respected"' (6 April 1916). The criteria for a great artist, particularly if she is female, preoccupied the *Evening Standard*:

> The fertile idea on which the play is based is that genius belongs of right to the people who 'don't care', to the people who are unnaturally set apart from their fellows and released from the ordinary conventions.
>
> (3 April 1916)

Ellen's dissociation from her body and from others has been productive for her art. The curing of her illness seems to have involved her recognition of her self in relation to others, which then disempowers her as 'The Don't Care Girl'. The dramatic action, instead of turning from hedonism to asceticism (as in *Godefroi and Yolande* and *Paphnutius*), is resolved in marriage.

The topical references were noticed by the *Sketch*, which reflected on 'the morality of real dancers' (12 April 1916: x). The *Globe* mused that 'We have seen so much of the neurotic dancer who can't dance during the past few years, the wonder is we have had to wait so long for a play about her' (3 April 1916). The allusion to 'real dancers' is elucidated by Marek Kohn's study of the involvement of dancers and performers in the drug underground, brought to public attention in 1916 with the trial of Willy Johnson (Kohn 1992: 37). Ellen Young's drug habit is therefore not an incidental feature in the play. As Kohn points out, from late 1915 the craze for drug-taking was covered in the press (Kohn 1992: 30). It is furthermore significant that Ellen Young is both a performer and working-class. While drug-taking had been fashionable and tolerated amongst the upper class,[55] when *Ellen Young* was performed by the Pioneer Players it was perceived to be particularly dangerous among certain groups. During the First World War all aspects of life were transformed, and anxieties were aroused by the realisation that Britain was a threatened and declining imperial power:

> Women, especially young women, were sensed to be the agents and beneficiaries of this transformation. Young women became exceptionally clearly defined as a distinct group in society, and drugs became one way in which anxieties about them could be articulated. Drug use was understood as a crisis of young womanhood; cocaine, especially, was a young women's drug.
> (Kohn 1992: 8)

Only three months after the production of *Ellen Young* another addition to DORA saw the criminalisation of the possession of cocaine and opium (Kohn 1992: 44). Kohn discusses the case of a music hall artiste, Billie Carleton, and it is likely that members of the Pioneer Players, if not reviewers, were aware of her drug-taking. Rumours about her were current in theatrical circles which intersected with those of the Pioneer Players in various ways. Carleton had taken the lead role from Ethel Levey in C. B. Cochran's show 'Watch Your Step', after which she joined André Charlot's revue where she was working in 1916. Ethel Levey had played the role of the dancer in *The Theatre of the Soul*, which André Charlot had banned from the Alhambra in 1915. Malvina Longfellow, a member of the Pioneer Players, was a cinema actress and a friend of Billie Carleton until they argued about Carleton's drug habit.[56]

The moral panic about drug-taking during the war focused anxieties about the changing social structure of society. It was feared because it was associated with women, theatre people and immigrants. Fears and legal action about drug-trafficking were fuelled by xenophobia.[57] In this context, the Pioneer Players were challenging conventional views of femininity in its production of plays which featured a female character who is a performer, in a strong central role, seen to be disruptive within the terms of the play and taking drugs.

The relationship between war-time anxieties about female dancers and anxieties about the regulation of female sexuality was made public two years after the Pioneer Players' production of *Ellen Young*. In 1918 J. T. Grein provided the financial backing for Maud Allan's libel case brought at the Central Criminal Court, at the Old Bailey on 29 May 1918 against Noel Pemberton-Billing after his publication on the front cover of the *Vigilante* on 16 February 1918 a reference to Allan's performance for Grein's production of Oscar Wilde's *Salome* under the heading 'The Cult of the Clitoris'. Dancing girls and cabinet ministers were claimed in Pemberton-Billing's article in the *Imperialist* on 26 January 1918 to be listed in a book in the possession of a German prince, identifying thousands of British citizens at the risk of blackmail from German agents (Sims 1992: 101). The court case concerned not just the libel against Allan's character but that of Grein. His language was referred to as that of a 'homosexualist' (*The Times*, 1 June 1918) and he was maligned for producing a play by Wilde. Even the typography of the advertisement for the play was subject to scrutiny: Oscar Wilde's name was announced in shamefully large print. The witnesses included drama critics, Mrs George Keppel, Lord Alfred Douglas[58] and several doctors. Dr J. H. Clarke asserted that the play 'might be produced in a medical theatre' but it belonged in a 'museum of sexual perversion'. During the trial it was implied that Maud Allan was guilty by association with her brother, William Durrant, who had been executed in San Francisco for murdering and 'outraging' two young girls (*The Times*, 30 May 1918).

While the Pemberton-Billing case is widely known, and Showalter has elucidated the significance of Maud Allan as a dancer in the context of the production of Wilde's *Salome*, the role of J. T. Grein has received little attention. When Pemberton-Billing was acquitted by Justice Darling, Grein lost a considerable amount of money, and left the country for two years (Orme 1936: 263). Given Grein's involvement with Craig, and with the production of translated plays in London, the Pioneer Players had lost an important ally. Craig also lost the opportunity of becoming involved in Grein's plan to produce plays abroad. With J. T. Grein's War Players, she and Frederick Whelen were to produce propaganda plays in neutral countries,[59] presumably intended to increase support for Britain in the war. Grein's involvement with Maud Allan associated the Pioneer Players after 1918 with a court case that had publicly debated sexuality. This may have added to the decline in the society's membership which had already been affected by the society's changed agenda.

The economic effects of the war were also decisive for the Pioneer Players: the costs of organising theatre productions for a play-producing subscription society and the rising cost of living for an audience required to pay subscriptions were considerable. The fate of the Pioneer Players was finally sealed when the British Drama League (BDL) was founded after the armistice at a conference during the summer festival at Stratford, 2–30 August 1919 (programme; ECD). The BDL aimed to foster a nationwide interest in the drama with a view to healing the scars of the war (*The Times*, 9 April 1919: 15). These aims were comparable with the belief in the morally uplifting effects of literature shared by I. A. Richards and others.[60] Edith Craig and Christopher St. John were involved individually in the BDL.[61] The Pioneer Players was represented at the conference in August 1919 by Lady Maud Warrender and Christopher St. John (*PPAR 1918–19*: 7), while Edith Craig was present as a member of the BDL council.

The BDL's plan for sharing administrative expenses with other play-producing subscription societies, including the Stage Society, promised to save the Pioneer Players from an early grave at the cost of compromising the society's autonomy. The financial state of the society seemed stable in the short term only, with rising costs and falling membership, but the management regretted that 'there seems to be no corporate enthusiasm in the ranks of the Members' (*PPAR 1918–19*: 7–8). The society's freedom from the overheads and responsibility of a theatre building had become a liability:

> Miss Craig was obliged to work in circumstances which crippled her greatly. It was quite impossible to get a theatre for rehearsals, and the dress rehearsals had become a farce. Although she had made the Pioneer Players famous by the work she had done, it was impossible for her to be expected to go on working under such conditions.
> (*PPAR 1918–19*: 9)

Christopher St. John considered possible ways of avoiding closing the society altogether: plays might be given in a less ambitious way in halls or rooms; subscriptions might be raised or a guarantee fund appealed for; the Drama League Amalgamation Scheme might be supported (*PPAR 1918–19:* 10). In the event the BDL's scheme was rejected and the society's activities were suspended, but there seems to have been dissent in the society's executive. Christopher St. John and Irene Cooper Willis resigned their posts on the executive committee when the society was wound up, while Craig retained her position on the committee and remained closely associated with the BDL. This indicates that Craig was less concerned than other members of the executive that the society should not participate in the BDL's scheme.

The increasing financial difficulties and the apathy of the society's members noted in the final annual report were not the only problems. At the end of 1919 a new practice was introduced. A production committee was formed, with a different chair person at each meeting.[62] Although the society produced annual reports it is clear from some correspondence that these reports did not document all the society's difficulties. The circumstances of the society's production of H. F. Rubinstein's play,[63] for instance, gave rise to some internal disputes. Rubinstein wrote to Christopher St. John from his RAMC camp at Blackpool that he was happy that the play went well, but regretted 'the many unpleasantnesses involved for which I feel solely responsible' (unpublished letter from H. F. Rubinstein to Christopher St. John, 4 June 1918; 3.580, ECCF). According to Rubinstein, there was a possibility that the production might have been cancelled:

> Would you convey to Miss Craig my undying admiration for her marvellous tact in keeping the show together, when shipwreck seemed inevitable – also my very very sincere thanks for her brilliant stage direction, of which I hear glowing accounts on all sides....
>
> And I have yet to acknowledge the greatest – your championship of the play, on the proposal to abandon it in despair. My feelings on that subject perhaps scarcely require expression!
>
> (Unpublished letter from H. F. Rubinstein to Christopher St. John, 4 June 1918; 3.580, ECCF).

The society's minutes of the casting committee, although incomplete, provide an insight into the problems faced in 1920. The society had intended to produce only two plays by Chekhov, together with 'The Swan Song' by a Mr Stayton. The brief report of the meeting presents 'Reason for substituting "The Bear" for "The Swan Song",'[64] in first performance. This report records Christopher St. John's suggestion that the ending of 'The Swan Song' should be altered. It is possible that some form of internal censorship may have been at work in the society.[65]

The society's war-time repertoire reflects the diversity of opinions of members of the society. The plays produced and the statements in annual reports (as well as to apparently ephemeral data such as advertisements in play programmes) have shown that the Pioneer Players' response to the war was not clearly defined. The Pioneer Players were unconventional in refraining from taking one definite stance as regards the war. Furthermore, by representing the experiences of non-combatants (in *Luck of War*) and of Americans (in *The Quitter*) the society was inviting understanding rather than snap judgments and resisting the dominant emphasis on the combatants' experience of the war. The society courted controversy in producing plays that dealt with uncomfortable topics. While some productions were explicitly patriotic the society accommodated among its members several pacifists. These contradictions in the society's history confirm the importance of examining theatre as a social practice, inevitably subject to pressures, from within and without, to conform or to deviate from the expected.

8
Towards an Art Theatre

In December 1915 the Pioneer Players announced their intention to establish an art theatre in London. This was a significant change in the society's agenda from its earlier aim to produce the 'play of ideas' and it led to the society's most successful productions. Other critics who have recognised that the society changed have described this change in negative terms as reactive and pragmatic. These interpretations have been shaped by critics' difficulty in reconciling the two phases of the Pioneer Players' work as a society which was involved in both suffrage-related drama and art theatre. The change in the Pioneer Players' agenda can now be dated precisely, not to the outbreak of war (although this had important implications as was seen in Chapter 7), but to December 1915 with the pivotal and controversial production of Nikolai Evreinov's expressionist play, *The Theatre of the Soul*. The Pioneer Players has suffered from the same kind of critical perspective which is often applied to the visual art of suffragists. It is seen as '[t]oo "artistic" for the interests of political history, it was too political (and too ephemeral) for the history of art' (Tickner 1987: ix). The Pioneer Players' experiments in art theatre concerned the production of plays translated and adapted from other languages. They prioritised form and production technique and signified the rising status of theatre. These changes had a significant effect on the representation of women in the plays and as authors, and interpretations of the society's feminist commitment.

The Pioneer Players did not declare the change of agenda in their annual reports, but in an advertisement in a play programme for the December 1915 production of Evreinov's *The Theatre of the Soul*. Other critics have consequently not identified this public declaration of the society's change in agenda and they have interpreted the society's commitment to diversity and experiment as a pragmatic response to changing social conditions rather than the result of a specific aesthetic decision.

Julie Holledge suggests that pragmatism explains the changes in the Pioneer Players' work:

> Edy and her company were quick to realise that their audience would not be interested in plays about the oppression of women while the newspaper headlines were filled with the atrocities of war. They found themselves in the ridiculous position of having lost an audience while being one of the few theatre companies in the country not reduced to chaos by young men dashing to the front.
>
> (Holledge 1981: 137)

Holledge's appraisal of the effect of the war on the society's reserve of actors and its plays needs to be re-examined (PPAR 1915–16: 7); her emphasis on the 'loss' which the outbreak of war signified for the society remains unsubstantiated. The society's membership, never constant, changed drastically in 1915 with a significant increase in the number of aristocratic members rather than the loss of members which Holledge seems to suggest. She notes the society's need to 'build up a new audience with a new repertoire of plays' (137). Nina Auerbach interprets the change in the society as signifying a loss of women's participation, but this privileges the role of the writer over the director and the performer:

> Feminists regretted Edy's abandonment of women, but the Pioneer Players remained vital by broadening their scope, and Edy strengthened herself when she brought male as well as female visions into her little empire.
>
> (Auerbach 1987: 426)

Holledge also noted that the society's commitment to women's writing waned:

> Although the company created excellent work for actresses, it increasingly neglected women playwrights. Over half of all the plays produced in the pre-war repertoire were written by women, but by 1921 the proportion had fallen to less than one-third.
>
> (Holledge 1981: 144)

The reasons for this proportionate decrease in the number of plays written by women are not simple. The women's suffrage movement had encouraged women to write; and several of the society's early plays were products of this enthusiastic period. The change in priorities and diversion of energies meant that for many writers, such as Laurence Housman and Cicely Hamilton, the act of writing during the war became problematic. The women whose plays the Pioneer Players had produced were using their skills in other fields during the war. Edith Lyttelton, for instance, organised a motor-car parade of 'Girls on the Land' as war-time 'street propaganda' (Kingston 1937: 71–2); Margaret Wynne Nevinson worked as a masseuse for wounded Belgian soldiers (Nevinson 1926: 246).

Although the number of plays written by women diminished, the fact that the Pioneer Players continued to provide 'excellent work for actresses' should not be underestimated. The society's earlier commitment to women working in the theatre had taken the form of producing women's writing. This was later concentrated on the support of women working as actresses, and, in Craig's case, as a director. The decrease in the number of plays written by women should not necessarily be seen as a drastic change in direction for the society. It conforms to a strategy which many suffragists favoured before and increasingly during the war. As Christopher St. John said of Dr Christine Murrell, women who excelled in a particular profession were encouraged to prove the talents of women through working rather than divert their attentions to militant missions (St. John 1935: 57). The play programme design, executed by Pamela Colman Smith for the society's pivotal December 1915 production of Evreinov's play (Plate 7), emphasises women at work, reflecting the significance of this production in establishing the society's determination to continue working. The borders of the design are filled with numerous women, conventionally dressed and conventionally fulfilling a serving role. But they fill the page and their physical strength is much in evidence; they are carrying, with ease, towering piles of plates for the soldiers' and sailors' buffet. Women's physical strength was an issue concerning the role women's work played during the war. This design emphasises women working (in whatever capacity) during the war, which was the stance adopted by the Pioneer Players.

Holledge does, however, indicate that the change in the society was at the level of dramatic form. The society's experiments with any one dramatic form were never sustained. Saint-Georges de Bouhelier described the Pioneer Players' 'struggle against conventions' which was a consistent position whether in terms of dramatic form or the representation of issues relating to social reform (De Bouhelier 1949: 60–1).

The Pioneer Players' commitment to form and techniques of production was fuelled by the desire to demonstrate that a theatre society organised by women could produce excellence in theatrical experiment. This entailed the appropriation, or (less comfortably) capitulation to, the values of the male-dominated art theatres rather than, as Laurie Wolf has suggested, an attempt to establish a feminist aesthetic entailing a deliberate move into the 'mainstream' (Wolf 1989: 245). Although the Society's attempt to establish an art theatre may signify the excellence of women in the theatre it does not in itself constitute a feminist position.

While other critics have overstated the role of pragmatism in their understanding of the society's change, the financial constraints on experimental theatre must not be underestimated. This affected the extent to which the society could afford – quite literally – to develop its performance techniques. Mary Watson has argued that, 'Whereas the most conspicuous feature of the Stage Society's performances had been the acting, the great strength of the Pioneer Players' work lay in the overall presentation of the play, in the production' (Watson 1970: 130). The standard of acting in some of the society's productions was affected by lack of rehearsals and time to work on the production in the theatre. Claudel's *Exchange*, for instance, was criticised for the extent to which the actors relied on the prompter (*Stage*, 6 May 1915: 23). Another reviewer attacked the acting in a production of Claudel's *The Hostage*:

> The Pioneer Players, with their scratch company and limited rehearsals, added to its original defects a large number of new ones. It is an astonishing thing that a society which devotes itself to the encouragement of modern drama, and which prides itself, I understand (though there was little sign of the fact in this play), on its modern ideas of stage decoration, should apparently never have grasped the vital necessity for reforming the technique of its actors.
> ('M. Claudel and the Pioneer Players', *Athenaeum*, 4 April 1919: 146)

However, the society did show an understanding of the position of the actor and the importance of encouraging new talent. With some satisfaction in having brought George Elton's talents to the attention of the public in the society's production of *The Quitter*, the Annual Report declared:

> the Pioneers can do more than produce new plays – they can produce new actors, or, rather can give actors opportunities for showing their

art in a new aspect. This often means that for the first time they meet with the recognition which they have long deserved, and are hailed as 'new' actors.

(*PPAR 1916–17:* 9)

In order to consolidate the success of 1916–17, to maintain the standards of its stage design and production, the executive called for increased financial security at the annual general meeting:

> But we have reached a stage in our existence when the difficulties of continuing our performances on the same lines are every day increasing, and we have to adapt ourselves to the situation. The precise manner in which this is to be done must be determined by the number of people whom we can reach who believe that art is necessary to life at its fullest, that there is *an art of the theatre*, and that all worthy experiments in it which have taken root should be jealously protected, since they are rare and slow-growing plants not easily cultivated in this country [my emphasis].
>
> (*PPAR 1916–17*: 12)

Consistently deprived of sufficient funds for its experimentation, the society was forced to 'adapt'. When funds dictated, the number of plays produced was cut.[1]

The Pioneer Players made an important contribution to the attempts to raise the status of theatre in Britain, and was one of the few English contributors to an experimental theatre widely recognised in Europe, as J. Fisher White acknowledged in his praise of the society's production of Claudel's *The Hostage*:

> I think you are doing work which is absolutely essential for the health, even for the life, of the theatre; & work which cannot be done otherwise, seeing that we have no subsidised or endorsed theatre here.
> (Unpublished letter from J. Fisher White to Edith Craig and Christopher St. John, 31 March 1919; 3.763, ECCF)

The plays produced were diverse because they wanted to represent the variety of experiments initiated abroad, and because their insecure financial position prevented a commitment to a sustained experiment dependent on a permanent theatre building and company of actors.

The society was constrained by the use of minimal props and scenery, even though Craig used these economically and to great effect. The continuities which may be discerned in retrospect from the society's diverse repertoire are to be found neither in the work of particular dramatists (although the predominance in later years of Paul Claudel's drama is significant) nor in the production of one dramatic form. It is rather the director's approach to the staging of the plays which emerges as a characteristic of the Pioneer Players' new phase of work from 1915 onwards, as Mary Watson has noted (Watson 1970: 131). Craig's inventive use of brilliantly coloured curtains in *Paphnutius*, for instance, was praised: 'Critics were quick to find echoes of Bakst and Beardsley' (Watson 1970: 134). The society's prioritisation of the director over the dramatist, read by Holledge and Auerbach in negative terms, may be understood as conforming to contemporary tendencies in the theatre.

This shift of focus, from the dramatist or the drama to the director, conforms to developments in many European theatres of which the Pioneer Players were well informed. On one occasion, for instance, the Japanese playwright, Torahiko Kori, whose drama the Pioneer Players introduced to the British stage with a production of *Kanawa* in 1917, sent reports to Craig of theatre news abroad:

> On the whole, however, German theatres are disappointing when one thinks of their pre-war days, although they still have some dignified theatres alone among European countries, & dramas as far as writers are concerned only exist there. For the present Hauptmann & his literary plays are enjoying a sort of revival, but the main current of the movement of the younger generation is unmistakably classic in its severest sense (not that kind of dilettante lyricism of 20 years ago a la Hofmannsthal) in curious conformity with other art movements in Paris & elsewhere.
> (Unpublished letter from Torahiko Kori to Edith Craig, 16 June [?];
> 3.411, ECCF)

The Pioneer Players' 'art theatre' was not to be drawn exclusively from English drama. The numerous translated plays performed by the Pioneer Players offered opportunities for exploring innovative techniques and interpretations: verse form; lighting to suggest atmosphere; dance, music and minimal props; and the transgression of the fourth wall of naturalism. This invites comparison between the Pioneer Players' concept of an art theatre with that of, amongst others, Vsevolod Meyerhold, Max Reinhardt, Edward Gordon Craig and Adolphe Appia.

Edith Craig's methods as a director have been associated with a challenge to naturalism shared by many European theatre practitioners; in the opinion of Saint Georges de Bouhelier, Craig was comparable with these leading (male) directors of art theatres during her lifetime (de Bouhelier 1949: 59). Later in her career Craig was most vocal about her ideas for transforming theatrical conventions. Many of her statements reveal a distinctly anti-naturalist bias. She argued against the fourth wall of naturalism, urging the need for new theatre spaces which, liberated from the constraints of the proscenium stage, might unite performer and audience: 'The audience should be an integral part of the play, and feel that it is in it, and not merely looking on' ('Troubles of the Theatre', *Liverpool Post*, 1 March 1935; ECD). It is likely that these views developed while Craig directed for the Pioneer Players, but her method was not confined to productions of anti-naturalist plays. One critic described Craig's production of Herman Heijermans' *The Good Hope*: 'The staging expressed everything one has learnt to expect from Miss Edith Craig, and made of the production a series of perfectly lighted and perfectly harmonised pictures' (*Votes for Women*, 8 November 1912).

The society's staging techniques, largely the responsibility of Edith Craig, attracted contemporary critics' attention. Craig's 'art as a producer' was drawing considerable attention and praise (*PPAR 1916–17:* 10). Christopher St. John summarised Craig's method as the achievement of a combination of 'pictorial effect with dramatic significance' (St. John 1949: 28). Craig was a polymath, skilled as a director, musician, actress, costumier and fencer. This enabled her to experiment with the interdisciplinary approach to theatre favoured in Europe. Through the productions of drama by Echegeray, Claudel and Chekhov, Edith Craig and the Pioneer Players are linked directly with Lugné-Poe and the Théâtre de l'Oeuvre. Edith Craig shared with Meyerhold an insistence that the audience use its imagination, an interest in Japanese and Chinese theatre, and an attempt to draw the audience and performers together. Meyerhold's use of lighting to heighten mood followed Adolphe Appia who advocated (as early as 1895) a theatre of atmosphere, constructed through lighting and its effects on the imagination of the spectators (Roose-Evans 1989: 48).

The Pioneer Players' experiments with lighting were the most frequently noted by reviewers. The production of Claudel's *Exchange* was praised by the *Stage* for the coastal setting indicated 'by the beautiful and artistically-managed lighting in vogue at the Little' (*Stage* 6 May 1915: 23). Gertrude Kingston recalled that her Little Theatre was the first to use 'dimmers' (invented in America) (Kingston 1937: 192). In 1915–16 the Little Theatre was appropriated by the YMCA, depriving the Pioneer Players of a venue well suited to these characteristic experiments with lighting (*PPAR 1915–16:* 9). The problems of securing a venue increased and this affected the extent to which Craig was permitted to experiment with lighting effects. Unlike Meyerhold,[2] Craig was never given financial support and a theatre in which to explore her ideas. In spite of these practical difficulties, unusual lighting effects were a significant feature of many of the society's productions. In 1918 Craig experimented with lighting in the Pioneer Players' dramatisation of Pierre Louys' short story *The Girl and the Puppet*. The society committed most of its funds to this production, determined to produce this rather than several less expensive plays. It provided an opportunity to experiment with lighting through gauzes to simulate the nudity of the dancing woman in Louys' story (Asquith 1987: 411).

Like Meyerhold, Craig rejected the heavy and elaborate scenery and stage furniture of naturalism, liberating the play for suggestion and metaphoric interpretation. The use of minimal props, while convenient and necessary for low-budget productions, demanded the use of the imagination. The Pioneer Players' production in 1916 of Evreinov's *A Merry Death*, for instance, was praised for the setting and costumes which exemplified 'how easily brains beat money in the matter of production' (*Westminster Gazette*, 4 April 1916). According to the *Era*, 'The colour scheme was exquisite' (*Era*, 12 April 1916: 9). The society's production of Andreiev's *The Dear Departing* was the first in Britain,[3] and its considerable demands on imaginative stage design is typical of the symbolist drama. Andreiev's play was described as a grim comedy, and only Craig's interpretative skills ensured that the humour was focused on exposing the sensation-seeking characteristic of many tourists, *Baedeker* in hand. The play is set in the mountains, where a man is clinging precariously to a cliff and attracts a large crowd, waiting to see him fall. The whole impending disaster has been staged to make money from the tourists. The *Stage* praised Craig's organisation of the crowd scene and the way in which the man hanging precariously on a cliff was contrived: 'he was shown clinging apparently for dear life to the rock, in a white orifice in a black curtain' (*Stage*, 10 February 1916: 23). Craig employed contrasting colours in draped cloth and lighting to suggest height and depth.

The Pioneer Players' triple bill of Chekhov in 1920 was fashionable.[4] The *Stage* noted, 'There seems to be a boom in Tchekov...just at present, vague obscure, and amorphous though the plays of this Russian dramatist may be' (*Stage*, 29 January 1920: 20). Craig's treatment of *On the High Road* (the first production in this country),[5] avoided current tendencies in what she later referred to as 'lighting the stage like a saloon' ('Leeds Leads!', *Daily News*, 7 August 1924; ECD). Instead, this and *The Wedding*,[6] were remarkable for the atmospheric lighting to heighten the tragic mood of the play. *On the High Road* was described by a critic as an

> episodical picture of Russian life, much more sombre in nature, and performed in such murky gloom both on the stage and in the auditorium that it was difficult to follow the details of a quasi-tragic dénouement. Otherwise, Miss Edith Craig's production of these last two pieces was as skillful and effective as her work is wont to be.
>
> (*Stage*, 29 January 1920: 20)

Craig's method was becoming recognised for its unique style. *The Times* referring to the production of Claudel's *The Tidings Brought to Mary*, noted: 'Miss Edith Craig stages this sort of thing better than anyone' (*The Times*, 24 March 1919: 15).[7] In the published edition of Cecil Fisher's *The Great Day*, the author referred prospective directors to Edith Craig's method, as if this were widely known. The play was

> conceived in the realist vein and should be played accordingly.... the reaction on the various characters alone should provide the right dramatic effect without recourse to theatrical artifice. At any rate that was the way the play was originally produced by Miss Edith Craig for the Pioneer Players' Society, and I think the result showed that her method was the right one.
>
> (Fisher 1925: iv)

Craig's method is difficult to analyse in any detail because of limited photographic evidence. However, it seems fair to conclude that her interest was in combining the visual with the verbal, giving equal attention to both elements of the production. In this respect she could be seen to differ from her brother, whose concept of an art of the theatre, published in 1905 emphasised the visual to the extent that actors were perceived as *'ubermarionettes'*, seemingly of less significance in his productions than the looming screens and the architectural swathes of light and darkness. For Auerbach, Edith Craig's approach to the theatre was rooted in the nineteenth century, influenced more by Henry Irving than Gordon Craig's technical innovations:

> The communities of her stage had nothing to do with the technology that was invading the theater's humanness. At their best, they per-

formed a dream of the human estate where community and glory were one, and each actor had the power to play out her elected destiny. In Edy's theater, the leading actors were women, but they were closer to Irving's kings and cardinals, devils and saints, than Gordon Craig's marionettes would ever be. In their small compass, the Pioneer Players, like the imperial Lyceum, allowed audiences to imagine that their lives were grand.

(Auerbach 1987: 426)

This does not account for those plays which explicitly challenged the possibility of 'humanness', foregrounding an alienated and artificial experience. One such example is Evreinov's *The Theatre of the Soul*, and another, more directly associating Craig and the Pioneer Players with Gordon Craig's concept of a dehumanised marionette theatre, is Torahiko Kori's *Kanawa*.

In the author's prologue to Kanawa, delivered by Kori on the occasion of the Pioneer Players' production, the actors were identified as 'poor marionettes', who may 'catch and draw the marionettes that are in you too' (Kori 1934: 856). The play dramatises the ritual performed by a wife to exact revenge on her unfaithful husband and his lover. The characters, as 'marionettes', are seen to be driven by uncontrollable desires, the destructive effects of which are regulated through the enactment of an ancient belief system. This treatment of the unconscious was met with cynicism. The *Sketch*, for instance, remarked: 'we rather regretted it was not played by [marionettes]. With flesh-and-blood players, it was rather heavy and unimpressive' (*Sketch*, 26 December 1917: xiv). Kori's praise of the production suggests the extent of Craig's influence on the production:

I feel I must congratulate you on your most successful production last Sunday. As far as my little effort is concerned I cannot help expressing my satisfaction at the way it was done. It chanced to be the very first Japanese dramatic work produced outside Japan, not to speak of European stage. And considering all the difficulties both technical and due to circumstances that naturally accompany such an enterprise your production has really opened the way to an immense field of possibility.

(Unpublished letter from Torahiko Kori to Edith Craig, 19 December 1917; 3.405, ECCF)

In view of the dramatist's claim that the Pioneer Players' was the first production of a Japanese play in Britain,[8] and the influence of Japanese drama on writers such as W. B. Yeats, their 1917 production of *Kanawa* was a significant event.[9]

Craig's attitude to the role of the actor differed from her brother's in that, although often frustrated by their limitations, she regarded the actors' function as central to the production. A comparative study of the careers of Edith Craig and her brother would establish precisely the points of similarity and difference in their approaches to theatre. This has not hitherto been considered worthwhile since so little has been known about Edith Craig's work. Edith Craig's suffrage theatre directing should be considered as an integral part of her career. Comparisons between Craig and her male contemporaries help to disrupt the exclusive androcentric canon of theatre history, but any such comparisons should take into account the different conditions in which women and men were working, including different economic positions and opportunities. Contemporary reviewers tended to qualify their praise by automatically attributing Craig's talents to her family relationship instead of placing her work in the context of European directors such as Meyerhold and Reinhardt. Regarding Craig's scene designs for Claudel's *The Tidings Brought to Mary*, the *Stage* considered that 'the beauties of production by Miss Edith Craig, [were] quite Gordon Craigesque in the matters of simplicity of outline and of effects' (*Stage*, 14 June 1917: 7), while the *Sketch* concluded: 'The leper's cave was a great piece of work, exhibiting, no doubt, the influence of Gordon Craig' (*Sketch*, 20 June 1917: f).

The status of reviews needs to be considered. Reviews were usually anonymous, edited and constructed for a particular paper's readership. Extant letters provide evidence of their problematic nature, even when the critic can be identified. William Archer's praise for Edith Craig's treatment of the cave scene in *The Tidings Brought to Mary* was edited from the published review, apparently without his permission:

> I am disgusted to say that the wretched Star people have cut out of my notice of last night's performance what I said about your production. I thought the cave scene one of the most ingenious and beautiful things I had ever seen on the stage.
> (Unpublished letter from William Archer to Edith Craig, 11 June 1917; 3.008, ECCF)

Sybil Thorndike, whose performances in Claudel's drama for the Pioneer Players were important to her career, was quick to support Craig, and criticise Archer's review of the play:

I should always jump quite selfishly at the chance of being produced by you because you teach me such a lot, I wish I had more work with you – I loved the play too, & I feel very disappointed that Mr Archer didn't like it more. Perhaps he didn't feel very well – or something was wrong with him somehow!
(Unpublished letter from Sybil Thorndike to Edith Craig, nd; 3.699, ECCF)

Thorndike's response is to blame the reviewer, demonstrating the conventional ignorance of editorial interventions.

Many of the innovations in art theatre were challenging disciplinary boundaries, attempting to fuse music, song, dance and dialogue. The Pioneer Players used dance in several of their productions, benefiting from the skills of professional dancers such as Margaret Morris, Ethel Levey and especially Mrs Christopher Lowther (Ina Pelly) who were sometimes responsible for arranging dances.[10] Craig's training as a musician meant that she was able to arrange music herself.[11] The use of music in Pioneer Players' productions, such as the antiphons in *Paphnutius* and the experiments with cantillation in 'Death and the Lady', compare with Tairov's work at the Kamerny Theatre, founded in 1914, and in some respects explain the society's interest in Claudel's drama. Claudel described his work as 'musical drama' which, as Christopher Innes notes, used music as a 'structural analogy' in order 'to amplify character and dramatic situation' (Innes 1993: 101). It was through his productions of Claudel's drama that Jean-Louis Barrault developed his concept of 'total theatre' in France in the 1940s and 1950s (Innes 1993: 100). Claudel's plays have been attractive to other art theatre practitioners for their exploration of the subjective, and for the alternative values they offer in contrast to the 'materialism and rationalism' which typified the experience of modernity for many modernists.[12] In this sense, the production of Claudel's drama by the Pioneer Players signifies more than an endorsement of Catholicism, and places the society's approach to an 'art theatre' in the company of the symbolists and, more recently, the work of Barrault and Peter Brook.

The participation of visual artists in the Pioneer Players' productions, producing costumes and play programmes, is significant for the multimedia potential nature of art theatre and its emphasis on the visual. One important member of the Pioneer Players was the symbolist artist Pamela Colman Smith who explored the relationship between art and music. She practised a form of synaesthesia (the interpretation of music in painting), and had worked with Craig since the turn of the century.

Smith, a member of the Pioneer Players' executive 1915–18, designed some costumes for the society as well as the programme cover for the 1915 production of Evreinov's *The Theatre of the Soul*. Several other artists, including George Plank and Clare Atwood, worked in managerial or administrative roles in the Pioneer Players, as well as contributing artwork. Atwood, a member of the New English Art Club, and one of the few women to be commissioned as a war artist, was Play Secretary for the society, and was responsible for making such properties as the crucifix for Claudel's *The Hostage* in 1919. The performance of Evreinov's play in 1916 introduced the talents of another artist, George Plank, whose work was seen on the covers of *Vogue*.[13] Plank not only designed the costumes worn by Mrs Christopher Lowther in 'Death and the Lady' (*PPAR 1916–17*: 11), and for Evreinov's *A Merry Death*, but also became a member of the society's council in 1919–20.[14] The Pioneer Players did not make use of all available artistic talent. Hope Joseph and Louise Jopling Rowe, former members of the Suffrage Atelier like Craig and Colman Smith, were not used.

When the Pioneer Players turned their attention to art theatre, the acting space was being reconsidered by many theatre workers as affecting the relationship between performers and audience. The society was confined, for most productions, to the use of theatres lent or hired, and it therefore accepted, or worked within, the constraints of the conventional stage. In 1925, the society attempted to stage its last production – Susan Glaspell's *The Verge* – at the Botanical Gardens at Kew, but were told that the 'laboratory accommodation... would [not] be sufficient for your purpose' (unpublished letter from J. F. Chipp, on behalf of the Director to Edith Craig, 6 March 1925; 3.143, ECCF). Craig was interested in producing plays in unusual venues; the production of plays in churches was to occupy an important part of her work in the 1920s and 1930s.[15] Craig's interest in religious drama began with the works of Hrotsvit and Claudel and bears comparison with Reinhardt, who was concerned to revive the sense of community attributed to Greek drama.

The range of dramatic forms with which the Pioneer Players experimented may have made its audience uneasy. The 'fourth wall' of naturalism was disrupted with an ironic direct address to the audience in the Pioneer Players' productions of Evreinov's *The Theatre of the Soul* and *A Merry Death*.[16] In *A Merry Death*, once the curtain falls, Pierrot emerges, addresses the audience and speaks of the author's belief that life should not be taken seriously. Since the society continued to produce some naturalist drama, its audience would be wary, prepared for the unexpected.

The formal innovations discussed above were instigated by the Pioneer Players' change of image, launched with the production in 1915 of Evreinov's monodrama, *The Theatre of the Soul*, which will be discussed in detail.[17] The Pioneer Players' advertisement in the play programme for this production provides important evidence of the society's redefinition of its aims. The advertisement welcomes new members and, although it is not made explicit, the society's aims are presented in different terms from those given in its annual reports:

> In their choice of plays the Society have always tried to avoid limiting their field of action to any particular school, and have refrained from proclaiming that revolutionary aesthetic formulae, as such, have any value. What they ask of any play which they produce is some dramatic quality, and they attempt to give it a *mise-en-scene* which shall create a dramatic atmosphere by means of colour, form and lighting.
> (Play programme, 3 December 1915, Shaftesbury Theatre; ECD)

This declaration emphasises the society's concern with formal diversity and the artistic production of its plays. The rejection of 'revolutionary aesthetic formulae' shows its refusal to tie its flag to any limiting theory.

St. John's introduction to the play establishes both Evreinov's and St. John's own influence on the Pioneer Players. She compares the drama of Evreinov with that of Chekhov, and particularly identifies Evreinov's self-consciously antagonistic attitude to these theatre practitioners who were keen to establish a theoretical approach or method. Evreinov parodied both Edward Gordon Craig and the approaches of the Moscow Art Theatre in his production of Gogol's *Inspector-General*. The first act of this play was produced by Evreinov

> several times in one evening in the different styles of modern stage production – after the Art Theatre, Moscow, after Gordon Craig, and so on. In this satirical venture Evreinof [sic] was hitting out at the cranks who want to reform the theatre or make a new thing which shall be more artistic than the theatre.... He is in the position of being a rebel against the rebels, and is no more in sympathy with the Art Theatre, Moscow, and all similar enterprises than with the ordinary commercial theatre.
> (St. John 1915: 8)

180 *Women and Theatre in the Age of Suffrage*

For Evreinov and the Pioneer Players theatre was life; there were to be no distinctions between the transformations effected on stage and those possible off-stage.[18]

If, for St. John, Gordon Craig was a crank, the Pioneer Players took Evreinov's stance of 'a rebel against the rebels', refusing to be categorised and declining to produce a definitive manifesto of revolutionary aesthetics. The production in 1915 of *The Theatre of the Soul* is formally striking as a monodrama which attempts to present the action entirely from the point of view of the protagonist.[19] Both the setting and the actors present the perspective of a man faced with a choice between staying with his wife or leaving her for a dancer with whom he is in love. This seemingly banal story is given a striking treatment by situating the action entirely in the mind of the protagonist. His body becomes the scene and his different selves (the rational and the emotional) are embodied by actors, as are the selves' differing perceptions of both wife and dancer. The 'eternal self' or soul of the man is presented as a traveller, who leaves for Everyman's Town at the end of the play, which coincides with the death of the self.

One of the most defamiliarising devices in the play is the treatment of time. The action, taking place over 18 seconds, attempts to reproduce on stage the intricacies of a moral decision in the mind of a man. This compares with the futurist *syntesi* or synthetic theatre, described in one manifesto, *Futurist Synthetic Theatre* (1915) as performances which 'deliberately consisted of brief, "one idea" performances' (Goldberg 1988: 26). Several features of *The Theatre of the Soul* are comparable with futurist theatre: the violence of the characters appearing as puppets or machines, the use of discordant sound effects,[20] the anomaloys treatment of time and space.

Edith Craig's staging of the play was admired and although no photograph of the performance is extant, St. John's descriptions and an extant lighting plot offer some indication of her treatment. The heart of the man was conveyed by a red pulsating light cast on the back of the set, and the scenes were presented almost entirely in darkness, an effect comparable with Samuel Beckett's *Not I* (1972). During the violent struggle between the emotional and rational selves, the nerves are conveyed by percussion instruments. This device, which compares with the futurists' interest in noise, is repeated in Evreinov's *A Merry Death*, when Harlequin's deteriorating state of health is dramatised by sounds: his rapid heart beats are suggested by a drum, and his laboured breathing by a bellows. In *The Theatre of the Soul*, the alienating experience of modernity is suggested by the use of the telephone to represent communication between the different selves, which ends in the man's decision to commit suicide.

The society gained its greatest critical acclaim, not for the diversity of its productions,[21] but for its production of the poetic drama of Paul Claudel. Claudel's *The Tidings Brought to Mary*,[22] one of the most expensive of the year's productions,[23] was 'the most adventurous enterprise which we have yet undertaken' because it was a poetic drama, and:

> Worse still, from a point of view which has to be taken into account, it is a religious drama. Professor Gilbert Murray's dictum that there is something about a poet which produces resentment in the ordinary human being applies with tenfold force to a religious poet like Claudel. Moreover the unusual dramaturgy of this author demands that his audience should listen with a patient concentration which is rare in the theatre.
>
> (*PPAR 1916–17*: 9)

This sustained the commitment to Claudel's drama announced the previous year when it produced *The Exchange*, only one year after its publication in French:

> This was the first time that Claudel, one of the most notable figures in modern French literature, had ever been acted in England, and although the play did not please everyone, it was everywhere acknowledged that its production was true pioneer work. The Committee may, without boasting, congratulate themselves on having put this play on the stage, and the members of the Society on having appreciated a poet's fearless excursion into the *théâtre de l'âme*.
>
> (*PPAR 1914–15*: 10)

If Claudel was 'fearless', the Pioneer Players' choice of plays was brave. They was not dependent on a need to placate their audience with the familiar or expected, and seem to have favoured the obscure, the difficult and the unknown. By 1920 the society was, for Virginia Woolf, associated with the exploration of subjectivity. These expectations were, however, disappointed in the society's production of M. E. M. Young's naturalist play, *The Higher Court*:

> Pioneers – a subscription performance – Sunday evening – the very name of the play – all conspire to colour one's preconceptions. We are not going to enjoy ourselves comfortably all over (that is the shade of

it); we are going to be wrought into a sharp nervous point. How queer the Strand will look when we come out; how sharp and strange will be our contact with our fellows for the whole of Monday morning and a considerable part of the afternoon! In short, we are going to be scraped and harrowed and precipitated into some surprising outburst of bitterness against – probably the Divorce Laws. On the other hand, there is the new Bastardy Bill, and Dr Freud may very well have discovered something entirely new and completely devastating about children's toys. What, when you come to think of it, is a Teddy bear?

(Woolf 1988).

The Pioneer Players' exploration of the split subject was most apparent in plays such as *The Level Crossing, The Great Day, The Verge* and *The Duel*, which attribute the cause of the protagonist's instability to the difficulty of conforming to dominant gender roles. The representation of the split subject is therefore grounded in a social context which exposes the material determinants of its subjection. This treatment is confined neither to the work of women writers nor to the representation of female characters. The society's interest in subjectivity and its interest in formal experiments which seem to have little relevance to the representation of women, bear some similarities to the changes apparent in women's writing in the late 1920s as described by Virginia Woolf in 'Women and Fiction' and discussed below.

When Woolf attended the performance of Young's play she had expected the Pioneer Players' production to display an 'outburst of bitterness'. Woolf argued that the changes in women's position in society affected women's writing. Women were finding the freedom to 'occupy themselves more than has hitherto been possible with the craft of letters' (Woolf 1979: 50–1). Although these changes occurred in the novel and not the field of theatre, her memorable example of the constraints on women as artists is Judith Shakespeare, a dramatist. Even in 1929, Judith Shakespeare for Woolf is non-existent, only a possibility contingent on a revolution in thinking. Woolf overlooked the women dramatists whose work was produced by the AFL and the Pioneer Players; she also overlooked the role of the theatre director-as-artist. The role of the artist in the Pioneer Players was no longer occupied by the writer but by the director. The society was indeed resisting the 'temptation to anger', and in its attention to form it was experimenting with the 'craft of letters', which was largely male-authored.

The Pioneer Players' attitude to their audience had changed. The audience, often 'scraped and harrowed', as Woolf suggests, was also moved to reflect, rarely allowed a passive role. When the society produced Claudel's *The Tidings Brought to Mary*, a highly demanding play for an audience which does not share Claudel's religious convictions, one member of the audience reported that even though the subject matter was abhorrent, the formal treatment was stimulating:

> I hated the play – of course *only* for its abominable ethics – but *your* work is really magnificent. It's so simple & direct & logical – & every play I *see* produced by you gives me intense satisfaction – Thank you.
> (Unpublished letter from Rosina Filippi to Edith Craig, 25 March 1919; 3.243, ECCF)

This exemplifies the conflict between formal innovation and representation.

Many reviewers criticised the length of the play. The endurance of some spectators was tested to the limit and they abandoned their seats before the end of the performance:

> That the afternoon was one of almost unrelieved tedium will hardly be denied, except by a few benevolent critics who think it their duty to foster the flickering spark from which shall spring a regenerate English stage. But if this is to be the breed of our phoenix, we had better strangle it at birth.
> ('M. Claudel and the Pioneer Players,' *Athenaeum,* 4 April 1919: 145)

The reviewer criticised the 'academic' style of acting, and makes the criticisms more specific:

> Miss Edith Craig seems to have made no attempt to cope with such acting, and had even supported it by a production as full of stage tricks as the acting itself. In particular, she imposed on the critical moments of the play that incredible slowness of action which is supposed to heighten the 'effect', but which in reality drives the audience almost to despair.
> (ibid.)

J. T. Grein seems to have been aware of the significance of Craig's interest in Claudel's drama for the ritualised performance techniques required, which were later to attract Barrault. Grein gives a very different impression of both play and production techniques:

Of all the things worth doing which we owe to Miss Edith Craig, this production of Claudel's 'Hostage' is perhaps the most valuable. In the spirit of the part she has created the atmosphere of intense religiousness, of exalted feeling, of super-human sacrifice; she has imbued her actors with the ethereal meaning of the play; she has framed the story in such simple grandeur, anon in such grand display, as makes for impressiveness.
('The Pioneers', *Arts Gazette* (9) 29 March 1919: 129)

The disagreements about the merits of this production exemplify the challenge which Claudel's plays posed to critics used to naturalist and even expressionist drama. The solemnity and ritualised performance style used in these poetic dramas contrast greatly with the ironic, self-consciously alienating tone of Evreinov's play which, in turn, evoked a suspicious response from the critics and launched the society's into art theatre. These differences in form and style are, however, typical of the heterogeneous nature of modern drama, which is difficult to categorise because of its 'range of divergent, even contradictory, tendencies' which resist any 'single direction' (Fletcher and McFarlane 1991: 507).

The rejection of the rigid constraints of conventions, subverting, reversing and combining seemingly disparate features in order to produce a different way of seeing is, however, an important characteristic of modern drama. To this the Pioneer Players made a significant contribution. This diversity confounded some reviewers. When the Pioneer Players produced Nikolai Evreinov's *A Merry Death*, critics were unsure of their frames of reference. Evreinov shows the stock characters of the *commedia dell'arte* tragically constrained by repeated behaviour and responses, typifying Evreinov's view of the automatizing modern experience.[24] One critic praised George Plank's 'Good baroque costumes' (*Pall Mall Gazette* 3 April 1916), while for another critic late nineteenth-century symbolism provided the context for an understanding of the play, which was

one of those *chinoiseries* from the Russian which the French of the Second Empire, from Theodore de Banville downwards did so copiously and so much better. But, in the spirit of the Yellow Book, the scene and the costumes were charming to behold.
(*Sunday Times*, 9 April 1916)

The reviewers' difficulty in describing and contextualising the formal characteristics of some of the Pioneer Players' drama shows the extent to which many theatrical experiments were drawing on different, and sometimes contradictory, influences and sources. The form of 'Death and the Lady', 'the traditional ballad', which dramatised the death of a mother at her daughter's wedding feast, for instance, confounded one reviewer's powers of description:

> A quaintly archaic setting, with fine tapestry and rich dresses, and a well-contrived combination of miming, dancing, and a sort of chanted recitative marked Miss E. Craig and Mrs C. Lowther's production, in stage form, of the traditional ballad, 'Death and the Lady,' the measured phrases of which were uttered with impressive effect (cantillated is the word, we think) by Mr. William Stack as Death, with pallid visage and black robe and hood, and by Mrs Lowther.
> (*Stage*, 17 May 1917: 15)

This is an example of new forms pioneered by Edith Craig, which the society described for its 'Italian Renaissance setting... which gave pleasure to those of our members who have an eye for beautiful decorative effects' (*PPAR 1916–17*: 9). The *Sketch* describes this as 'chiefly notable for the remarkably picturesque setting contrived by Miss Edith Craig with simple means'.[25]

Although the Pioneer Players never defined their work in terms of one particular form, many of the plays produced after 1915 were influenced by symbolism or expressionism. Raymond Williams summarises the characteristics of symbolic abstraction as rejecting the rationality and the social emphasis of naturalism in preference to the 'mysterious, inexplicable and ungraspable' (Williams 1983: 173), drawing on myth, legend and religion, reviving older forms of masque, chorus and verse drama. The society's productions of Claudel's plays and of Marjorie Patterson's *Pan in Ambush* and Herman Sudermann's *The Last Visit*, exemplify experiments in these modes. The best known of the expressionist plays the society performed are Nikolai Evreinov's monodrama, *The Theatre of the Soul* and Susan Glaspell's *The Verge*. The technique of rendering the 'non-communication' of characters in three plays by Chekhov signified the isolation of the individual. In some plays produced by the society, the isolation of a female character is a result of the loss of shared meaning between women and men, figurimg a breakdown in society.[26]

In formal terms, the influences on the society's work are distinguishable. One is a symbolist influence, emphasising ceremony and ritual, poetic drama, the implicit, suggestive of mood and atmosphere, a highly formalised 'intimate theatre' for the discerning minority audience, reviving older forms of drama which promised more closely to effect a communion between performer and audience. In her study *Ancient Art and Ritual* (1913), Jane E. Harrison examined the correspondence between some modern approaches to drama, such as that of the Futurists, and that of ancient Greek theatre. Both insisted on the representation of the contemporary experience in order to revive the fundamentally social and ritualistic function, 'the social, collective element in art' (Harrison 1913: 241).

The second influence on the Pioneer Players' productions is Futurism and expressionism. The significance of Futurism to the Pioneer Players' work may be less obvious than that of expressionism, since the society produced several expressionist plays. The description of several members' costumes at a Pioneer Players' costume ball in 1913 as 'Futurist', however, indicates at least the supposition on the part of one newspaper that the society was interested in Futurism. The society may have become interested in Futurism through Margaret Wynne Nevinson.[27] The emphasis on representing the contemporary experience as alienated is effected by a violent rejection of theatrical illusion, an antagonistic attitude to the audience. Marinetti argued that 'Futurists must teach authors and performers to despise the audience' (Goldberg 1988: 16). The idea of art as sacred and solemn was to be superseded by a 'serio-comic-grotesque' art (Goldberg 1988: 29). The symbolists' 'theatre of beauty', ceremony and ritual, reviving older dramatic forms, was rejected by the Futurists. If naturalist drama attempted mimesis, the symbolists were attempting to mirror the beauties of the soul, while the Futurists and Expressionists offered a crooked or broken mirror to reflect the fragmented self.

The Pioneer Players' productions promised a variety of significant formal initiatives which were never sustained. There was insufficient funding to produce plays requiring sophisticated technical equipment or long rehearsal periods which might allow the development of a performance style. Some of the society's experiments were, however, pursued by others. Evreinov's *The Theatre of the Soul,* for instance, is cited as a precursor of the drama of Ionesco and Beckett (Esslin 1991: 554). It was the Pioneer Players as a society and Edith Craig as a director who first produced the drama of Evreinov and Claudel in Britain.

By excelling in their chosen profession, women were proving their eligibility for enfranchisement. This is typical of the political significance attached by many suffragists to exemplary women.[28] While the Pioneer Players affiliated to an art theatre practice which was emerging in Europe, the society was in some ways developing the symbolist approach to theatre established in The Masquers, a theatre society formed by Edith Craig in London in 1903. In spite of Craig's insistence on working with diverse dramatic forms, both naturalist and anti-naturalist plays, Craig's 'pictorial effects' should refer us to the symbolist attempts to cross disciplinary boundaries, to render the musical, or pictorial, in the verbal.

9
On the Verge

After five years of inactivity, the Pioneer Players was revived for a production of Susan Glaspell's *The Verge*. Activities had been suspended in October 1920 as a result of increasing costs of both administration and staging plays. Although their work had been critically acclaimed, they were losing rather than gaining members year by year. The penultimate production, Saint Georges de Bouhelier's *The Children's Carnival* in June 1920,[1] 'met with a very hostile reception from the London critics' (*PPAR 1919–20*: 6), which may have helped precipitate the society's decline. The play concerns a dying woman whose last moments of life are witnessed by her distressed children. Some reviewers were appalled by this. In the *New Age*, the reviewer remarked: 'It was the powerful acting of the child...that made the play seem so unnecessarily brutal; for once, I find myself in agreement with Mr William Archer, and revolted by the torture of the child.' Although since 1915 the Pioneer Players had produced few plays written by women, the final play was Susan Glaspell's second play to be performed. Its reception shows that the Pioneer Players still commanded interest for their experimental activities. The society's closure was ostensibly a result of financial insecurity, but it also symbolised the difficult relationship between women and the role of the artist as defined by existing male institutions.

Ironically a sense of rivalry with the Stage Society was partly responsible for the Pioneer Players' last production. Sybil Thorndike[2] had bought the performance rights for the play (conveniently within the budget of the Pioneer Players' remaining funds). In addition to this financial incentive, she tempted Craig thus: 'The Stage Society is sure to bag it if you don't – & it would be sickening' (unpublished letter from Sybil Thorndike to Edith Craig, nd; 3.704, ECCF). A different version of events appears in Thorndike's later account when she claims to have been persuaded by Craig, who was desperate to produce the play (Thorndike 1949: 82). Craig did indeed know Glaspell's work before Thorndike brought *The Verge* to her attention in 1924 – Glaspell's *Suppressed Desires*[3] had already been produced at the Everyman Theatre, Hampstead to which Craig had devoted her energies for a time when the Pioneer Players failed to provide her with the financial security which her experimentation required.

The protagonist in *The Verge* had more in common with the Pioneer Players than the Stage Society. Claire Archer is both an explorer and a creator; she is a pioneer, inspiring awe and disapprobation. Claire's commitment to the success of her pioneering experiments drives her to the verge of madness. Obsessed with creating a new species of plant, she is not interested in the role of mother, having rejected her daughter, Elizabeth. Her experiments both with the new plant, 'breath of life,' and the three men (Tom, Dick and Harry) with whom she has had relationships, all end violently. Claire attacks Elizabeth because she is too conventional, destroys the Edge Vine (which has failed to become sufficiently different) and at the end of the play kills Tom. In this respect the play compares with other expressionist drama in which the primacy of the New Man was based on a violent denigration of the feminine (Esslin 1991: 537).

Claire is obsessed with boundaries, with abnormality and differences. She insists that she is not producing new species because they are better, but because they are different and new. She is presented as 'a creative genius' and therefore not 'truly feminine', and in this respect she conforms to the image of the female artist as neurotic (Battersby 1989: 135). Claire's experiments prove to be destructive. As one review noted, 'it is the mad who are the pioneers' (*Sunday Pictorial*, 12 April 1925; ECD). The impasse in which Claire ends may help elucidate the reasons why the Pioneer Players were unable to sustain their art theatre experiments. The role of artist (and for the Pioneer Players, that of an art theatre) was differently available to women and men.

The actors were overwhelmed by Glaspell's play. Charles Carson's performance as Harry gave him 'a horrible sense of failure' (unpublished letter from Charles Carson to Edith Craig, 7 April 1925; 3.128, ECCF). Gertrude Kingston, as Adelaide, felt 'I could do so little to "make" anything, I could only be careful not to "mar" everybody else's part' (unpublished letter from Gertrude Kingston to Edith Craig, 3 April; 3.416, ECCF).

Reviews of *The Verge* were preoccupied with the revival of the Pioneer Players, which this production seemed to promise.[4] Una O'Connor, who had acted successfully in *Insurrection*, was delighted: 'It's good news that the Pioneers are starting again. I hope you havent [sic] quite forgotten one of the "Old Contemptibles" & that I may be enrolled again as an acting member' (unpublished letter from Una O'Connor to Edith Craig, 12 March 1925; 3.494, ECCF). The *Daily Herald,* at this time edited by a former Pioneer Players dramatist, announced: 'It is splendid news that the Pioneer Players have resumed work' (12 March 1925).[5] Others marvelled at the play's bizarre subject and the language of the protagonist. They speculated about the author's sanity and the kinds of plays written by women. They remarked on Thorndike's performance and her gratitude to the society for her appearance in Claudel's play in 1917. Much was made of the audience of 'wild-eyed young women with cropped heads and Chelsea uniform and an enormous number of rather grubby-looking young men with slouch hats and red ties' (*Daily Mirror*, 31 March 1925; ECD), Bohemians and Vorticists (*Scotsman*, 30 March 1925; ECD).

This wide publicity and encouraging response show that the Pioneer Players could have resumed activities. The reasons for their failure at this point to establish an art theatre in London were complicated and cannot be attributed to lack of talent or to mismanagement. Rather, changes in the society played an important part in its demise. According to its official statements, the society's interests turned from propaganda to art theatre and it is this transition which created contradictions and tensions in the society's relationship with its audience. The transition from pioneering women's suffrage discourse to 'the category of the aesthetic' (Eagleton 1990: 3) was too problematic.

Instead of using its success in 1916–17 to promote women's writing for the stage, the Pioneer Players committed themselves to formal experimentation irrespective of the gender of the dramatist. Although recently critics have claimed the Pioneer Players as a feminist or women's theatre, they never unambiguously identified their work in this way and did not sustain the impetus of women's engagement in writing for the stage which the women's suffrage movement had initiated. The society was interested in formal innovation and, following the position of many women formerly active in the women's suffrage movement, were concerned to prove women's abilities in organising theatre.

The Pioneer Players' change in policy in 1915 therefore reveals more than a hitherto overlooked field of the society's work. It has implications for the relationship between women and art, and specifically the ways in which women who had been involved in cultural practices as a result of the women's suffrage movement failed to sustain their commitment to women's writing and came to understand this break with what has subsequently been regarded as an important moment in women's cultural history, due to the society's increasingly aesthetic stance. Since the Pioneer Players' work prior to 1915 has given it an important place in the history of women in the theatre, the society's change in policy has implications for the debates about the relationships between women and art and the difficulty of the role of artist for women (as writer, director and performer). The standard of Craig's work was excellent and ground-breaking, but unlike male directors in Europe, Craig did not secure financial or critical support. Women faced difficulties in achieving the role of the artist in economic and cultural terms.

Elisabeth Bronfen's study of the female muse and the relationship between death and femininity in cultural representations traces an important problematic which, in her references to Virginia Woolf's invocation of Judith Shakespeare as muse (Bronfen 1992: 396), offers an illuminating perspective on the Pioneer Players' relationship with art theatre and representations of women. Bronfen argues that the significance of Judith Shakespeare has been overlooked, and that it should be seen as reversing the model adopted by many other writers:

> While the poets discussed used the death of a historical woman so as to turn her into the rhetorical figure of the muse, the death of this imagined figure is seen to engender actual women's poetic gift.... Woolf's model also grounds writing in the death of a woman, yet the paradox that emerges in her anecdote is that, having inspired the writing of other women, the dead woman poet as muse will come into being again, for the first time.
>
> (Bronfen 1992: 398)

Woolf's model of the female muse in women's writing is paradoxical. She invokes a dead woman writer who has never existed but will 'come into being again' through the writings of women. Judith Shakespeare is presented by Woolf as a poet and a dramatist. It seems surprising that Woolf failed to acknowledge the many female dramatists who were writing for the suffrage movement. While Bronfen's analysis of the problems for women writing engages, like many other poststructuralist accounts, with the difficulty for women of achieving a subject position in language, in the case of Woolf's reference to Judith Shakespeare it fails to situate Woolf's writing historically.

When we consider that Woolf's Judith Shakespeare was imagined in 1929, after the intensely productive period of women's writing inspired by the women's suffrage movement another paradox becomes apparent. Woolf ignored the existence of many actual women writers, and (specifically when we consider the Pioneer Players) many women dramatists. Woolf expected the Pioneer Players to produce an 'outburst of bitterness' associated with writing which pleaded a special cause, or 'disability'. Such writing was deemed to be inartistic compared with an impersonal art in writing. Woolf's attitude towards actual women writers was therefore ambivalent. Her views on art were shaped by a privileged position ultimately shared by the Pioneer Players, whose interest in art theatre similarly involved the prioritisation of form over the significance of the sex of the writer. As Bronfen points out, Woolf's position entails the following assumptions:

> Any women's writing is worthwhile, she claims, even when written in poverty and obscurity, for 'I maintain that she would come if we worked for her'. The birth of the originary, effaced woman poet here requires that feminine subjectivity has already attained a space within the symbolic order of culture.
>
> (Bronfen 1992: 397)

The Pioneer Players' experiments were similarly grounded in the assumptions that women had already found a voice. Edith Craig's directorial voice was articulated through formal experimentation but this experimentation was largely dependent on producing plays written by men. This signals a departure from the society's earlier support of women's writing for the theatre and the importance of recovering the lives of women of the past.

The society's shift of concern from the sexual politics of the author to matters of form should be seen in the context of modernism, the theoretical work of T. S. Eliot and the later New Critics. It can also be understood in terms of the changing political attitudes of women previously involved in the women's suffrage movement. They optimistically regarded many struggles for women as already won. In 1913, Cicely Hamilton, for instance, wrote:

> Quite a number of women of late have shown themselves capable of taking a hand in the administrative work of the theatre; and more would have done so, had more opportunity offered. So at least we

believe; and, because we believe it, we are seeking to prove it by experiment. Women stage-managers and women business-managers, we think, are still regarded with suspicion; we wish to show there is no cause for it. Once the actress was in the same boat; and, not so very long ago, the woman playwright. Some seven years past I was asked not to affix my Christian name to a one-act play – my first – lest its chances should be damaged by the admission that I was a woman. Now -who worries about the sex of a writer of plays?
(Souvenir programme, Women's Theatre Inaugural Week, qtd. in Wolf 1989: 62)

Hamilton, like Craig, regarded her own immediate successes as part of the cumulative effect which, it was thought, individual remarkable women would exert on the wider social and cultural domain. This over-optimistic, liberal faith in the individual depended too much on the examples set by the talented few; the relatively undistinguished woman was effectively written out of the cultural debate. The Pioneer Players' work has subsequently sunk into obscurity. Even in 1929, Virginia Woolf overlooked Cicely Hamilton and many of her contemporaries. It seems, therefore, imperative to consider the historical context of women's involvement in cultural practices.

The Pioneer Players' interest in experiment signalled their attempts to engage with theatre as art. In so doing they seem to have broken their ties with the female tradition to which their earlier work was committed. This break in 1915 can be understood as a response to the changing role of cultural practices in the women's suffrage movement; it resulted in the Pioneer Players adopting an alternative rather than oppositional role in relation to the dominant culture. In some respects, however, it signifies a re-emergence of some aesthetic concerns and formal experimentation with which Craig, and others, had been involved over a decade earlier in The Masquers, a theatrical venture influenced by symbolism rather than modernism.

The Pioneer Players' were committed to innovation. Initially aligned with the women's suffrage movement, their *primary* concern was never political. The society prioritised the production of plays over any single political campaign. In this respect, the Pioneer Players were little different from other modernist cultural formations which tended to be male-dominated. The Pioneer Players failed to align their aesthetics with a clearly defined political position or programme. Both the Pioneer Players and the Stage Society were concerned with revitalising the theatre. Their interests in art theatre coincided with the professionalisation of theatre as a field of employment. This served to elevate the status of theatre since the category of the aesthetic denies the economic determinants of cultural practice by distinguishing art theatre from commercial theatre. Art theatre is perceived to operate autonomously, rising above the mundane and inescapable problematics of paying actors and hiring venues.

Terry Eagleton has argued that the category of the aesthetic reduces cultural practice to art, 'conveniently sequestered from all other social practices, to become an isolated enclave within which the dominant social order can find an idealized refuge from its own actual values of competitiveness, exploitation and material possessiveness' (Eagleton 1990: 9). While art theatre denied its place in the social and cultural moment it could also provide an opportunity for challenge and change, particularly for those 'dispossessed' and 'politically oppressed' (Eagleton 1990: 321). The aesthetic therefore 'provides an unusually powerful challenge and alternative to these dominant ideological forms, and is in this sense an eminently contradictory phenomenon' (Eagleton 1990: 3). The Pioneer Players' understanding of the aesthetic is significant: how could a theatre society which had been so vociferously (and successfully) committed to challenging conventional attitudes to gender dispense with drama written by women in favour of formally innovative, but in some cases, misogynistic drama written by men? In some ways, the Pioneer Players shared Cicely Hamilton's view that priorities had changed: 'Now – who worries about the sex of a writer of plays?... Women stage-managers and women business-managers, we think, are still regarded with suspicion; we wish to show there is no cause for it' (Wolf 1989: 62).

The difficulties faced by the female dramatist have been given more attention than that of the director. According to Michelene Wandor, the constraints imposed on women writing for the theatre are greater than those for the novelist or poet since the theatre is a very public cultural practice:

> It seems that women playwrights become prominent when there is some kind of fundamental social change which involves morality or sexual ideology: for example, during the Restoration; at the turn of the century, coinciding with the movement for female suffrage; and again in recent years, alongside the new feminism. As the political movements settle and lose their radical or revolutionary momentum, so women recede again from participation in the professional theatre as writers. There is a very real symbiotic relationship between the

state of sexual mores, the presence of a feminist movement and the appearance of women playwrights; and the political struggle always comes first.

(Wandor 1990: 106)

Wandor's argument that women write for the theatre in the context of a movement for political agitation is exemplified by both the Pioneer Players and the AFL. Wandor's description addresses the dynamics of culture, in that social changes will affect the positions available to women in the theatre, but suggests the inevitability that women 'recede' once the political movement loses its impetus.

The Pioneer Players' transitional place in this scheme is important, and cannot be explained in Michelene Wandor's terms. Several of the female dramatists whose plays were produced by the society wrote only one play,[6] inspired by their participation in women's suffrage politics. It is likely that Jess Dorynne and Margaret Wynne Nevinson may not have considered themselves primarily as dramatists, and therefore they did 'recede again from participation in the professional theatre as writers' (Wandor 1990: 106). Since the Pioneer Players usually performed a play only once and never more than twice, it is therefore not surprising that they did not revive the plays by Dorynne and Nevinson. It is significant, however, that the work of these, like that of other female dramatists who wrote plays in the wave of the suffrage movement, was marginalised because it was perceived to be 'propaganda'. This supports Wandor's argument that 'the political struggle always come first' in prompting women to write for the theatre, but the ways in which their plays are subsequently perceived should also be considered. Women writers find that when their work is not associated with 'propaganda' it becomes marginalised because it is not perceived to be 'artistic'. The construction of the political/aesthetic opposition effectively devalues women's writing and it is one to which women such as Virginia Woolf and Rebecca West have subscribed. Unfortunately the changes in the Pioneer Players are not explained by women writers simply receding, but rather by women actively engaged in the idea of an aesthetic which is bound to exclude them. While the Pioneer Players' relationship with women writers and with empowering parts for women in the plays produced was problematic, it was typical of prevailing priorities. Hamilton and other women in theatre regarded the organisation of theatre by women as managers (and in Craig's case as a director) as the next step in challenging prejudices in the theatre. Interestingly, critics such as Loren Kruger (1995) have more recently arrived at a similar position. Suffragists had widely accepted the burden of proof that women could excel in various fields of work. The move towards an art theatre for the Pioneer Players therefore proved that art theatre was open to women who had already excelled in the production of politically driven plays. This both–and logic was baffling to those bound within the exclusionary binary of aesthetics or politics.

By examining the society's relationships both to women's suffrage and, more briefly, to art theatre this study has placed the Pioneer Players in relation to 'matrilineal and patrilineal lines of influence and response' (Battersby 1989: 152). This has made it possible to understand the significant 'faultline' in the Pioneer Players' history: the shift from explicitly political drama to art theatre. Although this research has developed within literary studies, its interdisciplinary scope has attempted to reassess the plays produced within the institutional contexts in which the Pioneer Players were working. The significance of the Pioneer Players' work lies not solely in the production of plays written by women but in the organisation by women of the production of plays, irrespective of the sex of the dramatist. Thus, Karen Laughlin's warning is relevant for both the Pioneer Players and its critics: 'the limits of a purely text-based aesthetics come into view as we begin to envision feminist practices in relation to the material aspects of production' (Laughlin 1995: 18).

The demands of the women's suffrage movement were demands for inclusion and on many occasions suffragists subscribed to the demand that they prove their entitlement to enfranchisement. This was the spirit in which Cicely Hamilton devised with Edith Craig *A Pageant of Great Women*, signalling the beginnings of the Pioneer Players. In some respects the Pioneer Players' attempt to establish an art theatre in London was another demand for inclusion. For Edith Craig the role of director in this scheme promised a means of professional achievement and it concurred with Christopher St. John's belief in the need for exemplary women as role models, sign-posting the achievements of women in different professions (St. John 1935).

In trying to establish itself as an art theatre, the Pioneer Players was daring to claim a space for women to organise, to direct, and to perform. The female artist had become the theatre practitioner and not the dramatist. The society's past associations with a dissident femininity mobilised through a feminist political movement excluded it from the aesthetic. As Eagleton suggests, the aesthetic conventionally divorces itself from the material determinants of art production. The organic metaphor used by the Pioneer Players to describe art theatre, 'rare and slow-growing plants not easily cultivated in this country'

(*PPAR 1916–17*: 12), significantly recalls Claire Archer in *The Verge* and introduces the profound conflict in which the society was caught up. Although the society may have understood its demand for inclusion as radical, its challenge to the terms of the aesthetic were limited.

Edith Craig believed that in the theatre women and men were judged according to their individual merit, but this transient equality was produced because the theatre was a different 'country':

> A man, when he comes on the stage, steps into a country where men and women are equal if they are equally able, and where the woman who is good at her work is thought infinitely more of than a man who is not good. Men quickly find their level on the stage, and perhaps for this very reason some who are not much good like to think that once outside the stage doors they have a fictitious importance.
>
> ('Miss Edith Craig', *Vote*, 12 March 1910: 323)

In Craig's opinion, the stage offered a free space in which equality might be played out. Her assumption that the theatre is a different country is founded on the aesthetic, denying the social and material determinants of theatre which ultimately deprived Craig and the Pioneer Players of work.

As one of very few female directors, Craig represented a challenge to the institution of theatre, but changes in that institution could only be effected by the Pioneer Players if they adopted a practice which was representative of all women, rather than of the exceptional woman. Ironically in the society's first production, St. John's *The First Actress* adopted similar spatial metaphors to those used later by Craig. But the play was concerned not with one woman's plight but with the systematic economic and ideological oppression women have experienced in the theatre. Margaret Hughes is only able to sustain her pioneering role because the actresses of the future appear to support her as a group. Unfortunately, the Pioneer Players' female majority failed to learn this lesson from an earlier female pioneer.

Although suffrage commentators had recognised the need to address the economic determinants of theatre, debating performers' low pay for instance, the Pioneer Players did not develop these arguments. The Pioneer Players were most radical when they challenged the separate-spheres ideology by representing women as workers, by representing the dissenting female (pioneer) as *both* rational *and* desiring, as *both* claiming citizenship *and* challenging conventional ideas about femininity including motherhood. However, in adopting the category of the aesthetic from 1915, the Pioneer Players failed to take responsibility for the space they moved into, failed to acknowledge it as already occupied. The Pioneer Players demanded acceptance as an art theatre without revising its terms. The basis of art theatre was at odds with the Pioneer Players' political past. Karen Laughlin has suggested that, 'feminist aesthetics means denying the notion of the aesthetic as a uniquely privileged, autonomous realm. It means seeing the aesthetic as political and feminist aesthetics as a political "way of seeing", and as a vision that is necessarily as diverse and contradictory as feminism itself' (Laughlin 1995:19). The society could not sustain a feminist position because it was unable to identify the need to challenge the exclusive and exclusionary practices of art theatre. In almost every other respect the Pioneer Players was successful, repeatedly achieving the impossible.

Appendix I Pioneer Players' Productions

All plays directed by Craig unless otherwise stated. Numbers of subscription performances follow information from play programmes and annual reports. Non-subscription performances are shown in italics.

8 February 1911, Cicely Hamilton and Christopher St. John, How the Vote Was Won, *Royal Albert Institute, for Windsor and Eton Branch of London Society for Women's Suffrage*

4 May 1911, Cicely Hamilton, A Pageant of Great Women, *Mechanics Hall, Nottingham*

FIRST SEASON

FIRST SUBSCRIPTION PERFORMANCE: 8 May 1911, Kingsway Theatre, 3 pm
Margaret Wynne Nevinson, *In the Workhouse;* Christopher St. John, *The First Actress;* Cicely Hamilton, *Jack and Jill and a Friend* (directed by author)

SECOND SUBSCRIPTION PERFORMANCE: 11 June 1911, Garrick Theatre 8.30 pm
Ellen Terry's lecture on Shakespeare's Triumphant Women (reception by committee)

November 1911, Mrs J. M. Harvey, Baby, *Small Public Hall, Croydon; Croydon WFL*

THIRD SUBSCRIPTION PERFORMANCE: 26 November 1911, Savoy Theatre 8 pm
Laurence Housman, *Pains and Penalties* (directed by author and Craig)

28 January 1912, Savoy Theatre, Christopher St. John and Charles Thursby, The Coronation; *George Bernard Shaw,* The Man of Destiny; *International Suffrage Shop*

2 February 1912, Cicely Hamilton, A Pageant of Great Women, *Philharmonic Hall, Liverpool; WSPU*

FOURTH SUBSCRIPTION PERFORMANCE: 21 April 1912, King's Hall, 8.15 pm
H. Hamilton Fyfe, *Race Suicide;* Christopher St. John, *Macrena;* Jess Dorynne, *The Surprise of His Life*

30 April 1912, Florence Edgar Hobson, A Modern Crusader, *King's Hall; NFRA*

FIFTH SUBSCRIPTION PERFORMANCE: 5 May 1912, King's Hall
J. Sackville Martin, *Nellie Lambert;* Christopher St. John, *Macrena*

SIXTH SUBSCRIPTION PERFORMANCE: 16 June 1912, King's Hall, 8 pm
George Bernard Shaw, *Mrs Warren's Profession*

18 June 1912, George Bernard Shaw, Mrs Warren's Profession, *King's Hall, 2 pm*
Estelle Burney, The One Thing Needful, *Court Theatre*

SECOND SEASON

SEVENTH SUBSCRIPTION PERFORMANCE: 3 November 1912, King's Hall, 8.15 pm
Herman Heijermans, *The Good Hope*

13 November 1912, Charlotte Perkins Gilman, Three Women

EIGHTH SUBSCRIPTION PERFORMANCE: 15 December 1912, Little Theatre, 8.15 pm
Hugh de Selincourt, *Beastie*; Edith Lyttelton, *The Thumbscrew*; H. M. Harwood, *Honour Thy Father*

NINTH SUBSCRIPTION PEFORMANCE: 9 February 1913, Little Theatre, 8.15 pm
Cicely Hamilton, *A Matter of Money*

11 February 1913, Little Theatre, 2.30 pm Cicely Hamilton, A Matter of Money

TENTH SUBSCRIPTION PERFORMANCE: 9 March 1913, King's Hall, 8 pm
William Shakespere, *Hamlet* (directed by Louis Calvert)

ELEVENTH SUBSCRIPTION PERFORMANCE: 18 May 1913, Little Theatre, 8 pm
Cecil Fisher, *The Great Day* (directed by Leonard Craske); Herman Sudermann, *The Last Visit* (directed by Ben Webster); Salvatore di Giacomo, *The Month of Mary*, trans. Constance Hutton

THIRD SEASON

TWELFTH SUBSCRIPTION PERFORMANCE: 30 November 1913, Little Theatre, 8 pm
Antonia R. Williams, *The Street*; Norreys Connell, *The King's Wooing* (directed by author)

THIRTEENTH SUBSCRIPTION PERFORMANCE: 11 January 1914, Savoy Theatre, 8.30 pm
Hrotsvit, *Paphnutius*, translated by Christopher St. John
12 January 1914, Savoy Theatre, 3 pm Hrotsvit, Paphnutius, *trans. Christopher St. John*

FOURTEENTH SUBSCRIPTION PERFORMANCE: 1 March 1914, King's Hall, 8 pm
A. D'Este Scott, *The Daughters of Ishmael*, based on novel of same title by Reginald Wright Kauffman

FIFTEENTH SUBSCRIPTION PERFORMANCE: 3 May 1914, Ambassador's Theatre, 8.30 pm
Conal O'Riordan, *The Patience of the Sea* (directed by author)

SIXTEENTH SUBSCRIPTION PERFORMANCE: 21 June 1914, Little Theatre, 8 pm
Harcourt Williams, *The Duel*, adapted from Guy de Maupassant; Mrs Herbert Cohen, *The Level Crossing*; Magdalen Ponsonby, *Idle Women*

22 June 1914, Little Theatre, 3 pm
Harcourt Williams, *The Duel*; Mrs Herbert Cohen, *The Level Crossing*; Magdalen Ponsonby, *Idle Women*

FOURTH SEASON

SEVENTEENTH SUBSCRIPTION PERFORMANCE: 7 March 1915, Little Theatre, 8 pm
Isi Collin, *Sisyphus and the Wandering Jew*, trans. by a member
Edmond Rostand, *Two Pierrots*, trans. Edith Lyttleton (directed by Patrick Kirwan and Craig)
Nikolai Evreinov, *The Theatre of the Soul*, trans. Marie Potapenko and Christopher St. John
Constance Campbell, *A Dilemma*

EIGHTEENTH SUBSCRIPTION PERFORMANCE: 2 May 1915, Little Theatre, 8.30 pm
Paul Claudel, *Exchange*, trans. Dr. Rowland Thurnam

NINETEENTH SUBSCRIPTION PERFORMANCE: 30 May 1915, the Playhouse, 8 pm
Laurence Irving, *Godefroi and Iolande*; Laurence Irving, *The Terrorist*; H. B. Irving read Laurence Irving's 'Drama as a Factor in Social Progress'

3 December 1915, Nikolai Evreinov, The Theatre of the Soul, *Shaftesbury Theatre, Lady Randolph Churchill's matinee in aid of Countess of Limeric's Free Refreshment Buffet for Soldiers and Sailors at London Bridge Station and the Pioneer Players' Society.*

FIFTH SEASON

FIRST SUBSCRIPTION PERFORMANCE: 5 December 1915, Royalty Theatre, 5.15 pm Edward Knoblauch, *Mouse* (directed by author and Craig)

SECOND SUBSCRIPTION PERFORMANCE: 6 February 1916, Court Theatre, 5 pm
Delphine Gray, *The Conference*; Marjorie Patterson, *Pan in Ambush*; Leonid Andreiev, *The Dear Departing*, trans. Julius West

THIRD SUBSCRIPTION PERFORMANCE: 2 April 1916, Savoy Theatre, 5 pm
Gabrielle Enthoven and Edmund Goulding, *Ellen Young*; Nikolai Evreinov, *A Merry Death*, trans. C. Beckhoffer

FOURTH SUBSCRIPTION PERFORMANCE: 28 May 1916, Criterion Theatre, 5 pm
Michael Orme, *The Eternal Snows*

SIXTH SEASON

FIRST SUBSCRIPTION PERFORMANCE: 4 February 1917, Queen's Theatre, 3 pm
Jose Echegeray, *The Cleansing Stain*, trans. Manuel Gonzalez and Christopher Sandeman
Preceded by William Archer's address on Echegeray

SECOND SUBSCRIPTION PERFORMANCE: 25 March 1917, St. Martin's Theatre, 3 pm
Sholom Alechem, 'Gymnasie', trans. Helena Frank; Herman Heijermans, *The Hired Girl*, trans. Christopher St. John

THIRD SUBSCRIPTION PERFORMANCE: 13 May 1917, Kingsway Theatre, 5 pm
Gwen John, *Luck of War*; Sewell Collins, *The Quitter* (directed by author); 'Death and the Lady', arranged by Edith Craig and Mrs Christopher Lowther

FOURTH SUBSCRIPTION PERFORMANCE: 10 June 1917, Strand Theatre, 8 pm
Paul Claudel, *The Tidings Brought to Mary*, trans. Louise Morgan Sill

SEVENTH SEASON

27th SUBSCRIPTION PERFORMANCE: 16 December 1917, Criterion Theatre, 8 pm
Torahiko Khori, *Kanawa* (directed by author and Craig); W. F. Casey, *Insurrection*; George Bernard Shaw, *The Inca of Perusalem*

28th SUBSCRIPTION PERFORMANCE: 17 February 1918, Princes Theatre, 5 pm
Pierre Louys and Pierre Frondaie, *The Girl and the Puppet*, trans. Dr. Chalmers Mitchell

29th SUBSCRIPTION PERFORMANCE: 14 April 1918, King's Hall, 5 pm
Gerolamo Rovetta, *Romanticismo*, trans. F. M. Rankin

30th SUBSCRIPTION PERFORMANCE: 2 June 1918, King's Hall, 5 pm
H. F. Rubinstein, *The Earlier Works of Sir Roderick Athelstane: A Biographical Fragment in 3 Acts*

EIGHTH SEASON

31st SUBSCRIPTION PERFORMANCE: 9 February 1919, King's Hall, 4 pm
Constance Holme, *The Home of Vision;* Miles Malleson, *The Artist*, from a story by Anton Chekov

Christopher St. John, *Nell'Est*, translated into Italian by F. Ferraro and P. Ramella; Susan Glaspell, *Trifles*

32nd SUBSCRIPTION PERFORMANCE: 23 March 1919, Scala Theatre, 2 pm
Paul Claudel, *The Hostage*, translated by Pierre Chavannes

33rd SUBSCRIPTION PERFORMANCE: 1 June 1919, Lyric Opera House, 3 pm
Herman Heijermans, *The Rising Sun*, trans. M. V. Salvage and Christopher St. John

NINTH SEASON

34th SUBSCRIPTION PERFORMANCE: 25 January 1920, St. Martin's Theatre, 3 pm
Anton Tchekov, *The Bear* (directed by A. E. Filmer); Anton Tchekov, *On the High Road;* Anton Tchekov, *The Wedding*

35th SUBSCRIPTION PERFORMANCE: 11 April 1920, Strand Theatre, 8 pm
M. E. M. Young, *The Higher Court*

36th SUBSCRIPTION PERFORMANCE: 20 June 1920, Kingsway Theatre, 8 pm
Saint Georges de Bouhelier, *The Children's Carnival*, trans. Christopher St. John

21 June 1920, 2.30 pm, Saint Georges de Bouhelier, The Children's Carnival, t*rans. Christopher St. John; for Serbian Children, Save the Children Fund and Serb-Croat-Slovene Children's Welfare Association.*

38th SUBSCRIPTION PERFORMANCE: 29 March 1925, Regent Theatre, 8 pm
Susan Glaspell, *The Verge*

Appendix II Subscription Performances – Plays and Dramatists. Statistical Analysis of Data from Annual Reports

Season/Year	Plays	One-act	Three-act	Four-act	Other	Not specified	Lectures	Female dramatists	Male dramatists	Anon
1st/1911 12	9	6	1	2	1 (harpsichord concert)	0	1	4	4	0
Two plays by Christopher St. John performed					One play repeated (*Macrena*)					
2st/1912 13	9	6	0	1	0	1	0	2	7	0
One plays repeated (*A Matter of Money*)										
3st/1913 14	8	4	2	0	2 (13 scenes/6 episodes)	0	0	4	4	0
Two plays repeated (*Paphnutius/Idle Women*)										
4th/1914 15	7	0	0	0	0	7	1	1	5	0
Two plays by Laurence Irving performed										
5th/1915 16	7	0	0	0	0	7	0	4	4	0
One collaboration (one female, one male dramatist)										
6th/1916 17	6	0	0	1 (ballad)	6	1	1	1	5	1
7th/1917 18	6	0	0	0	6	0	0	0	6	1
One collaboration (two male dramatists)										
8th/1918 19	6	0	0	0	6	0	3	3	3	0
9th/1919 20	5	0	0	0	5	0	1	1	2	0
Three plays by Anton Chekhov performed										

NB. The annual reports 1911–20 do not list the final subscription performance in 1925 of Susan Glaspell's *The Verge*. All four plays repeated are female-authored. Total number of subscription-performance: plays = 63; lectures = 3; harpsichord concert = 1; ballad = 1.

Subscription Performances – Dramatists
Statistical Analysis of Data from Annual Reports

Season/year	Female dramatists	Male dramatists	Anon
1st/1911–12	4	4	0
2nd/1912–13	2	7	0
3rd/1913–14	4	4	0
4th/1914–15	1	5	0
5th/1915–16	4	4	0
6th/1916–17	1	5	1
7th/1917–18	0	6	1 [male]
8th/1918–19	3	3	0
9th/1919–20	1	2	0

Total number of subscription performance dramatists listed in annual reports = 62
Of which, female = 20
Of which, male = 40
Of which anon = 2

Sex ratio of dramatists

For four years of the society's existence the sex ratio of subscription-performance dramatists is equal.

For five years of the society's existence the work of male rather than female dramatists is favoured; in one of these five years, no female dramatist's work is performed.

Notes

1 Introducing the Pioneer Players

1. Christopher St. John (d. 1960) translated this play by Hrotsvit (c. 930–c. 990).
2. The Pioneer Players are considered from the perspective of Craig's career in Katharine Cockin, 1998. *Edith Craig (1869–1947): Dramatic Lives*, London: Cassell.
3. Edith Craig's mother, Ellen Terry (1847–1928) and her brother, Edward Gordon Craig (1872–1966), have received considerable critical attention from theatre historians.
4. The society arranged for translation if this was necessary. On one occasion a play was translated into Italian from English.
5. See Holledge, 1981; Spender and Hayman, 1985; Gardner, 1985; Wolf, 1989; Stowell, 1992.
6. Miles Malleson (1888–1969) was a prolific actor on stage and film, distinguished for his plays such as *The Fanaticks* (1927) and his adaptations of Moliere, as well as his political activism.
7. Craig's headed notepaper with the legends 'Suffrage Plays' or 'Propaganda Plays', would also alert correspondents to this position, as I have argued elsewhere (Cockin 1991).
8. The plays performed for subscription productions which have not been located are: Nellie Lambert; The Daughters of Ishmael; Death and the Lady; The Early Works of Sir Roderick Athelstane; The Girl and the Puppet.
9. W. B. Yeats, *The King's Threshold*, Sygmunt Krasinski, *The Undivine Comedy*.
10. Nikolai Evreinov (1879–1953) subsequently became known for his mass spectacle, The Storming of the Winter Palace (Carnicke 1989; Cockin 1994; Golub 1984).
11. Malcolm Bradbury and James McFarlane address this in their anthology *Modernism: A Guide to European Literature 1890–1930* (1991 rept).

2 The Costs of a Free Theatre

1. Raymond Williams uses the concept of a 'class fraction' to analyse the Bloomsbury Group (Williams 1989).
2. Neither Harley Granville Barker nor Elizabeth Robins was a member of the society.
3. The International Suffrage Shop did not perform this play (Fisher 1995). Rather the shop was the recipient of the funds raised by the performance.
4. Many of its plays have therefore survived in the Lord Chamberlain's play collection.
5. The AFL performed *Change of Tenant* and *The Maid and the Magistrate* on Monday 27 February [1911?] at the Eustace Miles Restaurant. This was

organised by Beatrice Filmer on behalf of the Women Sanitary Inspectors and Health Visitors' Suffrage Group (AFL Half Yearly Report of the Play Dept; FL).
6 Harley Granville-Barker's play *Waste*.
7 See St. John's introduction to *The Theatre of the Soul* by Nikolai Evreinov; documents, copies of letters and press cuttings relating to this controversy (ECD); Cockin 1994.
8 None of these 15 men was titled, and the longest serving man on the committee was E. Harcourt Williams, a member for seven years (1912–19). Ten of the 51 women were titled.
9 They include Radclyffe Hall, Una Troubridge, Mabel Batten, Cynthia Asquith, Elizabeth Robins and Harley Granville Barker.
10 See unpublished letter from Basil Rathbone to Edith Craig, 13 November 1919; 3.551, ECCF.
11 In 1917–18, income from subscriptions totalled £527 4s from which Entertainment Tax of £73 11s was paid.
12 It is also clear from this 'Note to Authors' that Holledge's assertion that 'each play was restricted to a single "matinee"' is incorrect (Holledge 1981: 126).
13 See Appendix II.
14 Conal O'Riordan's *The King's Wooing* and Sewell Collins' *The Quitter*.
15 Ben Webster directed *The Last Visit*, and Louis Calvert directed *Hamlet*.
16 Travelling expenses (possibly from the non-subscription performances of *Pageant* in Liverpool for the WSPU and in Camberley and Windsor) were incurred in its first year, £28 18s 11d (*PPAR 1911–12:* 12).
17 Edith Craig's headed notepaper lists a number of plays for which she held the rights.
18 See letter from George Bernard Shaw to Florence Farr, 19 April 1904 (Bax 1951: 35–7).
19 The Stage Society had produced Street's *Great Friends* at the Royal Court in 1905 (Woodfield 1984: 184).
20 The Pioneer Players shared some of the Stage Society's dramatists (H. Hamilton Fyfe, Hugh de Selincourt, Miles Malleson, George Bernard Shaw) and some members (Florence Edgar Hobson, Charlotte (Mrs) Shaw, Pamela Colman Smith, Magdalen Ponsonby).

3 The Feminist Play and the Art of Propaganda

1 The term 'pioneer' derives from '*pionnier*', meaning foot soldier, who digs trenches in the front-line or avant-garde, preparing ground for the following army (*OED*). Figuratively 'pioneers' have been innovators or explorers, those breaking new ground spiritually or ideologically.
2 Although Dymkowski has claimed like the contemporary review in the *Morning Post* that there was 'nothing in its rules to suggest that it is mainly concerned with the position of women', the society's annual reports referred to supporting movements of interest.
3 The *Daily Herald* 'originated as a printers' strike sheet in 1911' (Thompson 1992: 242).

4. The *Freewoman*, edited by Dora Marsden and Mary Gawthorpe, both formerly involved in WSPU, ran from November 1911 to May 1912 and had some 300 subscribers (Garner 1984).

5. A database was used to collect data from one of the two scrap books of newspaper reviews collected for the society, possibly by Gabrielle Enthoven, whose own collection of theatre memorabilia was donated to the V & A Museum.

6. Incidences of reference to suffrage or votes for women were 12: 108 or 11 per cents; feminism 5: 108 or 5 per cent; and propaganda 14: 108 or 13 per cent.).

7. Thus 'the very being or legal existence of the wife is suspended during the marriage or at least incorporated and consolidated into that of the husband under whose wing, protection and cover she performs everything' (Lewis 1987: 3).

8. Scenes from Acts I and III were performed in a programme of events for the AFL at the Lyceum Theatre.

9. Gail Finney has cited *Candida* as typifying George Bernard Shaw's representation of New Woman as madonna.

10. Selincourt's play *Life's Importance* was performed by the Stage Society in 1909–10. Edith Ellis was an ordinary member of the Pioneer Players 1912–13; the society discussed the possibility of staging her play *The Pixey* (Minutes of the Casting Committee; ECD). Emmeline Pethick Lawrence was a member of the Pioneer Players who knew both De Selincourt and Edith Craig (Pethick Lawrence 1938: 318).

11. These Acts were introduced in 1864 to control the spread of Contagious Diseases by forcibly examining and controlling women thought to be prostitutes. They were not repealed until 1886.

12. Some prominent actors performed in the Pioneer Players' production of Delphine Gray's *The Conference*. Edith Evans played Lady Frances Ponsonby, Inez Bensusan played the Dowager Duchess of Westhampton, Mary Jerrold and Elaine Sleddall played her daughters.

13. Conal O'Riordan who sometimes wrote under the pseudonym Norreys Connell had worked at the Abbey Theatre.

14. Kingston also acted in the role of Queen Caroline in the Pioneer Players' production of Laurence Housman's *Pains and Penalties*.

15. George Bernard Shaw's vegetarianism was a life-long commitment.

16. Edith Craig directed Jones' *The Liars* on 13 March 1933 at the Garrick Theatre in aid of the Fellowship of St. Christopher for Unemployed and Homeless Boys (handbill; ECD).

17. Evreinov's *The Theatre of the Soul*, Cecil Fisher's *The Great Day* and Harcourt Williams adaptation of Guy de Maupassant's *The Duel*.

18. Licensed for production on 4 May 1914 (not 3 May) at the Ambassador's, suggesting that there may have been two performances.

19. Allan Monkhouse's *Nothing Like Leather* was performed at the Gaiety Theatre on 29 September 1914 (Pogson 1952: 157). Gilbert Cannan's *Dull Monotony* was performed for the Stage Society on 20 May 1909 at the Hotel Cecil (Woodfield 1984: 186).

20. Fyfe's play *A Modern Aspasia* was performed by the Stage Society in the year 1908–9.

21 The play was licensed for production at the Gaiety Theatre Manchester on 16 September (produced on 23 September) 1912, five months after the Pioneer Players' production at the King's Hall (ADD LCP 1912/39).
22 The Lord Chamberlain's report describes it as dealing with the 'futilities of social science' (ADD LCP 1914/18; BL).
23 Charlotte Despard, leader of the WFL, was a theosophist. In late 1909 she and Mrs Pankhurst met Gandhi who particularly endorsed Despard's 'spiritual resistance' (Mulvihill 1989: 86).
24 There was an impressive cast for this production which Edith Craig directed. Mary Jerrold performed Lady Ditcham of Drury 'with much success' and the other characters were 'admirably sustained' (*Stage*, 25 June 1914: 22).
25 The cast lists in the annual report and the minutes of the casting committee for this production do not include the character of Flannery O'Hooligan, suggesting that the character was cut for the Pioneer Players' production.
26 In the play programme for *Mouse* (5 December 1915) the society advertised lectures by Inayat Khan, the leader of a Sufi group with which Edith Ellis was involved in 1916 (Grosskurth 1985: 269).
27 Such as Paula Tanqueray in A. W. Pinero's *The Second Mrs Tanqueray*, Mrs Ebbsmith in Pinero's *The Notorious Mrs Ebbsmith* and Mrs Dane in H. A. Jones' *Mrs Dane's Defence* (Clarke 1989: 43).

4 Pioneers Perform Politics

1 Elizabeth Howe makes a case for Anne Marshall, dating the first performance by an actress on a London stage as 8 December 1660 (Howe 1992: 24). However, St. John cites 1661.
2 In her collection *Mirrors and Angles* (1931), Friedlander includes a short poem, 'Swan-song of Any Pioneers'.
3 Stanley has suggested a comparison with Gertrude Colmore's short stories which are similarly episodic and enigmatic (Stanley and Morley 1988: 97).
4 See Sage 1986.
5 Sowon Park's discussion of the Women Writers' Suffrage League and the professional writer does not adequately address the challenges to aesthetic value and the professional which were pressing cultural concerns in the movement.
6 I have discussed the association between Edith Craig, the AFL and the Pioneer Players elsewhere (Cockin 1991).
7 Mrs Drummond, possibly Flora Drummond, a leading WSPU activist; Edith Craig active in the Suffrage Atelier and WFL; Christopher St. John and Cicely Hamilton, both members of the Women Writers' Suffrage League; Marie Lawson, editor and formerly co-editor with Cicely Hamilton of the *Vote*; Mrs Cavendish Bentinck; Isabella O. Ford, socialist and suffragist; Sime Seruya, founder of the International Suffrage Shop; and Laurence Housman, founder of the Men's League for Women's Suffrage and Suffrage Atelier member.
8 For further information on Craig's work for the movement, see Cockin 1998a.

9 The Play Actors produced several plays by Hamilton, including *The Sergeant of Hussars* and *Mrs Vance*. Further research may reveal the extent to which theatre societies such as the Play Actors were involved in the women's suffrage movement.
10 For further details of this play, see Cockin 1998a.
11 In Caryl Churchill's *Top Girls* (1982) 'characters form different worlds populate the "actual" world of the drama. They violate the convention of a fixed, time-bound place of action' (Aston and Savon 1991: 32).

5 Working women

1 Clemence Housman served a prison sentence for non-payment of taxes (Tickner 1987: 245). The Tax Resistance League was one of many suffrage organisations to which Edith Craig belonged.
2 Tickner points out that this evidence provides a general picture only. The suffragists' boycott of the Census in 1911 must have affected the data.
3 Cecil Fisher, *The Great Day* and Heijermans' *The Rising Sun* were published by the Labour Publishing Co. Ltd, in 1925 in the 'Plays for the People' series, ed. Monica Ewer. Gwen John's *Luck of War*, performed by the Pioneer Players and discussed in Chapter 7, was later performed by the Workers' Theatre Movement.
4 See Katharine Cockin, 'Charlotte Perkins Gilman's *Three Women*', in *Charlotte Perkins Gilman: Optimist Reformer*, (eds) Jill Rudd and Val Gough (University of Iowa Press, 2000), pp. 74–92.
5 See letter from J. J. Mallon to Edith Lyttelton (3 December 1912; ECD).
6 Emigration was proposed by the anti-suffragist, Sir Almroth Wright.
7 This racial stereotype may be compared with Stearn in *Honour Thy Father*, a play described by Holledge as 'offensively racist in the character of Stearn, the brutish, Jewish tradesman' (Holledge 1981: 131). There is no explicit reference in the play to Stearn's Jewish identity which may be inferred from his surname.
8 In Lyttelton's play *Nyanysa* (1911) the critique of arranged marriages is located in Africa, exposing the oppression of Zulu women but too readily associating dissent with white Christianity.
9 Lyttelton's play *Warp and Woof* (1904) exposed the conditions of the sweated labour of dressmakers which may have influenced Hamilton's *Diana of Dobson's*.
10 The Pioneer Players' performance of *The Coronation* and George Bernard Shaw's *The Man of Destiny* (performed by Margaret Halstan and Michael Sherbrooke, and 'a number of old songs' by Miss Sterling Mackinlay) on 28 January 1912 was not a subscription performance. Knowles incorrectly gives the date of first performance for this play as 1910, referring to a review in *The Times* of 29 January 1910 (Knowles 1934: 105).
11 Thursby played both George IV in Laurence Housman's *Pains and Penalties* and Prejudice in Cicely Hamilton's *A Pageant of Great Women*.
12 The coronation of George V in 1910 raised expectations of a new social order and had prompted suffrage processions.

13 The author's note states that the play was written from personal experience. Conflicting dates of performance are given in the published play (15 May 1913) and the Annual Report (18 May 1913).
14 First performed in Britain by the Stage Society, Imperial Theatre, 1903, translated by Christopher St. John, directed by Max Behrend.
15 J. Sackville Martin's *Nellie Lambert* which has not been located.
16 Radclyffe Hall and Ladye (Mabel Batten) attended this performance, although they were never members of the society (Baker 1985: 49).
17 This play was adapted from a novel of the same title, but the play has not been located.
18 Kauffman wrote several articles for *The Freewoman* which ran adverts for his novel in almost every issue. Holledge incorrectly cites the author as Richard Wright Kauffman (Holledge 1981: 132).
19 In this performance, the central character was played by Marjorie Patterson, the author of *Pan in Ambush* which was later produced by the Pioneer Players.
20 A poem by S. Gertrude Ford, 'Houseless By Night', published in *Vote*, expressed the plight of homeless women (*Vote* 17 June 1911: 91). Ford's work appears in Reilly 1989.
21 St. John was to give a lecture on Hrotsvit to the Catholic Women's Suffrage Society at the Suffrage Club on 18 February 1915.
22 Case regards the plays of Hrotsvit as a prototype for feminist drama (Case 1988: 34).
23 The play programme for *Paphnutius* includes an advertisement for Christabel Pankhurst's *The Great Scourge and How to End It* and announces the Pioneer Players' forthcoming production of *The Daughters of Ishmael*.
24 St. John's translation was published the same year as that of H. J. W. Tillyard (Wilson 1984: 60).

6 Outside Marriage

1 Mark Sheridan, 'In the Times That Are Going Bye and Bye' (1909), *Blaze of Day*, Pavilion Records, 1992.
2 A. E. Filmer, rather than Edith Craig, directed this play for the Pioneer Players.
3 Claude Rains was considered for the part of Bortsov (Minutes of the Casting Committee; ECD).
4 The performance was given in Italian as *N'ell Est (On The East Side)*; the Italian script has not been located.
5 These were: Agatha (governess); Molly (writer), Christine (proprietor of dressmaking business); Maudie (comic actress); and Lizzie (landlady).
6 Edith (Mrs) Garrud who ran the WFL Athletic Section, gave demonstrations of Ju-Jitsu (*Vote*, 4 June 1910: 63).
7 See for instance A. Mollwo, *A Fair Suffragette*, 1909; Edith Zangwill, *The Call*, 1924; Evelyn Sharp, 'The Women At the Gate', 1915
8 One reviewer was as perplexed as Emily's father, describing the play as 'in a light vein, although...it is not easy to see where the "humour" lies' (*Pall Mall Gazette*, 13 April 1912: 5).

9 Salvatore di Giacomo's play was one of three translated plays produced in the Pioneer Players' second season, two years after Nevinson's *In the Workhouse*.
10 The standard of acting was criticised in the *Pall Mall Gazette* (19 May 1913: 7) and the *Sketch* (28 May 1913: 256). *The Times* praised the translation by Constance Hutton and performances by Annie Schletter and Mrs Ivan Berlyn (19 May 1913: 10).
11 Very few of the actors considered by the casting committee performed in the play (Minutes of the Casting Committee; ECD).
12 This was co-directed by Craig and Housman, one of the many instances of Craig's collaborations.
13 The bill of 'pains and penalties' was 'a special procedure in the House of Lords... which provided a way of punishing a person without legal trial' (Davidoff and Hall 1988: 150).
14 This follows the conventional interpretation of Caroline's trial as 'symbolizing the corruption of the political system' (Davidoff and Hall 1988: 151).
15 Whitelaw cites a published edition of *A Matter of Money* which I have been unable to locate.
16 Ben Webster played Dr Channing, and his wife was played by May Whitty.
17 *A Matter of Money* was described as 'a strong play with a curious vein of grim humour in the last act' (*Sketch*, 19 February 1913: 204).
18 In this respect, Mrs Herbert Cohen's play *The Level Crossing* may have been influenced by Hamilton's *A Matter of Money*.
19 The earlier production of this play under the title *The Cutting of the Knot* at the Royalty Theatre, Glasgow on 13 March 1911, associates the Pioneer Players with the provincial repertory theatres (*PPAR 1911–12*: 8).
20 The *Referee* noted that Young's play was 'practically a re-writing of "The Great Adventure"', in which Pioneer Player Wish Wynne had starred.
21 The motion was defeated by 134 votes to 91 on 14 April 1920 (*Referee*, n.d.).
22 Leprosy features in Laurence Irving's *Godefroi and Yolande* performed by the society in 1915.
23 See, for instance, the work of Flaubert and the male quest romances analysed by Showalter (1990).
24 Sarah Moore Grimké, the American suffragist, had translated from French a biography of Joan of Arc (1876) (Warner 1981).
25 The suffragist martyr is explored by Nevinson ('A Calvary of Womanhood,' *Vote*, 14 May 1910: 30).
26 De Musset was satirised in Marjorie Patterson's *Pan in Ambush*, produced by the Pioneer Players.
27 Although in July 1911 the CWSS resolved to approach St John to speak to their society, it was not until 14 June 1912 that they wrote to her requesting a performance of this play (records of the Catholic Women's Suffrage Society; FL).
28 In December 1912 St. John was made a member of the committee of the CWSS, and on 11 March 1914 she gave a lecture on 'Woman Suffrage from the Catholic Point of View' at the Suffrage Club, at which the Ranee of Sarawak was in the chair. The Ranee of Sarawak was on the advisory committee of the Pioneer Players from 1914–15.
29 Weedon states an alternative reading of subject positions typically constructed through Catholicism: 'sex is defined as naturally heterosexual and procreative and femininity is implicitly masochistic' (96).

7 The Luck of War

1. Whitelaw states incorrectly that the Pioneer Players folded when the war began (Whitelaw 1990: 125). However, the Play Actors suspended its activities from 1915–1920 (Watson 1970: 152).
2. Lady Randolph Churchill and Mrs Claude Beddington were commended for their recruitment of new members (*PPAR 1915–16*: 11).
3. More aristocratic women, who had attended Lady Randolph Churchill's matinée the previous year, joined the society (*World*, 7 December 1915: 575). In addition, the society raised £163 13s in donations, probably from the fund-raising function of Lady Randolph Churchill's charity matinée at which the Pioneer Players' produced Nikolai Evreinov's *The Theatre of the Soul*.
4. Laurie Wolf claimed that since the acting membership was largely female this was not a problem (198).
5. During the war the Pioneer Players offered four seasons of plays, falling short of its promised five annual productions. In total 26 plays were produced, of which only six were written by women. In the fourth season (1914–15) it managed to produce only three productions, although this was increased to four in the remaining three seasons.
6. The society intended to produce Van Leerberghe's *Pan* and Paul Claudel's *Proteus*. Van Leerberghe's *Pan* had been produced by Komisarjevsky (Sayler 1923: 182). These plays have not been located.
7. The society produced Gerolamo Rovetta's *Romanticismo* at the King's Hall instead of the Princes Theatre because of 'the new Government restrictions on Electric Lighting making Sunday performances in a licensed theatre impossible for the present' (printed note [to be inserted with tickets] n.d; ECD).
8. These included: Lena Ashwell; Cicely Hamilton (although she remained a member of the executive until 1919); Laurence Housman; Marie Lawson; Nigel Playfair.
9. Of the 28 military-titled men, there were 17 captains, 5 lieutenants, 4 majors, 1 major-general and 1 ensign.
10. In 1924 Dr. Christine Murrell became the first female member of the Council of the British Medical Association and in 1923 of the General Medical Council of Great Britain.
11. See Whitworth (1951: 118). Gertrude Forbes Robertson thanked Craig for her work at the Shakespeare Hut (unpublished letter from Gertrude Forbes Robertson to Edith Craig, 26 April 1917; 3.258, ECCF).
12. Mary Sheepshanks, secretary of the International Woman Suffrage Alliance and editor of *Jus Suffragii*, was an ordinary member of the Pioneer Players from 1916 to 1918.
13. An advertisement for the *Workers' Dreadnought* was carried in the play programme for *Ellen Young*.
14. From 1915 to 1919 it produced 23 plays and two ballets, of which 21 were written in English and only two were translated (Watson 1970: 92).
15. In 1916 the Pioneer Players introduced an entrance fee of 10s 6d. In 1917–18 £73 11s was paid in Entertainments Tax from an income of £527 4s subscriptions, that is 12% of its income for the year.

16 In the NFRA annual reports of 1914–18, only one member of the original NFRA committee remained, Charles E. Hecht, as secretary. Women were well represented on the committee which included Mrs Waymouth of the British Women's Patriotic League.
17 The FES participated in the Patriotic Thrift Campaign, supported the Ministry of Food's Communal Kitchens and helped the catering of the YMCA Huts at home and abroad.
18 Such as the National League for Health, Maternity & Child Welfare, the Charity Organisation Society, and the Federation of Women's Institutes.
19 When the premises of the FES were requisitioned by the Ministry of Food in September 1917, the government rehoused the society at Danes Inne House, 265 Strand.
20 Its publications included: *Facts for Patriots* (November 1914), *Diet for Brainworkers*, *Rearing an Imperial Race*, *The Feeding of Children in Wartime and After*, and *Life Without Servants*. The FES sold its publications at the Eugenics Education Society's summer school at Cambridge in August 1919.
21 The plot resembles Somerset Maugham's *Home and Beauty* (1919) although John's play is not a comedy. I am grateful to Dr Richard Foulkes for this information.
22 Holledge mistook the dramatist for the artist (Holledge 1981: 137). A photograph of the dramatist was published in the *Bookman* June 1917.
23 The play was licensed for performance at the Palace Theatre, Manchester on 21 May 1917, but the Pioneer Players' performance on 13 May 1917 seems to have been unlicensed.
24 Other dramatists who directed their own plays were Cicely Hamilton and Torahiko Kori.
25 The *Stage* compares the character of Cecil Ames, as an American joining the British Army in the RAMC, with Harold Chapin (17 May 1917: 15). Harold Chapin was an acting member of the Pioneer Players from 1911 to 1915.
26 This review compares the play with Mr Macdonald Hastings' 'fine comedy' *The New Sin* (Sketch 23 May 1917: xii).
27 The Stage Society produced Shaw's *Augustus Does His Bit* on 21 January 1917 at the Royal Court, and *O'Flaherty VC* on 19 December 1920, at the Lyric, Hammersmith.
28 Previously performed on 7 October 1916 at the Birmingham Repertory Theatre and on 14 November 1916 at the Neighbourhood Playhouse, New York.
29 Passages marked for deletion, were those referring to King Edward, to King George's abstinence from wine, and a reference to the Empress's marriage.
30 Licensed for production at the Little Theatre on 20 November 1915 (ADD LCP 1915/32; BL). If this performance was given, it pre-dates the first production in 1916 at the Birmingham Repertory Theatre cited by Trewin (1963: 190).
31 See *The Times* 17 December 1917: 11; *Sketch* 26 December 1917: xiv.
32 The plays produced were Isi Collin, *Sisyphus and the Wandering Jew*, Edmund Rostand, *Two Pierrots*, Nikolai Evreinov, *The Theatre of the Soul* and Constance Campbell, *A Dilemma*.
33 The play was translated by Miss F. M. Rankin, who had translated Guiseppe Giacosa, *The Rights of the Soul* for the Stage Society production 1908–9.

34 The same play performed in Italian by the Italian Players on 12 March 1918 was directed by Ugo Catani.
35 Unpublished letter from Frederick Whelen to Edith Craig, 21 February 1918; ECD.
36 Craig organised with Whelen for the payment of expenses to certain members of the English Players (copy of letter from Edith Craig to Frederick Whelen, 20 March 1918; ECD).
37 The Italian Play Society also produced Salvatore de Giacomo's *Mese Mariano*, Sem Benelli's *La cena delle beffe* and Gabriel d'Annunzio's *La figlia di iorio*.
38 Unpublished letter from Frederick Whelen to Edith Craig, 1 March 1918; ECD.
39 Unpublished letter from Frederick Whelen to Edith Craig, 13 March 1918; ECD.
40 *On the East Side* was, like *The Good Hope* and *Godefroi and Yolande*, a revival from Craig's earlier productions. *On The East Side* had been produced by Craig at the Royal Court in July 1908 in aid of the East London Hospital for Children, Shadwell in Miss Granville's matinee (*Sketch* 11 July 1908; William Archer's Press Cuttings, BTA).
41 J. T. Grein was Honorary President of The French Players, based at 30 New Bond Street: 'A society formed for the production of French plays in London' (play programmes for *The Cleansing Stain* and *The Hired Girl*; ECD). See Schoonderwoerd (1963: 190).
42 Unpublished letter from Acton Abbas to Edith Craig and Christopher St. John, 3 June 1919; 3.000, ECCF.
43 The short stories 'The Artist', 'The Duel' and 'The Girl and the Puppet' and the novel *The Daughters of Ishmael* were adapted for dramatisation.
44 The translated adaptations used in the performances of 'The Daughters of Ishmael' and 'The Girl and the Puppet' are not extant.
45 For recent theoretical work on ways in which 'the translation involves the transfer of a culture, which is inscribed as much in words as in gestures' (Pavis 1992: 155).
46 The play was licensed for performance on 16 September 1920, and was, according to J. C. Trewin, a financial disaster (Trewin 1963: 60).
47 It is described as 'poor stuff, but there is no possible objection to it' (ADD LCP 1920/23; BL).
48 There were several advertisements for Russian events in the society's play programmes.
49 The Pioneer Players' play programme for *Romanticismo* advertised an Elsie Fogerty-Ruby Giner [sic] Season at the Royal Court on 11–23 March (1918) for plays, mimes dances, to include Debussy's 'La Boite a Joujous' and 'The Suminda River' an episode in the No manner (ECD).
50 The Defence of the Realm Act was introduced to control the dissemination of information pertinent to the war but additional regulations were added during the course of the war (Kohn 1992: 29).
51 The Pioneer Players' play programme for *Ellen Young* advertised the *Woman's Dreadnought* only days before Sylvia Pankhurst's Workers Suffrage Federation (reorganised from the East End Federation of Suffragettes in March 1916) held an anti-war rally in Trafalgar Square on 8 April 1916 (Taylor 1993: 39).

52 The Pioneer Players sponsored dancers in the play programme for *The Dear Departing*. An advert appears for Rose Benton, teacher of Raymond Duncan's system of Greek Rhythmic Movements and waving at 86 Ladbroke Road (play programme; ECD).
53 This production cost £122 2s, much more than the usual expenditure, possibly facilitated by Lady Randolph Churchill's donation of funds from *The Theatre of the Soul* (*PPAR 1915–16:* 12).
54 The society secured a venue at the Savoy Theatre at the last minute, thanks to H. B. Irving's generosity (*Era* 12 April 1916: 9).
55 Lady Diana Manners, a member of the Pioneer Players un 1917–18, was taking drugs in 1915 (Kohn 1992: 32–3).
56 Miss M. Longfellow was an ordinary member of the society from 1913–14 and an acting member from 1913–15.
57 This was apparent in the 1920s concerning the public images of 'dope kings' Brilliant Chang and Edgar Manning but the fears regarding drugs were articulated in racist terms much earlier (Kohn 1992: 125).
58 Douglas was a witness for Billing and used the trial as an opportunity to present himself as Wilde's victim. Douglas's obscene sonnet had cited Margot Asquith 'bound with Lesbian fillets' (Sims 1992: 100).
59 Advertised in Pioneer Players' play programmes (Schoonderwoerd 1963: 189–92).
60 For a discussion of the ways in which the study of poetry was perceived to have a morally improving effect see Baldick.
61 Christopher St. John spoke as representative of the Foreign Drama Committee at the BDL dinner of Council and Committees headed by Lord Howard de Walden on Sunday 30 November 1919 at the Florence Restaurant, W1 (Menu; ECD).
62 On 10 December 1919 the first meeting was held with Mrs Ellis, Miss Craig, Miss St. John, Miss Atwood, Mr Ellis (Chairman) Mr Plank, Mr Kirwan and Mr Knoblock present (Minutes of the Casting Committee; ECD). The powers of this committee may have encroached on Craig's powers as honorary director.
63 H. F. Rubinstein was a prolific writer and lawyer. He defended Radclyffe Hall in the trial for obscenity of her novel *The Well of Loneliness* (1928).
64 The name 'Stayton' has been added later to the Minutes of the Casting Committee. However, in the play programme for the Chekhov triple bill on 25 January 1920, forthcoming productions were announced, including 'a new play by Frank Stayton,' *Abraham* (dramatist not stated) and Mrs Kennedy Fraser's *The Seal Woman*. A copy of the latter is held at ETMM.
65 The meeting was held on 2 February 1920 with Miss Craig, Miss St. John, Miss Atwood, Mr Ellis, Mrs Ellis, Mr Kirwan and Mr Plank present.

8 Towards an Art Theatre

1 At an extraordinary AGM, members agreed to accept three instead of five annual subscription performances (*PPAR 1914–15* 11). In 1917–18 the society could not afford to produce Zygmunt Krasinski, *The Undivine Comedy*. The

society announced its intention to produce Yeats, *The King's Threshold* which but this was never realised.
2 Meyherhold was director at Vera Komisarjevskaya's theatre until 1908 when he was replaced by Nikolai Evreinov (Roose-Evans 1989: 22).
3 Trewin incorrectly dates the first British performance of *The Dear Departing* as 1923 by the Birmingham Rep (Trewin 1963: 194).
4 Other recent productions included: *The Seagull*, the Glasgow Repertory, 1909 and the Little Theatre, London, 1912; *The Cherry Orchard*, 1911 and *Uncle Vanya*, 1914 produced by the Stage Society.
5 The Pioneer Players' Minutes of the Casting Committee show that Claude Rains was considered for the part of Bortsov (ECD).
6 *The Wedding* had been performed in Britain in May 1917 at the Grafton Galleries (*Stage* 29 January 1920: 20).
7 This play was produced by Lugne-Poe in 1912, later 'performed with Appia's settings and Dalcroze's collaboration in the same summer festival at Hellerau' (Innes 1993: 49); the Provincetown Players also produced the play (Field 1983: 129).
8 *Kanawa* was written in English by Kori.
9 Kori was to benefit from his relationship with Craig, since her production of his *The Toils of Yoshitomo* in 1922 enabled him to prove his talents to the Japanese government when he was considered for the poet's pension (unpublished letter from Torahiko Kori to Edith Craig, 16 June [?]; 3.411, ECCF).
10 Lowther arranged the dances for the society's production of Evreinov's *A Merry Death*, while the music was produced by Christopher Wilson.
11 Lady Maud Warrender assisted with music in several productions.
12 Innes understands the interest in religious drama such as that of Claudel shown by avant-garde practitioners such as Barrault and Brook, was part of a search for a 'secular religion' as Grotowski has said, 'To find a place where a communion becomes possible' (Innes 1993: 150).
13 Plank designed the programme cover for 'The Smokes for the Wounded' matinée on 7 April 1916 at the Savoy Theatre at which the Pioneer Players performed *The Theatre of the Soul*.
14 George Plank and Saba Raleigh were co-opted onto the council for 1919–20 to take the places of Miles Malleson and Torahiko Kori who had both resigned (*PPAR 1919–20*: 1).
15 Craig produced many nativity plays and Hugo von Hofmannsthal's *The Great World Theatre* (Cockin 1998a).
16 Evreinov's *A Merry Death* was written in 1908, and performed in 1909. The society may have learnt of the play when it was published in the *New Age* on 25 November 1915, five months before this performance. At the end of January 1920 it was produced by Komisarjevsky at the Wigmore Hall for LAHDA, a new Russian artistic society ('LAHDA', *Observer* 1 February 1920: 11).
17 One review lists some of the aristocratic members of the audience, including Baroness D'Erlanger, Lady Diana Manners, Lady Juliet Duff and Lady Cunard, who later became members of the society (*World*, 7 December 1915: 575).
18 Evreinov's views on theatre have been compared with the developments in transactional analysis (Carnicke 1989: 82), a comparison which links Evreinov's with the later experiments of Jerzy Grotowski and Peter Brook in the

218 Notes

relationship between acting and life, in the potential of theatre to transform the individual and to re-examine spiritual values.
19. This technique was adopted in Evgeny Vakhtangov's 1922 production in Berlin of Strindberg's *Erik IV*, where the court setting is presented as rusty and twisted, suggesting the distorted perspective of the mad king (Roose-Evans 1963: 36).
20. This was explored by Russolo in *The Art of Noises* manifesto (1913).
21. Gwen John's *Luck of War* was the only play written by a woman produced in that year and was one of several naturalist plays.
22. Louise Morgan Sill's translation was sold at the performance, a practice which was not an isolated one for the society and which helped to publicise a new play.
23. The production cost £110 17s 6d (*PPAR 1916–17*: 9).
24. It is not surprising to note that many of Evreinov's parodic productions defamiliarised the perceptions of audiences at the The Crooked Mirror cabaret theatre referred to by the Russian Formalist theorist, Boris Tomashevsky (Lemon and Reis 1965: 81).
25. Craig collaborated on dance with Mrs Christopher Lowther, with Christopher Wilson who arranged the music and with George Plank who designed Lowther's dress for this performance.
26. See *The Level Crossing*, *The Street*, *The Verge* and *Beastie*.
27. Nevinson enjoyed Marinetti's company although she disagreed with his views on women and worship of war: 'He admired English women, sympathising with our fight for freedom and political rights, and our disregard for convention and public opinion; his approval naturally went to the extreme left of the militant movement' (Nevinson 1926: 242).
28. This is exemplified by Cicely Hamilton's *A Pageant of Great Women*.

9 On the Verge

1. Edith Evans and Sybil Thorndike both performed in this play, Thorndike in the central role of the dying mother.
2. See unpublished letters in ECCF from Sybil Thorndike to Edith Craig: 9 September 1924 (3.705); n.d. (3.704); 14 October 1924 (3.707).
3. Produced on 4–29 October 1921 and 17–22 July 1922.
4. Cicely Hamilton does not mention this in her review of the play (*Time & Tide* 17 April 1925: 379; ECD).
5. The editor of this newspaper at this time was H. Hamilton Fyfe, author of *Race Suicide*, produced by the Pioneer Players.
6. For instance Jess Dorynne, *The Surprise of His Life* and Margaret Wynne Nevinson, *In the Workhouse*.

Bibliography

Archives and Libraries Consulted

Edith Craig Documents, Ellen Terry Memorial Museum, Smallhythe, Kent (ETMM).
Mander & Mitchenson Theatre Collection, Beckenham, Kent (M&MTC).
British Theatre Association Library (BTA), Theatre Museum.
Lord Chamberlain's Play Collection, British Library (LCP).
MSS Gilbert Murray, Bodleian Library, Oxford.
Fawcett Library, London (FL).
British Newspaper Library, Colindale.
Pioneer Players Newspaper Cuttings Albums: Theatre Museum; and University of Hull.
Arncliffe-Sennett Collection. Vol. 23, June 1913 – February 1914; BL.

These and Dissertations

Cockin, Katharine Mary, 1994. 'The Pioneer Players (1911–25): A Cultural History', Ph.D. thesis, Leicester University.
Gandolfi, Roberta. 1995. 'La Prima Regista: Le sfide di Edith Craig nel temp del suffragismo e della nuova arte scennica', Dipartimento di Musica e Spettacolo, Universita degli Studi di Bologna.
Heath, Mary T., 1986. 'A Crisis in the Life of the Actress: Ibsen in England', Ph.D. thesis, University of Massachusetts.
Holledge, Julie M., 1985. 'Women's Theatres – Women's Rights', Ph.D. thesis. Bristol University.
Watson, Mary Jane, 1970. 'The Independent Theatre in London 1891–1914', M. Litt Diss, University of Bristol.
Wolf, Laurie Jayne, 1989. 'Suffragettes of the Edwardian Theatre: Edith Craig and the Pioneer Players', University of California, Los Angeles.

Pioneer Players' Plays

Andreiev, Leonid Nikolaevich,1916. *The Dear Departing*, trans. Julius West, London: Hendersons.
Chekhov, Anton, 1916. *The Bear* in *Plays*, trans. Julius West, London: Duckworth.
——, 1916. *The Wedding* in *Plays*, trans. Julius West, London: Duckworth.
——, 1916. *On the High Road*, trans.Julius West, London: Duckworth.
Claudel, Paul, *The Hostage*, trans. Pierre Chavannes, New Haven: Yale University Press and Oxford University Press, MDCCCCXVII.
——, *The Tidings Brought to Mary: A Mystery*, trans. Louise Morgan Sill, London: Chatto & Windus, 1916.

——, 'Exchange', trans. Rowland Thurnam; BTA.
Cohen, Mrs Herbert, 'The Level Crossing'; LCP 1914/18.
Collins, Sewell, 'The Quitter'; LCP 1917/11.
Connell, Norreys, 1908. *The King's Wooing*, in *Three New Plays*, London: T. Werner Laurie; typescript LCP 1924/41.
Connell, Norreys, 'The Patience of the Sea'; LCP 1914/13.
De Bouhelier, St. Georges, 'The Children's Carnival', trans. Christopher St. John; typescript, ETMM.
De Selincourt, Hugh, 1911. 'Beastie', *The Open Window*, 12 September, pp. 294–317.
Di Giacomo, Salvatore, 'The Month of Mary'; prompt copy, 28 pp, BTA.
Dorynne, Jes, 'The Surprise of His Life'; typescript 20 pp. ETMM.
Echegeray, Jose, 'The Cleansing Stain'; LCP 1920/23.
Evreinof, N., 1915 (1926). *The Theatre of the Soul: A Monodrama in One Act*, trans. Marie Potapenko and Christopher St John, London: Hendersons; typescript, LCP 1915/31
——, 1915. 'A Merry Death: A Harlequinade', trans. C. E. Bechhofer, *The New Age*, 25 November, pp. 86–89; typescript LCP 1916/25
Fisher, H. Cecil, 1925. *The Great Day*, London: Labour Publishing Co.
Fyfe, H. Hamilton, 'Race Suicide'; LCP 1912/39.
Gilman, Charlotte Perkins, 'Three Women', *The Forerunner*, nd, pp. 115–34.
Glaspell, Susan, 1916. *Trifles*, New York: Frank Shay.
——, 1922. *The Verge*, Boston, USA: Small Mayward.
Gray, Delphine, 'The Conference', typescript, 13 pp. ETMM.
Hamilton, Cicely, 1910 (1948). *A Pageant of Great Women*, London: Marion Lawson.
——, 1911. *Jack and Jill and a Friend*, London: Lacy's; typescript LCP 1911/14.
Harwood, H. M., 1926. *Honour Thy Father* in *Three One-Act Plays*, London: Ernest Benn Ltd., pp. 27–57.
Heijermans, Herman, 1921. *The Good Hope: A Play in Four Acts*, trans. Christopher St. John, London: Hendersons.
——, 1925 (1929). *The Rising Sun: A Play in Four Acts*, trans. Christopher St. John, London: Noel Douglas.
Hobson, Florence Edgar, 1912. *A Modern Crusader*, London: A. C. Fifield, 1912.
Holme, Constance, 1932. *The Home of Vision* in *Four One-Act Plays*, London: Kirkby Lonsdale.
Housman, Laurence, 1911. *Pains and Penalties*, London: Sidgwick & Jackson.
Irving, Laurence, 'The Terrorist'; LCP 1911/11; typescript annotated, 34pp ETMM
Irving, Laurence, 1898. *Godefroi and Yolande*, London & New York: John Lane.
John, Gwen, 1922. *Luck of War*, London & Glasgow: Repertory Plays.
Knoblauch, Edward, 'Mouse'; LCP 1915/32.
Kori, Torahiko, 1934. *Kanawa: The Incantation* in *Fifty One Act Plays* (ed.) Constance M. Martin, London: Victor Gollancz, pp. 853–64.
Lyttleton, Edith, 1911. 'The Thumbscrew', *Nineteenth Century*, May 1911, pp. 938–60; prompt copy, ETMM
Malleson, Miles, 1918 (1929). *The Artist* in *Young Heaven and Three Other Plays*, London: George Allen & Unwin.
Nevinson, Margaret Wynne, 1911. *In the Workhouse*, London: International Suffrage Shop; typescript LCP 1911/12.
Orme, Michael, 'The Eternal Snows'; LCP 1928/5.

Patterson, Marjorie, 1921. *Pan in Ambush*, Baltimore: Norman Remington Co.
Ponsonby, Magdalen, 1914. *Idle Women*, London: A. L. Humphreys; FL; typescript LCP 1914/18.
O'Riordan, Conal, 1929. *The King's Wooing*, London & Glasgow: Gowans & Gray.
Rostand, Edmund, 'Deux Pierrots'; LCP 1917/26
Hrotsvit (Roswitha), 1923. *Paphnutius*, in *The Plays of Roswitha*, trans. Christopher St. John, London: Chatto & Windus, pp. 93–130.
Rovetta, Gerolamo, 'Romanticismo', trans. F. M. Rankin; LCP 1918/5.
Shaw, George Bernard, 'The Inca of Perusalem'; LCP 1915/32
Sholom-Alecheim, 1912. 'Gymnasie' in *Yiddish Tales* trans. Helena Frank, Philadelphia: The Jewish Publication Society of America, pp. 162–79.
St John, Christopher, *The First Actress*, London: Utopia Press, nd; typescript 17 pp. ETMM; typscript LCP 1911/14
——, 'Macrena'; typescript 22 pp. ETMM
——, 'On The East Side'; English version, LCP 1908/15
——, and Charles Thursby, 1911. *The Coronation*, London: International Suffrage Shop.
Sudermann, Herman, 1912. *The Last Visit*, in *Roses*, trans. G. Frank, London: Duckworth.
Williams, Antonia, 1908. *The Street*, London: T. Werner Laurie.
Williams, Harcourt, 'The Duel', typescript 14pp, BTA; typescript LCP 1914/20
Young, M. E. M. 1931. *The Higher Court*, London: Burns Oates & Wishbourne.

Works Cited

Adlard, Eleanor (ed.) 1949. *Edy Craig: Recollections of Edy Craig*. London: Frederick Muller.
Alberti, Johanna, 1989. *Beyond Suffrage: Feminists in War and Peace, 1914–28*. Basingstoke: Macmillan.
Apter, Emily, 1996. 'Acting Out Orientalism: Sapphic Theatricality in Turn-of-the-Century Paris', *Performance & Cultural Politics* (ed.) Elin Diamond, London: Routledge.
Asquith, Lady Cynthia, 1968 (1987). *Diaries 1915–18*, London: Century Hutchinson.
Aston, Elaine, 1992. 'The "New Woman" at Manchester's Gaiety Theatre', *The New Woman and Her Sisters: Feminism and Theatre 1850–1914* (eds) Viv Gardner and Susan Rutherford, Hemel Hempstead: Harvester Wheatsheaf. 205–20.
——, 1994. ' "Meeting the Outside": The Theatre of Susan Glaspell', *Difference in View: Women in Modernism*, (ed.) Gabriele Griffin. London: Taylor & Francis, pp. 155–67.
——, 1995. *An Introduction to Feminism & Theatre*, London: Routledge.
Aston, Elaine and Savona, George, 1991. *Theatre As Sign System: A Semiotics of Text and Performance*, London: Routledge.
Auerbach, Nina, 1987. *Ellen Terry: Player In Her Time*. London: Phoenix House, 1987.
Baker, Michael, 1985. *Our Three Selves: A Life of Radclyffe Hall*, London: Hamish Hamilton.

Baldick, Chris, 1987. *The Social Mission of English Criticism 1848–1932*, Oxford: Clarendon Press.
Barrett, Michèle, 1990. 'Feminism and the Definition of Cultural Politics', in *Feminist Literary Theory: A Reader* (ed.) Mary Eagleton, Oxford: Blackwells, pp. 160–3.
Bassnett-McGuire, Susan, 1980 (1991) *Translation Studies*, London: Routledge.
Battersby, Christine, 1989. *Gender and Genius: Towards a Feminist Aesthetics*, London: Women's Press.
Bax, Clifford (ed.) 1951. *Florence Farr, Bernard Shaw and W. B. Yeats*, Dublin: Cuala Press.
Belsey, Catherine, 1980. *Critical Practice*. London: Methuen.
Bland, Lucy, 1995. *Banishing the Beast: English Feminism & Sexual Morality 1885–1914*, Harmondsworth: Penguin.
Blunt, Wilfrid, 1962. *Lady Muriel: Lady Muriel Paget, Her Husband and Her Philanthropic Work in Central and Eastern Europe*, London: Methuen.
Bradbury, Malcolm and McFarlane, James (eds) 1976 (1991). *Modernism: A Guide to European Literature 1890–1930*, Harmondsworth: Penguin Books.
Braybon, Gail and Summerfield, Penny, 1987. *Out of the Cage: Women's Experiences in Two World Wars*, London: Pandora Press.
Britain, Ian, 1982. *Fabianism and Culture: A Study in British Socialism and the Arts c. 1884–1918*, Cambridge: Cambridge University Press.
Bronfen, Elisabeth, 1992. *Over Her Dead Body: Death, Femininity and the Aesthetic*, Manchester: Manchester University Press, 1992.
Carnicke, Sharon M., 1989. *The Theatrical Instinct: Nikolai Evreinov and the Russian Theatre of the Early Twentieth Century*, New York: Peter Lang.
Case, Sue-Ellen, 1988. *Feminism and Theatre*, Basingstoke: Macmillan.
Chiba, Yoko, 1996. 'Kori Torahiko and Edith Craig: A Japanese Playwright in London and Toronto', *Comparative Drama*, 30, 4, pp. 431–51.
Clark, Suzanne, 1991. *Sentimental Modernism: Women Writers and the Revolution of the World*, Indiana: Indiana University Press.
Clarke, Ian, 1989. *Edwardian Drama*, London: Faber and Faber.
Cockin, Katharine, 1991. 'New Light on Edith Craig', *Theatre Notebook*, XLV.3, pp. 132–43.
——, 1994. 'The Pioneer Players: Plays of/with Identity' in *Difference in View: Women and Modernism* (ed.) Gabriele Griffin, London: Taylor & Francis, pp. 142–54.
——, 1998a. *Edith Craig (1869–1947): Dramatic Lives*, London: Cassell.
——, 1998b. 'Suffrage Drama' in *The Women's Suffrage Movement: New Feminist Perspectives* (eds) Maroula Joannou and June Purvis, Manchester: Manchester University Press, pp. 110–22.
——, 2000. 'Charlotte Perkins Gilman's *Three Women*: Work, Marriage and the Old(er) Woman', in *Charlotte Perkins Gilman: Optimist Reformer* (eds) Jill Rudd & Val Gough, University of Iowa Press, pp. 74–92.
Colmore, Gertrude, 1912. 'The Nun', *Vote*, 26 June, p. 175.
Counts, Michael, 1988. *Coming Home: The Soldier's Return in Twentieth Century American Drama*, New York: Peter Lang.
Davidoff, Leonore, 1973 (1986). *The Best Circles: Society Etiquette and The Season*, London: The Cresset Library, Century Hutchinson.
Davidoff, Leonore and Catherine Hall, 1987 (1988). *Family Fortunes: Men and Women of the English Middle Class 1780–1850*, London: Hutchinson Education.

Davies, Andrew, 1987. *Other Theatres: The Development of Alternative Experimental Theatre in Britain*, Basingstoke: Macmillan.

Davis, Jill, 1992. 'The New Woman and the New Life', in *The New Woman and Her Sisters: Feminism and Theatre 1850–1914* (eds) Viv Gardner and Susan Rutherford, Hemel Hempstead: Harvester Wheatsheaf, pp. 17–36.

Davis, Tracy, 1989. 'Questions for a Feminist Methodology in Theatre History', in *Interpreting the Theatrical Past: Essays in the Historiography of Performance* (eds) Thomas Postelwait and Bruce A. McConachie, Iowa City: University of Iowa Press, pp. 37–58.

——, 1990. 'The Independent Theatre Society's Revolutionary Scheme for an Uncommercial Theater', *Theatre Journal*, 42, 4, pp. 447–54.

——, 1991. *Actresses as Working Women: Their Social Identity in Victorian Culture*, London: Routledge.

——, 1994. *George Bernard Shaw and the Socialist Theatre*, London: Greenwood Press.

De Bouhelier, Saint-Georges, 1949. 'Edith Craig', in *Edy: Recollections of Edith Craig* (ed.) Eleanor Adlard, London: Frederick Muller, pp. 59–66.

Despard, Charlotte, 1910. *Woman in the New Era*, London: Suffrage Shop.

Dodd, Kathryn (ed.) 1993. *A Sylvia Pankhurst Reader*, Manchester: Manchester University Press.

Dodd, Philip, 1987. 'Englishness and the National Culture', in *Englishness: Politics and Culture 1880–1920*, (eds) Robert Colls & Philip Dodd, London: Croom Helm, pp. 1–28.

Dollimore, Jonathan, 1984 (1989). *Radical Tragedy: Radical Tragedy: Religion, Ideology and Power in the Drama of Shakespeare and His Contemporaries*. Hemel Hempstead: Harvester Wheatsheaf.

——, 1991. *Sexual Dissidence: Augustine to Wilde, Freud to Foucault*, Oxford: Clarendon Press.

Donawerth, Jane L. and Kolmerten, Carol A. (eds) 1994. *Utopian and Science Fiction by Women: Worlds of Difference*, Liverpool: Liverpool University Press.

Dukes, Ashley, 1911. 'The Illusion of Propagandist Drama', The *Freewoman*. 23 November 1911, pp. 13–14.

Dymkowski, Christine, 1992. 'Entertaining Ideas: Edy Craig and the Pioneer Players', *The New Woman and Her Sisters: Feminism and Theatre 1850–1914* (eds) Viv Gardner and Susan Rutherford, Hemel Hempstead: Harvester Wheatsheaf.

Eagleton, Terry, 1990. *The Ideology of the Aesthetic*, Oxford: Basil Blackwell.

Esslin, Martin, 1976 (1991). 'Modernist Drama: Wedekind to Brecht', in *Modernism: A Guide to European Literature 1890–1930*, (eds) Malcolm Bradbury and James McFarlane, Harmondsworth: Penguin, pp. 553–7.

Fenton, S. H, 1910. 'Street "Vote" Selling', *Vote* 9 April, p. 286.

Field, Andrew, 1983. *Djuna: The Life and Times of Djuna Barnes*. New York: G. P. Putnam & Sons.

Finney, Gail, 1989. *Women in Modern Drama: Freud, Feminism and Modern Theater at the Turn of the Century*, Ithaca and London: Cornell University Press.

Ferris, Lesley, 1995. 'The Female Self and Performance: The Case of *The First Actress*', in *Theatre and Feminist Aesthetics*, (eds) Karen Laughlin and Catherine Schuler, Cranbury, New Jersey: Associated University Presses, pp. 242–57.

224 Bibliography

Findlater, Richard, 1967. *Banned! A Review of Theatrical Censorship in Britain*, London: MacGibbon & Kee.
Fisher, James, 1995. 'Edy Craig and the Pioneer Players' Production of Mrs Warren's Profession', *Shaw: The Annual of Bernard Shaw Studies*, 15, pp. 37–56.
Fletcher, John and McFarlane, James, 1991. 'Modernist Drama: Origins and Patterns', in *Modernism: A Guide to European Literature 1890–1930* (eds.) Harmondsworth: Penguin, pp. 499–513.
Forster, E. M. 1908 (1978). *A Room With a View*, Harmondsworth: Penguin.
Foucault, Michel, 1976 (1990). *The History of Sexuality Volume One*, trans. Robert Hurley, Harmondsworth: Penguin.
——, 1975 (1991). *Discipline and Punish: The Birth of the Prison*, trans. Alan Sheridan, Harmondsworth: Penguin.
Frank, Arthur W., 1991. 'For a Sociology of the Body: An Analytical Review', *The Body: Social Process and Cultural Theory* (eds) Mike Featherstone, Mike Hepworth and Bryan S. Turner, London: Sage, pp. 36–102.
Fraser, Flora, 1996. *The Unruly Queen: The Life of Queen Caroline*, London & Basingstoke: Macmillan.
Friedlaender, V. H. 1910. 'The Master Joy', *Votes for Women*, 19 August, p. 763.
Gardner, Viv (ed.) 1985. *Sketches From the Actresses' Franchise League*, Nottingham: Nottingham Drama Texts.
Gardner, Viv and Rutherford, Susan (eds) 1992. *The New Woman and Her Sisters: Feminism and Theatre 1850–1914*, Hemel Hempstead: Harvester Wheatsheaf.
Gilbert, Sandra & Gubar, Susan, 1988. *No Man's Land Volume 1*, New Haven & London: Yale University Press.
Gilder, Rosamund, 1931. *Enter the Actress*, London: Harrap & Co.
Glasgow, Joanne, 1990 (1992). 'What's A Nice Lesbian Like You Doing in the Church of Torquemada? Radclyffe Hall and Other Catholic Converts', in *Lesbian Texts and Contexts: Radical Revisions* (eds) Karla Jay and Joanne Glasgow, New York: New York University Press, pp. 242–54.
Glendinning, Victoria, 1988. *Rebecca West: A Life*, London: Papermac.
Goddard, F. 1918. 'The Pioneer Players', *The Future* March 1918, pp. 104–5.
Goldberg, RoseLee, 1979 (1988) *Performance Art: From Futurism to the Present*, London: Thames & Hudson.
Green, Barbara, 1997. *Spectacular Confessions: Autobiography, Performative Activism, and the Sites of Suffrage 1905–1938*, New York: St. Martin's Press.
Griffin, Gabriele, 1993. *Heavenly Love*. Manchester: Manchester University Press.
Grosskurth, Phyllis, 1985. *Havelock Ellis: A Biography*. New York: New York University Press.
Hamilton, Cicely, 1935. *Life Errant*, London: J. M. Deutsch & Son.
Harding, G. L., 1911. 'Feminism and the Propagandist Drama', The *Freewoman*, 14 December, pp. 76–8.
Harrison, Jane Ellen, 1913 (1918). *Ancient Art and Ritual*, London: Williams and Norgate.
Hawthorn, Jeremy, 1996. *Cunning Passages: New Historicism, Cultural Materialism and Marxism in the Contemporary Literary Debate*, London: Arnold.
Hill, Lesley, 2000. 'The Suffragettes Invented Performance Art', in *The Routledge Reader in Politics and Performance* (ed.) Lizbeth Goodman and Jane de Gay, London: Routledge.

Hirschfield, Claire, 1985, 'The AFL and the Campaign for Women's Suffrage 1908–14', *Theatre Research International*, 10, 2, pp. 129–53.
——, 1987. 'The Suffragist as Playwright in Edwardian England', *Frontiers*, IX, 2, pp. 1–6.
——, 1991.'The Suffrage Play in England 1907–1913', *Cahiers Victoriens et Edouardiens*, 33, pp. 73–85.
Holledge, Julie, 1981. *Innocent Flowers: Actresses in the Edwardian Stage*, London: Virago.
Holroyd, Michael, 1988. *Bernard Shaw Volume I 1856–1898: The Search For Love*, London: Chatto & Windus.
——, 1989. *Bernard Shaw Volume II 1898–1918: The Pursuit of Power*, London: Chatto & Windus.
Housman, Laurence, 1910. 'The Anti-Suffrage Point of View', *Vote*, 12 March, pp. 238–40.
——, 1937. *The Unexpected Years*, London: Jonathan Cape.
Howe, Elizabeth, 1992. *The First English Actresses: Women and Drama 1660–1700*, Cambridge: Cambridge University Press.
Hunt, Hugh, 1978. *The Revels History of Drama in English: Volume II 1880 to the Present Day*, London: Methuen.
Hurd, Michael, 1962. *Immortal Hour: The Life and Period of Rutland Boughton*, London: Routledge & Kegan Paul.
Innes, Christopher, 1992. *Modern British Drama 1890–1990*. Cambridge: Cambridge University Press.
——, 1993. *Avant Garde Theatre 1892–1992*, London: Routledge.
Jeffreys, Sheila, 1985. *The Spinster and Her Enemies: Feminism and Sexuality 1880–1930*, London: Pandora Press.
Jerome, Jerome K., 1926. *My Life and Times*, New York & London: Harper and Brothers.
Joannou, Maroula, 1995. *Ladies Please Don't Smash These Windows*, Oxford: Berg.
Joannou, Maroula and Purvis, June (eds) 1998. *The Women's Suffrage Movement: New Feminist Perspectives*, Manchester: Manchester University Press.
John, Angela, 1995. *Elizabeth Robins: Staging a Life 1862–1952*, London: Routledge.
Kaplan, Joel and Stowell, Sheila, 1994. *Theatre and Fashion: From Oscar Wide to the Suffragettes*, Cambridge: Cambridge University Press.
Keating, Peter (ed.) 1976. *Into Unknown England 1866–1913: Selections From the Social Explorers*. Manchester: Manchester University Press.
Kelly, Katherine E., 1994. 'The Actresses' Franchise League Prepares for War: Feminist Theater in Camouflage', *Theatre Survey*, 35, 1, pp. 121–37.
Kent, Susan Kingsley, 1987 (1990). *Sex and Suffrage in Britain 1860–1914*, London: Routledge.
Kershaw, Baz, 1992. *The Politics of Performance: Radical Theatre as Cultural Intervention*, London: Routledge.
Keyssar, Helen, 1984. *Feminist Theatre: An Introduction to Plays of Contemporary British and American Women*, London: Macmillan.
Kingston, Gertrude, 1937. *Curtsey While You're Thinking*, London: Williams & Norgate.
Knoblock, Edward, 1939. *Round the Room: An Autobiography*, London: Chapman and Hall.

Knowles, Dorothy, 1934. *The Censor, The Drama and The Film*, London: George Allen and Unwin.
Kohn, Marek, 1992. *Dope Girls: The Birth of the British Drug Underground*, London: Lawrence & Wishart.
Kruger, Loren, 1995. 'The (Dis)play's the Thing: Gender and Public Sphere in Contemporary British Theatre', in *Theatre and Feminist Aesthetics* (eds) Karen Laughlin and Catherine Schuler, Cranbury, New Jersey: Associated University Presses, pp. 40–65.
Landry, Donna and MacLean, Gerald (eds) 1993. *Materialist Feminisms*, Oxford: Blackwell.
Laughlin, Karen, 1995. 'Why Feminist Aesthetics?', in *Theatre and Feminist Aesthetics* (eds) Karen Laughlin and Catherine Schuler, Cranbury, New Jersey: Associated University Presses, pp. 9–24.
Lemon, Lee T. and Reis, Marion J. (eds) 1965. *Russian Formalist Criticism: Four Essays*, Lincoln & London: University of Nebraska Press.
Lewis, Jane (ed.) 1987. *Before the Vote Was Won: Arguments For and Against Women's Suffrage 1864–1896*, London: Routledge & Kegan Paul.
Litz, A. Walton, 1996. 'Florence Farr: A "Transitional Woman"', in *High and Low Moderns: Literature and Culture 1889–1939* (eds) Maria DiBattista and Lucy McDiarmid, Oxford: Oxford University Press, pp. 85–90.
Lutyens, Mary, 1990. *The Life and Death of Krishnamurti*, London: Rider.
Lytton, Lady Constance, 1914 (1988). *Prisons and Prisoners: The Stirring Testimony of a Suffragette*, London: Virago.
McCarthy, Desmond, 1918 (1940). 'The Girl and the Puppet', *Drama*, London: Putnam, pp. 136–40.
Merquior, J.G. 1991. *Foucault*, London: Fontana.
Morley, Ann and Stanley, Liz (eds) 1988. *The Life and Death of Emily Wilding Davison*, London: Women's Press.
Mulvihill, Margaret, 1989. *Charlotte Despard*, London: Pandora.
Nevinson, Margaret Wynne, 1926. *Life's Fitful Fever: A Volume of Memories*, London: A. & C. Black.
——, 1911. 'A Bewildered Playwright', *Vote* 3 June, p. 68.
Norquay, Glenda (ed.) 1995. *Voices and Votes: A Literary Anthology of the Women's Suffrage Campaign*. Manchester: Manchester University Press.
Offen, Karen, 1992. 'Defining Feminism: A Comparative Historical Approach', *Beyond Equality and Difference*, ed. Gisela Bock and Susan James, London: Routledge.
Orme, Michael, 1936. *J. T. Grein: The Story of a Pioneer 1862–1935*, London: John Murray.
Park, Sowon, 1997. 'The First Professional: The Women Writers' Suffrage League', *Modern Languages Quarterly*, 58, 2, pp. 185–200.
Pavis, Patrice, 1992. *Theatre at the Crossroads of Culture*, trans. Loren Kruger, London and New York: Routledge.
Pethick Lawrence, Emmeline, 1938. *My Part in a Changing World*, London: Victor Gollancz.
Petroff, Elizabeth, 1986. *Medieval Women Writers*, New York: University Press.
Phelan, Peggie, 1993. *Unmarked: The Politics of Performance*, London: Routledge.
Poggioli, Renato, 1968. *The Theory of the Avant Garde*, Trans. Gerald Fitzgerald, Cambridge, Massachusetts: The Belknap Press.

Pogson, Rex, 1952. *Miss Horniman: and the Gaiety Theatre, Manchester*, London: Rockliff.
Raitt, Suzanne, 1993. *Vita & Virginia: The Work and Friendship of V. Sackville-West and Virginia Woolf*. Oxford: Clarendon Press.
Reynolds, Kimberley and Humble, Nicola (eds) 1993. *Victorian Heroines: Representations of Femininity in Nineteenth-Century Literature and Art*, Hemel Hempstead: Harvester Wheatsheaf.
Roose-Evans, James, 1970 (1989). *Experimental Theatre from Stanislavsky to Peter Brook*, London: Routledge & Kegan Paul.
Rowbotham, Sheila and Weeks, Jeffrey, 1977. *Socialism and the New Life: The Personal and Sexual Politics of Edward Carpenter and Havelock Ellis*, London: Pluto Press.
Sage, Lorna, 1986. 'The Available Space', in *Women's Writing: A Challenge to Theory* (ed.) Moira Monteith, Brighton: Harvester Press, pp. 15–33.
St. John, Christopher, 1909. 'A Defence of the Fighting Spirit', *Votes for Women* 18 June, pp. 808–9.
——, 1910. 'Mrs Despard: An Impression', *Woman in the New Era*, by Charlotte Despard, London: Suffrage Shop.
——, 1912. 'The Morality of Speaking Out', *Votes for Women*, 7 June.
——, 1925 (1929). 'Introduction', *The Rising Sun: A Play in Four Acts*, by Herman Heijermans, trans. Christopher St. John, London: Noel Douglas.
——, 1935. *Christine Murrell, M.D.: Her Life and Work*, London: Williams & Norgate.
——, 1949. 'Close Up', in *Edy: Recollections of Edith Craig*, (ed.) Eleanor Adlard, London: Frederick Muller, pp. 16–34.
Samuel, Raphael *et al.* (eds) 1985. *Theatres of the Left*, London: Routledge & Kegan Paul.
Sayler, Oliver M., 1923. *The Russian Theatre*, London: Brentano's.
Schoonderwoerd, N. 1963. *J. T. Grein Ambassador of the Theatre 1862–1935: A Study in Anglo-Continental Theatrical Relations*, Assen, Netherlands: Von Gorcum.
Schreiner, Olive, 1890 (1993). 'Three Dreams in a Desert', in *Daughters of Decadence: Women Writers of the Fin de Siècle* (ed.) Elaine Showalter, London: Virago.
Sedgwick, Eve Kosofsky, 1985. *Between Men: English Literature and Male Homosocial Desire*, New York: Columbia University Press.
Sheppard, Alice, 1993. 'Suffrage Art and Feminism', in *Aesthetics in Feminist Perspective* (eds) Hilde Hein and Carolyn Korsmeyer, Bloomington & Indianapolis: Indiana University Presss, pp. 76–90.
Showalter, Elaine, 1987. *The Female Malady: Women, Madness and English Culture 1830–1980*, London: Virago.
——, 1991. *Sexual Anarchy: Gender and Culture at the Fin de Siècle*, London: Bloomsbury.
Sims, George, 1992. 'Rex v. Pemberton-Billing', *London Magazine*, 32, 3–4, pp. 99–108.
Smith, E. A., 1993. *A Queen on Trial: The Affair of Queen Caroline*, Stroud: Alan Sutton.
Spender, Dale and Hayman, Carole (eds) 1985. *How the Vote Was Won and Other Suffragette Plays*, London: Methuen.
Stokes, John, 1972. *Resistible Theatres: Enterprise and Experiment in the Late Nineteenth Century*, London: Paul Elk Books.

Stowell, Sheila, 1992. *A Stage of Their Own: Feminist Playwrights of the Suffrage Era*, Ann Arbor: University of Michigan Press.

——, 1993. 'Rehabilitating Realism', *Journal of Dramatic Theory and Criticism*, 6, 2, pp. 81–8.

Swears, Herbert, 1937. *When All's Said And Done*, London: Geoffrey Biles.

Taylor, Rosemary, 1993. *In Letters of Gold: The Story of Sylvia Pankhurst and the East London Suffragettes in Bow*, London: Stepney Books.

Thompson, Paul, 1975 (1992). *The Edwardians: The Remaking of British Society*, London: Routledge.

Tickner, Lisa, 1987. *The Spectacle of Women: Imagery of the Suffrage Campaign 1907–1914*, London: Chatto & Windus.

Trewin, J. C., 1963. *The Birmingham Repertory Theatre 1913–1963*, London: Barrie and Rockliff.

Vicinus, Martha, 1985. *Independent Women: Work and Community for Single Women 1850–1920*, London: Virago Press.

Wandor, Michelene, 1990. 'The Impact of Feminism on the Theatre', in *Feminist Literary Theory: A Reader* (ed.) Mary Eagleton, Oxford: Basil Blackwell, pp. 104–6.

Warner, Marina, 1981. *Joan of Arc: The Image of Female Heroism*, London: Weidenfeld & Nicolson.

Warrender, Lady Maud, 1933. *My First Sixty Years*, London: Cassell.

Webster, Margaret, 1969. *The Same Only Different: Five Generations of a Great Theatre Family*, London: Victor Gollancz.

Weedon, Chris, 1987. *Feminist Practice and Poststructuralist Theory*, Oxford: Blackwell.

Wells, H. G., 1909 (1993). *Ann Veronica*. London: Everyman.

West, Rebecca, 1912, 'A Modern Crusader', *The Freewoman*, 23 May, p. 8.

Whitelaw, Lis, 1990. *The Life and Rebellious Times of Cicely Hamilton*, London: Women's Press.

Whitworth, Geoffrey, 1951. *The Making of a National Theatre*, London: Faber & Faber.

Williams, Raymond, 1977. 'Social Environment and Theatrical Environment: The Case of English Naturalism', *English Drama: Forms and Development: Essays in Honour of Muriel Clare Bradbrook* (ed.) Marie Axton and Raymond Williams, Cambridge: Cambridge University Press. pp. 203–23.

——, 1977, *Marxism and Literature*. Oxford: Oxford University Press, 1977.

——, 1980 (1989). *Problems in Materialism and Culture: Selected Essays*, London: Verso.

——. (1980) 1989. 'The Bloomsbury Fraction', *Problems in Materialism and Culture: Selected Essays*, London: Verso. pp. 148–69.

——, 1981 (1983). *Culture*, London: Fontana.

——, 1983 (1985). *Writing in Society*, London: Verso.

Wilson, Elizabeth, 1985. *Adorned in Dreams: Fashion and Modernity*, London: Virago Press.

Wilson, Katharina M., 1984. 'The Saxon Canoness: Hrotsvit of Gandersheim', in *Medieval Women Writers* (ed.) Katharina M. Wilson, Manchester: Manchester University Press, pp. 30–63.

——, 1998. *Hrotsvit of Gandersheim: Her Works*, London: D. S. Brewer.

Woodfield, James, 1984. *English Theatre in Transition 1881–1914*, London: Croom Helm.

Woolf, Virginia, 1919 (1986). *Night and Day*, London: Grafton Books.
——, 1979. *Women and Writing* (ed.) Michèle Barrett, London: Women's Press.
——, 1988. 'The Higher Court', *New Statesman*, 17 April 1920, in *Essays of Virginia Woolf* (ed.) Andrew McNeillie. London: Hogarth Press, pp. 207–10.
——, 1929 (1993). *A Room of One's Own and Three Guineas* (ed.) Michèle Barrett, Harmondsworth: Penguin.
Zimmerman, Bonnie, 1986. 'What Has Never Been: An Overview of Lesbian Feminist Literary Criticism', in *The New Feminist Criticism: Essays on Women, Literature and Theory* (ed.) Elaine Showalter, London: Virago Press, 1986, pp. 200–24.

Index

A Chat with Mrs Chicky (Glover), 65, 91
'A Daughter of the Morning' (de Selincourt), 56
'A Defence of the Fighting Spirit' (St. John), 76
A Dilemma (Campbell), 124–5
A Doll's House (Ibsen), 16, 36, 45, 51–2, 158
A Fair Suffragette, 124
A Matter of Money (Hamilton), 122–3
A Merry Death (Evreinov), 155, 173, 178, 180, 184
A Modern Crusader (Hobson), 48, 50, 63, 64, 65, 144
'A Night Out' (Nevinson), 86
A Pageant of Great Women (Hamilton), 34, 68, 78, 79, 82, 83, 84, 86, 93, 121, 140, 196
A Room with a View (Forster), 113
Abbas, Acton, 138, 153
Abortion, 21, 22; *see also* contraception; pregnancy; single parenthood
Achurch, Janet, 7, 16
Actors
  class composition of, 26; *see also* class
  female, 26; *and see* sexual harassment in theatre; *and under* names of actors
  see also theatre, professionalisation of
Actors' Association, 2, 29, 30
Actresses' Franchise League, 8, 14, 27, 48, 68, 135, 136, 144
Adultery, 114
Agit-prop, 44
Alecheim, Sholom, 114
Alhambra Theatre, 23, 24, 161
Alice in Ganderland (Housman), 93
Allan, Maud, 157, 158, 159, 162, 163
Allegory, 71
Ambassador's Theatre, 32

Ancient Art and Ritual (Harrison), 186
Andreiev, Leonid, 5, 45, 155, 173
Ann Veronica (Wells), 72, 101, 103, 128
Anti-naturalism, 5, 172
Anti-realism, 5
Anti-Semitism (Jewish stereotypes), 95, 106
Anti-suffragism, 74–5, 88
Anti-Suffrage Waxworks (Hamilton), 82, 159
Anti-Sweating League, 94; *see also* sweated labour; working women
Antoine, André, 17
Appia, Adolphe, 171, 172
Archer, William, 154, 176, 188
Arnold, Matthew, 16, 66
Art theatre, chapter, 8 passim
Artists' Suffrage League, 76, 77
Ashwell, Lena, 31, 87, 91, 144
Asquith, Lady Cynthia, 20, 21, 121, 157–8
Asquith, Herbert, 4
Atwood, Tony (Clare), 8, 32, 115, 178
Auerbach, Helena, 27, 83
Avant-garde, 11, 35, 38, 45

Baker, Elizabeth, 29
Barnes, Djuna, 130
Barrault, Jean-Louis, 177, 183
Batten, Mabel (Ladye), 160
Beastie (de Selincourt), 53, 54–6, 61
Bellwood, Bessie, 23
Bensusan, Inez, 79
Bijou Theatre, 79
Black 'Ell (Malleson), 142
'Black Friday', 83, 118; *see also* violence against women
Blavatsky, Mme Helena, 68; *see also* theosophy
Breaking a Butterfly on a Wheel (Jones and Herman), 52; cf. *A Doll's House*
British Drama League, 163

Index 231

Brookfield, Charles (reader for Lord Chamberlain), 17, 19
Butler, Josephine, 100; *and see* Contagious Diseases Acts

Campaigns: against Insurance Act; working conditions; for divorce reform; legal reform, 47–8
Campbell, Constance, 124
Cannan, Gilbert, 62
Carleton, Billie, 161
Caroline of Brunswick (Queen Caroline), 4, 18, 121, 122; *and see* double standard; *Pains and Penalties*
Caroline Society, 19
Carpenter, Edward, 27, 58
Carson, Charles, 189
Casey, W.F., 149
Cat and Mouse (Prisoners Temporary Discharge for Ill Health) Act, 123, 140; *see also* self-sacrifice; violence against women
Catholic Women's Suffrage Society, 131–2
Catholicism, 109, 125–6, 132; *see also* martyr; nun, iconography of; religious discourse; self-sacrifice
Cavendish, Margaret, 71
Celibacy, 114, 127, 129, 132; *see also* marriage, rejection of; nun
Censor, Censorship, 2, 17–24, 34, 35, 47; *see also* Lord Chamberlain's Office; unlicensed plays
Charlot, André, 23, 24, 161
Charrington, Charles, 7
Chekhov, Anton, 5, 114, 164, 173, 185
Child care, 94
Churchill, Lady Randolph, 137, 160
Clarion, 90
Clarke, J.H., 162
Class, 60, 92
  class conflict, 55
  class tourism, 105
  middle-class women, 3, 89; *and see* Pioneer Players, class composition
  working-class women, 56, 88, 89, 91, 99
Claudel, Paul, 4, 14, 45, 126, 127, 169, 171, 177, 181, 186
Cohen, Mrs Herbert, 119, 120
Collaboration, 78–9
Collins, Sewell, 145
Colman Smith, Pamela, 168, 177–8
Colmore, Gertrude, 93, 129, 158
Comedy
  romantic, 66
  subversive, 54, 65; and see *Idle Women*; *Race Suicide*
Conciliation Bill, 76–7, 121
Contagious Diseases Acts, 58, 100, 157; *see also* Josephine Butler, Defence of the Realm Act, prostitution
Contraception, 62
Cooper Willis, Irene, 28, 142, 145, 164
Copyright, 2, 76
Coronation Society, 20
Court Theatre, 51
Coverture, 24, 116
Craig, Edith
  career of, 7
  charity work, 141–2
  comparisons with Edward Gordon Craig, 176
  as director, 7, 171–2, 172–4
  and female desire, 115
  founder of Pioneer Players, 1
  Pioneer Players committee member, 27
  as producer, 46
  and propaganda, 43
  staging techniques, 171–2
  and WFL, 79, 80
  and women's suffrage theatre, 6
  and see Pioneer Players passim
Craig, Edward Gordon, 117, 171, 176, 179, 180
Cranford (Gaskell), 71
Crippen, Dr, 123
Cross-dressing, 128; *and see* Joan of Arc

'D' Company (Malleson), 142
D'Este Scott, A., 21, 102
Dance, dancer, 157, 158, 160–1, 177

De Bouhelier, Saint-Georges, 5, 142, 168, 172, 188
De la Crus, Suor Juana Ines, 110
De Selincourt, Hugh, 54
'Death and the Lady', 177, 178, 185
Defence of the Realm Act, 157
Delia Blanchflower (Ward), 58, 128
Despard, Charlotte, 68, 69, 115, 130, 145
'Detained by Marital Authority' (Nevinson), 116
Di Giacomo, Salvatore, 119
Diana of Dobson's (Hamilton), 88, 91, 104
Divorce, 123, 124–6
divorce reform, 48
Dorynne, Jess, 101, 115, 117, 195
Double standard, 54, 56, 90, 92, 116, 118, 121
Douglas, Lord Alfred, 162
Dreams (Schreiner), 71
Dress reform, 39, 58
Drug-taking, 159, 161–2
Drummond, Flora, 27
Drury Lane Theatre, 83
Dukes, Ashley, 49
Dull Monotony (Cannan), 62
Durrans, William, 162

East London Federation of Suffragettes, 157; *see also* Sylvia Pankhurst
Easter Rising, 149
Echegeray, Jose, 115, 138, 150, 154
Edge O'Dark (John), 147
Eliot, T.S., 192
Ellen Young (Enthoven and Goulding), 159–61
Ellis, Edith, 29
Ellis, Havelock, 56, 116
Elton, George, 169
England's Holy War (Cooper Willis), 142
Englishness, 35; *see also* national identity
Enoch Arden (Tennyson), 145
Entertainments Tax, 31, 143
Enthoven, Gabrielle, 27, 159
Eristoff, Princess, 160
Eugenics, 3, 59, 62, 64, 145
satirised in *Race Suicide*, 63

Eugenics Education Society, 59
Everyman Theatre, Hampstead, 189
Evreinov, Nikolai, 4, 10, 21, 23, 142, 155, 166, 173, 179–80, 184
Experimentation, 17
Expressionism, 185, 186

Fabian Society, 39, 64
associated with Stage Society, 55
Fabianism, 60
Farjeon, Herbert, 47
Farr, Florence, 16
Fellowship of the New Life, 58
Female employment *see* working women
Female literary tradition, 36
Female muse, 191
Femininity
dissident, 17, 36
fashionable, 75
Feminist drama, 51
First World War, 33, 37, chapter, 7 passim
Fisher, Cecil, 47, 97, 174
Fisher White, J., 24, 120, 170
Fitzgerald, Hon. Mrs E., 28
Food Education Society, 144; *see also* vegetarianism
Formalism, 45
Forster, E.M., 13
Foucault, Michel, 82, 116, 122, 128
'Free theatre' movement, 14, 16, 17, 34, 35
Freewoman, 48, 49
Friedlander, V.H., 68, 69
Frondaie, Charles, 21
Fuller, Loie, 158
Futurism, 5, 180, 186
Fyfe, H. Hamilton, 34, 62, 63

Gaiety Theatre, Manchester, 34, 62, 79, 106
Galsworthy, John, 16
Garrud, Mrs, 104
Gaskell, Elizabeth, 71, 141
Gender, 60, 92, 123, 128
identity, 36
ideology, 21
Gerald, Queenie, 102

Ghosts (Ibsen), 18, 21
Gilman, Charlotte Perkins, 71, 93, 117, 120
'Girls on the Land', 168
Glaspell, Susan, 1, 115, 123, 178, 185, 188–9
Glover, Evelyn, 91
Goulding, Edmund, 159
Grand Theatre, Islington, 21
Granville-Barker Harley, 16, 19, 58, 66; satirised, 62
Gray, Delphine (pseud.) *see* Lady Margaret Sackville
Grein, J.T., 18, 30, 47, 152, 162–3, 183
'Gymnasie', 114

Hall, Radclyffe, 132, 133, 159, 160
Hamilton, Cicely, 6, 26, 29, 32, 36, 46, 49, 63, 67, 75, 79, 81, 83–4, 88, 91, 112, 115, 122, 139, 168, 192–3
Harding, G.L., 49, 50, 51
Harraden, Beatrice, 79
Harrison, Jane, 186
Harvey, Kate, 23
Harwood, H.M., 102
Heijermans, Herman, 4, 90, 97, 98, 138, 172
Herland (Gilman), 71
Herman, H., 52
Hobson, Florence Edgar, 48, 63, 64, 144
Honour Thy Father (Harwood), 99, 102, 103–5
Housman, Laurence, 18, 19, 27, 47, 93, 112, 115, 121, 149, 168
Housman, Clemence, 88
How the Vote Was Won (Hamilton and St. John), 6, 68, 79, 82, 85, 90, 116
Hrotsvit, 1, 4, 8, 107–10, 126, 130; *see also* Catholicism; nun; *Paphnutius*; prostitution; self-sacrifice
Hughes, Margaret, 4, 46, 67, 85–7, 91, 121

Ibsen, Henrik, 10, 16, 18
Idle Women (Ponsonby), 53, 62, 64
Illegitimacy *see* single parenthood
Independent Labour Party, 90
Imlay, Agnes, 79

Imperialism, 3
In the Workhouse (Nevinson), 24, 46, 47, 62, 78, 99, 115, 116–17
Incident at the Savoy, 19
Incorporated Stage Society, 37
Independent Theatre, 18, 21, 26, 32, 34, 91
Insurance Act, 97, 118
Insurrection (Casey), 149–50, 190
International Suffrage Shop, 19, 27, 39, 47
Irving, Henry, 46

Jack and Jill and a Friend (Hamilton), 32, 46, 56, 91–3, l56
Japanese drama *see* Torahiko Kori
Jerome, Jerome K., 30
Jerrold, Mary, 126
Jewish League for Woman Suffrage, 27
Joan of Arc, 97, 127, 128; *see also* martyr, militant
John, Gwen, 135, 145
Jones, H.A., 52, 60

Kamerny Theatre, 177
Kanawa (Kori), 115, 155, 171, 175
Kauffman, Reginald Wright, 102
Kennedy, Margaret, 80
Keppel, Mrs George, 162
King's Hall, National Sporting Club, 1, 2, 21, 102
Kingston, Gertrude, 19, 60, 101, 172, 189
Kingsway Theatre, 1, 31, 41, 87, 91
Knoblock, Edward, 21, 104, 105
Kori, Torahiko, 15, 155–6, 171, 175
Krasinksi, Zygmunt, 152

L'Estrange, Geraldine, 28
Lawson, Marie, 27, 28, 79
Legal status of women, 25
Lesbianism, lesbian identity, 114, 132, 159
Levey, Ethel, 161, 177
Liberal Party, opposition to female suffrage, 4
Licence to perform, 17–18; *and see* Lord Chamberlain's Office
Lion, Leon, 32

234 Index

Little Theatre, 2, 19, 60, 138, 150, 172
Lloyd George, David, 47, 97, 123
Lloyd, Marie, 23
Longfellow, Malvina, 161
Lord Chamberlain's Office, 17; *and see* Charles Brookfield; censorship; Ernest Radford; G.S. Street
Louys, Pierre, 20, 21, 157
Lowther, Mrs Christopher (Ina Pelly), 155–6, 177, 178, 185
Luck of War (John), 135, 145–7, 150
Lyceum Theatre, 7
Lysistrata, 112
Lyttleton, Edith, 47, 90, 94–6, 168
Lytton, Lady Constance, 72

MacArthur, Mary, 89
MacKaye, Hazel, 82
Macrena (St John), 130, 131, 132, 141
Macrena, Irena, 4, 101, 131; *see also* nun
Malleson, Miles, 6, 142
Mallon, J. J., 94
Manners, Lady Diana, 160
Marginalised voice, marginalisation, 4, 56
Marlborough, Duchess of, 144
Marriage
  as business exchange, 114
  economic determinants of, 122
  interclass, 59
  reform, 60
  rejection of, 113
Marriage as a Trade (Hamilton), 63, 112, 122, 130
Marsden, Dora, 48
Martyr, 114, 126
  militant, 130, 132–3
  see also self-sacrifice
Mathews, Rose, 30
Matriarchy, 128
Matters, Muriel, 94
Matterson, Marjorie, 159
Mayo, Winifred, 27, 79
Mazzini, 151
McCarthy, Desmond, 5, 137, 138, 158
McGowan, Margaret Slieve, 51–2
Men's League for Women's Suffrage, 27
Meyerhold, Vsevolod, 171, 172, 173

Miles, Eustace, 21
Militancy, 128
  militant nun, 130
  suffrage, 77
Mill, J. S., 3
Millenium Hall (Scott), 71
Modern Troubadors (Ashwell), 144
Modernism, 3, 10, 11, 45
Monkhouse, Allan, 62
Morris, Margaret, 177
Moscow Art Theatre, 179
Mother's Arms, 94; *see also* child care; Sylvia Pankhurst
Motherhood, mothers, 24, 64, 84, 116, 119
Mouse (Knoblock), 21, 22, 105, 114
Mrs Warren's Profession (Shaw), 28, 47, 100–1, 103, 120–3
Murrell, Christine, 140, 168
Music hall, 23

National culture, 34
National drama, 2
National Food Reform Association, 48, 144, 145
National Health Week, 144
National identity, 35, 82
National insecurity, 34
Naturalism, 5, 10, 45, 51, 171
  fourth wall of, 172, 178
Nepotism, male, 26
Nevinson, Margaret Wynne, 24, 47, 78, 79, 80, 86, 115, 116, 168, 186, 195
New Critics, 192
New Woman, 53, 54, 57, 58, 59, 60, 74; cf. *raisonneur*; Womanly Woman
No Conscription Fellowship, 142
Nordon, Florence, 28
Nothing Like Leather (Monkhouse), 62
Nudity, 158
Nun, 114, 126–7, 129–31; *see also* celibacy; rejection of marriage; self-sacrifice
NUWSS, 77

O'Connor, Una, 189–90
O'Malley, Ellen, 101
O'Riordan, Conal, 60, 61
Oldfield, Nancy, 67, 83

On the East Side (St John), 115, 152
On the High Road (Chekhov), 114, 173
"Ope' (Colmore), 158

Pacifism, 141, 142
Pageants, 68, 82
Paget, Lady Muriel, 23
Pain and Penalties (Housman), 18–19, 47, 121
Pall Mall Gazette, 102
Pan in Ambush (Patterson), 159, 185
Pankhurst, Christabel, 62, 102
Pankhurst, Emmeline, 77, 123
Pankhurst, Sylvia, 94, 142, 157
Paphnutius, 1, 8, 32, 107–10, 171
Parrott, Ruth, 79
Paterson Strike Pageant, 82
'Patrolling the Gutter' (Sharp), 90, 105
Patterson, Marjorie, 159, 185
Pemberton-Billing, Noel, 157, 162
Pethick Lawrence, Emmeline, 59–60, 72, 112, 151
Pethick Lawrence, Frederick, 59–60
Picadilly Flat Case, 106
Pioneer, symbolism of, 68–71
Pioneer Club, 73
Pioneer Players
  accused of gender bias, 46
  acting rights held, 34
  advisory committee, 37
  amateur actors, 30
  annual general meetings, 26
  annual reports, 9, 26
  antagonism in plays performed by, 43
  as art theatre, 14, chapter, 8 passim
  class membership of, 6, 34
  commitment to form, 169
  commitment to new plays, 1
  committee structure, 8–9
  directors, 32
  executive committee, 28
  finances, 30
  financial constraints, 169, 170
  iconoclasm of, 12
  lighting in productions, 172, 173–4
  membership and audience, 5, 9, 26
  membership rates, 29
  membership sex ratio, 27
  music, use of, 177
  non-subscription performances, 34
  openness of, 7
  play programmes, advertisements, 13
  play selection criteria, 5
  policy change, 189; *and see* art theatre
  political motivation, 6
  prioritisation of director, 171
  production techniques, 169
  professional actors, 29
  props and scenery, use of, 2, 173
  representation of gender, 6
  response to First World War, 136–7
  reviews, 46, 71
  stage design, 170
  vs. Stage Society, 38–9
  subscription performances, 10
  subscription rates, 14, 29
  visual arts, 177
  visual effects, 2
  women writers, support for, 31
  writers, sex ratio, 31–2
  see also Edith Craig, Christopher St. John *and under play titles*
Plank, George, 178, 184
Play Actors, 29, 79
'Play of ideas', 40, 49, chapter, 3 passim
Playfair, Nigel, 29
Ponsonby, Magdalen, 62, 64
Potapenko, Marie, 23
Poverty, 107
Power, appropriation of, 73
Pregnancy, 21
Press Cuttings (Shaw), 79
Price Hughes, Katherine, 151
Propaganda, 7, 38, chapter, 3 passim
Prostitution, 25, 99, 100–4, 105–7, 108–9

Quem Quaeritis, 110

Race Suicide (Fyfe), 34, 53, 61, 63
Radford, Ernest (reader for Lord Chamberlain), 17
Raisonneur, woman as, 53, 56, 60; cf. New Woman; Womanly Woman
Rape, 119, 131

Rathbone, Basil, 29
Realism, 45
Reinhardt, Max, 171
Religious discourse, 70, 114, 127
Religious drama, 178
Religious writing, 86
Richardson, Mary, 54
Robins, Elizabeth, 16, 19
Romanticism, 130
Romanticismo (Rovetta), 151, 152
Ross, Derek (*Daily Herald* reviewer), 94–5, 96, 98, 105
Rovetta, Gerolamo, 32, 115, 151
Rubenstein, Ida, 158
Rubinstein, H.F., 164
Russian Ballet, 108
Rutland, Duchess of, 160
Ryley, Madeleine Lucette, 80, 096

Sackville, Lady Margaret, 57
Sacrifice, 126, 130; *and see* self-sacrifice
Sado-masochism, 127
Salome (Wilde), 157, 158, 162
Same-sex desire, 114, 129, 132; *and see* lesbianism
Santley, Kate, 18
Savoy Theatre, 1
Schreiner, Olive, 56, 68, 71, 72, 85, 92, 93
Scott, Sarah, 71
Sedley, Sir Charles, 86
Self-defence, 118
Self-parody, 63
Self-sacrifice, 70, 72, 105, 126, 131
Separate-spheres ideology, 12, 15, 74, 85, 88–9, 99, 115, 133
Seruya, Sime, 27, 47
Sexual abuse, 131
Sexual choice, 21
Sexual desire, 158
Sexual harassment, 107
  in theatre, 26
Sexual independence, 128
Sexual intercourse, reference in theatre, 21
Sexuality, 21, 113, 128
Seyler, Athene, 39
Shakespeare, Judith, 182, 191–2
Sharp, Evelyn, 90, 105

Shaw, Charlotte, 27
Shaw, George Bernard, 49, 10, 16, 28, 29, 37, 47, 49, 51, 57, 66, 60, 79, 100, 148; Shaw satirised, 62
Sheepshanks, Mary, 142, 153
Shelley Society, 18
Sherbrooke, Michael, 114
Single parenthood, 60, 115, 117–19
Sleddall, Elaine, 120
Smith, Lady Sybil, 28
Smyth, Ethel, 54
Social Darwinism, 3
Social mobility, 58, 59
Socialism, fear of, 59
Society for the Study of Sex Psychology, 27
Society of Authors, 79
Spinster-suffragette, 114, 128; *and see* celibacy; marriage, rejection of
St. John, Christopher, 68, 19, 23, 27, 28, 47, 67, 75, 94, 96, 115, 130, 131, 132, 133, 139–40, 152, 163, 164, 196
Stage Society, 9, 26, 29, 36–9, 135, 143
Stainton, J.S., 113, 128
Stead, W.T., 102
Stewart, Nona, 28
Stopes, Marie, 62
Street, G.S. (reader for Lord Chamberlain), 17, 22, 38
Subjectivity, 73–4
Subscription societies, unlicensed performances, 18
Sudermann, Herman, 185
Suffrage
  campaign for, 3
  economic arguments for, 88
Suffrage activism
  as class tourism, 90
  as religious commitment, 127
Suffrage artists, 75
Suffrage Atelier, 27, 30, 76, 77
Suffrage drama, 2
Suffrage movement, 74–5
  as Cause, 113
  cross-membership of, 78
  imagery, 75, 89, 127
  militancy, 77

use of reversal and mimicry, 68, 75
Suffragettes, 3, 74, 85; *and see*
    'Black Friday'; militancy, suffrage;
    Emmeline Pankhurst;
    spinster-suffragette; suffrage
    movment
Suffragette Alphabet (Housman), 93
Suffragette Sally (Colmore), 93, 124
Suffragists, 77, 118
    appropriation of theatre, 7
    and see Emmeline Pethick
        Lawrence; suffrage
        movement; *Votes for Women*;
        WSPU
Suppressed Desires (Glaspell), 189
Swanwick, Helena, 141, 142
Swears, Herbert, 39
Sweated labour, 88, 91, 94, 95; *and see*
    working-class women
Symbolism, symbolic drama, 71, 130,
    173, 185, 186
Synthetic theatre, 180

Tax Resistance League, 88
Tennyson, Alfred Lord, 145
Terry, Ellen, 7, 27, 28, 46, 48–0
Terry, Olive, 27, 28
The Actress of Today, 87
The Apple (Bensusan), 79
'The Artist' (Malleson), 142
The Bear (Chekhov), 114, 164
The Call (Zangwill), 118
The Caroline Society, 19
The Children's Carnival (de Bouhelier),
    142, 188
The Cleansing Stain (Echegeray), 115,
    138, 150, 154–5
The Conference (Sackville), 53, 56, 57,
    58, 59
The Coronation (St. John and Thursby),
    19, 47, 94, 96–7, 138
The Daughters of Ishmael (D'Este Scott),
    21, 102–3
The Dear Departing (Andreiev), 155, 173
The Description of a New World
    (Cavendish), 71
The Divine Comedy (Kraskinksi), 152
'The Duel' (de Maupassant/Williams),
    154, 182

The Exchange (Claudel), 169, 172,
    181
The First Actress (St. John), 46, 67, 68,
    85–6, 91, 121, 159, 197; *see also*
    Margaret Hughes
The French Players, 152
The Girl and the Puppet (Louys and
    Frondaie), 20, 21, 152, 157,
    173
The Good Hope (Heyerman), 90, 97,
    98–9, 172
The Great Day (Fisher), 47, 97–8, 174,
    182
The Great Scourge and How to End It
    (Christabel Pankhurst), 62, 102
The Higher Court (Young), 47, 125–6,
    181–2
The Home Breakers (Stainton), 113, 128
The Hostage (Claudel), 169, 170, 178,
    184
'The Illusion of Propaganda Drama'
    (Dukes), 49
The Inca of Perusalem (Shaw), 148, 149
The Ladies Almanac (Barnes), 130
The Last Visit (Suderman), 185
The Level Crossing (Cohen), 119, 120,
    182
The Liars (Jones), 60–1
'The March of the Women'
    (Hamilton), 54
The Marrying of Ann Leete (Granville-
    Barker), 58
The Masquers, 187, 193
'The Master Joy' (Friedlander), 68, 69
The Month of Mary (di Giacomo), 115,
    119
'The Nun' (Colmore), 93, 129
The Parasites (Mathew), 30
The Patience of the Sea (O'Riordan), 53,
    56, 60, 64
The Quitter (Collins), 145, 147–8, 150,
    169
The Rising Sun (Heijerman), 138
The Street, 105, 106, 107
*The Suffrage Annual and Women's Who's
    Who*, 78
The Surprise of His Life (Dorynne), 99,
    101, 104, 115, 117, 118
'The Swan Song' (Stayton), 164–5

The Theatre of the Soul (Evreinov), 21, 23, 142, 159, 166, 175, 178, 179, 180, 186
The Thumbscrew (Lyttleton), 47, 90, 94–6, 99
The Tidings Brought to Mary (Claudel), 126, 127–8, 174, 176, 181, 183
The Verge (Glaspell), 1, 178, 182, 185, 188
The Vote, 7, 13, 27, 79, 116
The Wedding (Chekhov), 114, 174
The Well of Loneliness (Hall), 159
The Woman With The Pack (Vaughan), 127
'The Yellow Wallpaper' (Gilman),120
Theatre
 experimentation in, 2
 professionalisation of, 194
 status of, 166
 and see under names of actors, playwrights and theatres; *see also* anti-naturalism; antirealism; Edith Craig; expressionism; futurism; naturalism; Pioneer Players; realism; Stage Society; Suffrage Atelier; symbolism
Theatre Act 1843, 21
Theatre of atmosphere, 172
Theatre of Cruelty, 5
Théâtre Libre, 17
Theatre Licensing Act 1737, 17
 circumvention of, 20
Théâtre de l'Oeuvre, 172
Theosophy, 65, 69
Thorndike, Sybil, 39, 176–7, 188–9, 190
'Three Dreams in a Desert (Schreiner), 56, 68, 71, 73, 92, 93
Three Women (Gilman), 93, 117
Thompson Price, Louise, 81–2
Thursby Charles, 19, 47, 94, 96
Translations, 155–6, 166
Trifles (Glaspell), 1, 115, 123
Troubridge, Una, 160
Turner, Daisy, 115, 119

Universal suffrage, 90

Unlicensed plays, 18
Unmarried mother *see* single parenthood
Utopian writing, 71, 73, 86

Vaughan, Gertrude, 127
Veasey, Arthur, 28
Vegetarianism, 58, 60, 65
Vestris, Mme, 67
Violence, 60, 115, 118
 against women, 83, 118
 within marriage, 115
Virgin martyr, 126
Virginity, 110, 126, 129
Visibility, making visible, 83, 88–9
Votes for Women, 13, 42, 68

War Players, 163
War relief work, 141
Ward, Mrs Humphry, 58
Warrender, Lady Maud, 28, 141, 151, 160, 163
Waste, 36
Webb, Beatrice, 89, 145
Webster, Ben, 123
Wells, H.G., 72, 101, 128
West, Rebecca, 5, 48, 144
Westminster Gazette, 116
White slave trade, 102; *and see* prostitution
Whitty, May, 123
Wilde, Oscar, 157, 162
Williams, Harcourt, 154
'Woman and Fiction' (Woolf), 54
'Woman This and Woman That' (Housman), 112
'Woman: the Spoilt Child of Law' (Nevinson), 116
Woman
 images of in theatre, 12
 representations of, 84
 women's history, 83, 86
 women's role, 24
 writer, 81
 see also New Woman; prostitution; Womanly Woman; working women
Woman's Dreadnought, 142
Womanly Woman, 53, 54, 81, 84, 112

Index 239

Women and the New Era (St. John), 69
Women in the New Era (Despard), 68, 69
Women Writers' Suffrage League, 71, 91
Women's Freedom League, 68, 78, 80
Women's International League, 142, 145
Women's suffrage drama, 2, 45, chapter, 4 passim
sexual politics of, 12
Women's Theatre, 3
Camps Entertainment, 144
Women's writing, 167–8
Woolf, Virginia, 5, 10, 35, 54, 84, 125, 140, 181–3, 191–2

Workers' Suffrage Federation, 142
Workers' Theatre Movement, 44, 146
Working class, 61
class health of, 59; *and see* eugenics
women, 56, 88, 89, 91, 99
Working women, chapter, 5 passim
during First World War, 141
WSPU, 42, 48, 71, 76, 80, 90

Xenophobia, 162

Young, M.E.M., 47, 125, 181

Zangwill, Edith, 118